Starring Mandela and Cosby

Starring Mandela and Cosby

Media and the End(s) of Apartheid

RON KRABILL

The University of Chicago Press.
Chicago and London

Ron Krabill is associate professor in the Interdisciplinary Arts & Sciences Program at the University of Washington Bothell and a member of the graduate faculty in the Department of Communication at the University of Washington Seattle.

The University of Chicago Press, Chicago 60637
The University of Chicago Press, Ltd., London
© 2010 by The University of Chicago
All rights reserved. Published 2010
Printed in the United States of America

20 19 18 17 16 15 14 13 12 11 10   1 2 3 4 5

ISBN-13: 978-0-226- 45188-6 (cloth)
ISBN-13: 978-0-226- 45189-3 (paper)
ISBN-10: 0-226-45188-7 (cloth)
ISBN-10: 0-226-45189-5 (paper)

Library of Congress Cataloging-in-Publication Data
Krabill, Ron.
  Starring Mandela and Cosby : media and the end(s) of apartheid / Ron Krabill.
    p. cm.
  Includes bibliographical references and index.
  ISBN-13: 978-0-226-45188-6 (cloth : alk. paper)
  ISBN-13: 978-0-226-45189-3 (pbk. : alk. paper)
  ISBN-10: 0-226-45188-7 (cloth : alk. paper)
  ISBN-10: 0-226-45189-5 (pbk. : alk. paper)
  1. Cosby show (Television program : 1984–1992)—Influence. 2. Television broadcasting—Social aspects—South Africa—History—20th century. 3. Television and politics—South Africa—History—20th century. 4. Television viewers—South Africa—Attitudes—History—20th century. 5. Whites—South Africa—Attitudes—History—20th century. 6. Mass media and race relations—South Africa—History—20th century. 7. Apartheid—South Africa. 8. South Africa—Race relations—History—20th century. I. Title.
  PN1992.3.S57K73 2010
  302.2'3450968—dc22   2010005836

♾ The paper used in this publication meets the minimum requirements of the American National Standard for Information Sciences—Permanence of Paper for Printed Library Materials, ANSI Z39.48-1992.

for my parents and my children;
may we all learn from those who have gone before
and never lose hope;
a luta continua!

in memory of
Willard S. Krabill
April 25, 1926–January 6, 2009

CONTENTS

ACKNOWLEDGMENTS

A project of this scope—conducted over many years on two continents through multiple institutions with a variety of funding sources—accumulates significant debts of gratitude. The immense generosity of time and spirit that is represented in these acknowledgments leaves me in awe; the many individuals and groups named below have gone far above and beyond the call of obligation in both their intellectual and personal support of this book. Without these many people, *Starring Mandela and Cosby: Media and the End(s) of Apartheid* would not be before you now. Although it has become a truism in acknowledgments such as these, it nonetheless remains necessary to say: everyone named below has undoubtedly strengthened this book, while none of them should be held responsible for its flaws.

More than ten years ago I arrived on the doorstep of Jon Hyslop, whom my professor at the New School for Social Research, Kate Crehan, had suggested I contact. He generously invited me into his living room for an extended conversation regarding the scholarship of the anti-apartheid movements and the areas that remained underresearched. It was Jon who first suggested to me that the role of television could benefit from more attention in scholarship on the late-apartheid era, and the intellectual and theoretical trajectory of this book thus was set in motion; I am immensely grateful to both Jon and Kate for catalyzing that moment. Several years later, Keyan Tomaselli offered me a visiting lectureship at what was then called the Graduate Programme in Cultural and Media Studies at the University of Natal in Durban, South Africa. As my institutional home in 1999 and 2000, the Graduate Programme was a vibrant beehive of visiting scholars, brilliant graduate students from across Africa and beyond, and passionately committed people exploring media and culture in South Africa and throughout the continent in a global context. Both Keyan and Ruth

Teer-Tomaselli have been invaluable supporters and engaged critics during the entire lifespan of this project. The staff and students in the Graduate Programme at that time—especially Mashilo Boloka, Jerome Dube, Thato Foko, Farhana Goga, Susan Govender, Andy Mason, Bright Phiri, Jeffrey Mathethe Sehume, and Rene Smith—remain valued friends and colleagues. In addition to those connected to my time at what is now the University of KwaZulu-Natal, many others in South Africa have been remarkably generous with their time and ideas. I want to especially thank Sean Jacobs, as well as Eve Bertelson, Colin Bundy, Pieter Conradie, Lesley Fordred, Mandla Langa, John Matisson, Achille Mbembe, Sarah Nuttall, Steve Robbins, Karen Thorne, Daan van Vuuren, and Herman Wasserman. The interviews I conducted for this book have been supplemented by a number of additional interviews carried out by a research assistant, Heinrich Crouse, and I extend my gratitude for his work. I would also be remiss if I did not acknowledge the consistently helpful assistance of the staff and archivists at the South African Broadcasting Corporation, the National Archives of South Africa, the historical papers of the University of the Witwatersrand, and the Mayibuye Center.

Since arriving in Seattle, I cannot imagine a group of more curious and collaborative colleagues than those at the University of Washington. Faculty in the Interdisciplinary Arts and Sciences Program on the Bothell campus have provided an intellectual community that has allowed me to integrate my research and teaching through interdisciplinary methods in unique and meaningful ways that are all too rare in academia. In particular, Bruce Burgett has given perceptive feedback on every part of the manuscript at several stages of its development, in addition to providing endless assistance in navigating the worlds of publishing and research in the context of pursuing tenure in an unusual interdisciplinary program. Kari Lerum and Elizabeth Thomas deserve special mention as members of a writing group and as valued colleagues who arrived on campus at the same time I did. The University of Washington Bothell also provided financial support for this research through the Worthington Distinguished Scholar Award and a Collaborative Undergraduate Research grant from the Teaching and Learning Center. The latter provided the immense pleasure of working with some remarkable students as research assistants on this project: Katy Afruma, Melissa Cushman, Amanda Dailey, Tyler Pratt, Claire Scarbeary, and Dana Shaphren. Each of these students offered countless hours of intellectual engagement and their insights have undoubtedly strengthened the claims in the book.

One of the great advantages of being based at the University of Washington is the opportunity to associate with a wide variety of exceptional scholars based at all three campuses in Bothell, Seattle, and Tacoma. I am deeply indebted to Lynn Thomas of the African Studies Program and the History Department for her friendship, her insights into this project, and her specific suggestions on parts of the book. The Walter Chapin Simpson Center for the Humanities provided both financial and intellectual support through my participation in the 2007–2008 Society of Scholars. Miriam Bartha and Kathy Woodward from the Simpson Center have been ongoing supporters of the project, while all the faculty and graduate students involved in this dynamic group of research fellows served as thoughtful interlocutors. I particularly want to recognize Crispin Thurlow of the Department of Communication, also a participant in the Society, for his willingness to engage deeply and meaningfully with a research project that holds implications for both his personal experience and his scholarly pursuits. Phil Howard, also of the Department of Communication, gave suggestions and encouragement on parts of the manuscript. Graduate students Laura Newlon and Megan Styles transcribed many hours of interviews and also added their observations to the mix. The University's Friday Harbor Laboratories on San Juan Island provided an idyllic setting in which to write parts of the book.

Many scholars based in New York during my graduate work at the New School for Social Research have contributed their keen intellect and valuable time to *Starring Mandela and Cosby*. Faculty of the New School who were involved during various moments of this process included Paolo Carpignano, Jose Casanova, Kate Crehan, Jeff Goldfarb, Mike Hanagan, Eiko Ikegami, Courtney Jung, and Louise Tilly. Beyond the New School, Josh Gamson has been an inspiration, a mentor, and a friend, and Juan Battle, David Johnson, Tony Marx, and Chuck Tilly all assisted in forming the theoretical and methodological foundations of my research. The Politics, Power, and Protest workshop at New York University (particularly Jeff Goodwin) and the South African Reading Group (particularly Penny Andrews, Mark Sanders, and Tony O'Brien) were invaluable sounding boards in the early stages of this project. My writing group at the New School gave profound shape to an early version of the work on which *Starring Mandela and Cosby* is based: Kevin Bruyneel, Edmund Fong, Joe Lowndes, Priscilla Yamin, and in particular Cat Celebrezze, whose innumerable sessions of back-and-forth with me on media theory have made me a better thinker. Jeremy Farrall provided his helpful comments on the entire dissertation as well. The New School also supported this project financially through the New Social Science Training Fellowship of the Transregional Center for

Democratic Studies and a variety of fellowships through the Department of Sociology, the Committee on Historical Studies, the Office of Student Affairs, and Eugene Lang College.

Doug Mitchell and Tim McGovern have shepherded *Starring Mandela and Cosby* through the University of Chicago Press from initial conversations to final product with a delightful combination of professionalism and good humor. They have also provided a helpful interface between the Press and the University of Washington at crucial moments in the process. I am deeply grateful for all of the work Doug, Tim, and everyone at the Press—especially Natalie Smith, Joel Score, Therese Boyd, Joe Claude, and Rob Hunt—have done to make this book a reality.

Finally, *Starring Mandela and Cosby* would not have been possible without the love and support of my family. My parents, Willard and Grace Krabill, along with my entire family of origin, have always provided me with a warm and caring foundation from which to pursue my passions; they remain mainstays in my life. No one has sacrificed more than my partner, Nancy Chupp, in order to bring this work to print. She has relocated across hemispheres, discussed theoretical points late into the night, endured vicarious moments of intense stress, rearranged incredibly complicated work and social calendars, and tolerated long stints of solo parenting in order for this research to come to fruition. My children, Keyan and Annika, have inspired in me a renewed fervor for making this world more just and compassionate, along with opening my eyes to an overwhelming delight in the beauty of every day. With the recent death of my father, I am keenly aware of the inheritances of history and the responsibilities for the future that we all carry with us. It is with this awareness that I acknowledge everyone named above—and many who remain unnamed—not only for making *Starring Mandela and Cosby* possible, but for continuing to believe that ideas matter and that justice is worth pursuing.

ABBREVIATIONS

All acronyms originate in South Africa unless otherwise noted.

AMPS   All Media Product Survey

ANC   African National Congress

APLA   Azanian People's Liberation Army

AWB   Afrikaner Weerstandsbeweging (Afrikaner Resistance Movement)

BBC   British Broadcasting Corporation (United Kingdom)

Bop   Bophuthatswana

Bop-TV   Bophuthatswana Television

CCV   Contemporary Community Values Television

CIB   Campaign for Independent Broadcasting

CNN   Cable News Network (United States)

CODESA   Congress for a Democratic South Africa

COM   Campaign for Open Media

COSATU   Congress of South African Trade Unions

CP   Conservative Party

ECC   End Conscription Campaign

HBO   Home Box Office (United States)

HNP   Herstigte Nasionale Party

HRC   South African Human Rights Commission

HSRC   Human Sciences Research Council

IBA   Independent Broadcasting Authority

ICASA   Independent Communications Authority of South Africa

IDASA	Institute for Democracy in South Africa (formerly Institute for a Democratic Alternative in South Africa)
IFP	Inkatha Freedom Party
ITV	Independent Television (United Kingdom)
JMCs	Joint Management Councils
MDM	Mass Democratic Movement
MK	Umkhonto we Sizwe
M-Net	Electronic Media Network
MWASA	Media Workers Association of South Africa
NNTV	National Network Television
NP	National Party
PAC	Pan-Africanist Congress
PBS	Public Broadcasting Service (United States)
PWV	Pretoria-Witwatersrand-Vereeniging
SABC	South African Broadcasting Corporation
SACP	South African Communist Party
SATRA	South African Telecommunications Regulatory Agency
SSC	State Security Council
TRC	Truth and Reconciliation Commission of South Africa
TSS	TopSport Surplus
TV1	Television One
TV2/3	Television Two and Television Three
TV4	Television Four
UDF	United Democratic Front
UP	United Party
VF-FF	Vreiheitsfront (Freedom Front)

Media, Democratization, and the End(s) of Apartheid

For a lot of White South Africans *The Cosby Show* was an example of how black people could be, "given enough time and education" . . . in short, they were "okay" and non-threatening in comparison to Black South Africans who were uneducated, did not all speak English, and were communists and terrorists to boot. Hence, to a degree, classism, American culture and family values won out over racism—but only in the minds of White South Africans.

—Jill, a thirty-two-year-old White English-speaking South African

In the fifteen years since the end of formal apartheid in South Africa, the anti-apartheid struggle has come to be viewed as the archetypal fight of good against evil. Nelson Mandela and Desmond Tutu are Nobel Peace Prize laureates and internationally recognized as global icons of moral leadership and heroism, the Truth and Reconciliation Commission has been heralded (and copied) as a model for postconflict societies, and the term *apartheid* has come to be used as a rhetorical weapon to indicate a nearly incomparable form of evil in government policies. In short, South Africa and its history play a symbolic role in international and transnational politics that extends far beyond the highly ambiguous nature of South African politics and social life today.

The combination of four remarkable facts regarding the struggle against apartheid inspired this book from the beginning: first, at the height of apartheid's States of Emergency in the mid-1980s, the most popular television show among White South Africans was *The Cosby Show.*[1] Second, during this same time, Nelson Mandela had spent nearly a quarter of a century under what was known in South Africa as "the ban," making it illegal to publish his image. As a result, most South Africans could recognize

Bill Cosby's face, but almost no one knew what the figurehead of the anti-apartheid struggle actually looked like. Third, television as a medium was actively kept out of South Africa by the apartheid regime until 1976—after more than 130 other countries had launched a television service. And fourth, the advent of television coincided with a significant increase in protest against the state in that same year.[2] These four facts combine to indicate a specific, remarkable historical conjuncture that can and should continue to inform our thinking about politics and culture in multiple times and places.

Today, when globalization and transnational media flows dominate thinking about media and culture, these facts might strike one as either quaint throwbacks to a bygone era or profoundly counterintuitive. It seems hard to imagine a time when television was not almost universally available, and talk in both scholarly circles and the popular press was not yet focusing on new media and the eclipse of television as the most important medium in cultural production. Likewise, the idea that the iconic situation comedy of wholesome, heteronormative family life that was so intricately tied up with race in the United States—*The Cosby Show*—could be enjoyed without irony by White South Africans in the midst of the apartheid regime's most brutal moments seems equally difficult to comprehend. Yet the central questions embedded within these four facts speak clearly to today's driving concerns around media, politics, and globalization: How do various media facilitate or constrain political action? How do they shape everyday social and political life across the globe? How do transnational media flows operate in particular times and places? And how do the technologies of media shape our imaginations of ourselves and our places in the world? In the historical particulars of late-apartheid-era television, we find a wealth of insight regarding twenty-first-century media and culture. Taken together, these four observations provide a compelling entry point to problematize the interactions between transnational media flows and processes of democratization by engaging television, White South African identifications, and politics between the years of 1976 and 1994.[3]

Scholars of South Africa have long recognized the Soweto Uprising and its aftermath as a major turning point in the struggle against apartheid. The apartheid state had enjoyed over a decade of relatively little overt opposition within the country following the banning of the African National Congress (ANC), the Pan-African Congress (PAC), the South African Communist Party (SACP), and several other resistance organizations in the early 1960s, along with the imprisonment and exile of their leadership. Although the strike waves of the early 1970s seem, in retrospect, like the harbinger of further political protest against apartheid, the Soweto Uprising nonetheless caught both the government and activists unprepared. Initially a local protest organized by schoolchildren against the use of Afrikaans as the language of instruction, the Uprising quickly spread—with the help of television—beyond both Soweto and the schools after police opened fire on the unarmed children. While the government managed to quell the Uprising after several months of violence, it would never again hold the kind of control over the nation that it did prior to 1976. The Soweto Uprising marks the beginning of the end of apartheid.

In spite of (or perhaps in part because of) its concurrence with the Soweto Uprising, scholars have paid scant attention to another significant event that took place in 1976: the introduction of television into South Africa. Very few places in the world have simultaneously experienced massive social unrest and the creation of a large-scale, state-of-the-art national television infrastructure as did South Africa in that year, thus begging the question of whether one conditioned the other in any way. Although this book shows that television had little, if any, *direct* impact on the Soweto Uprising itself, the coincidence of the two provides a unique starting point from which to trace the increasingly intertwined relationships between television and politics in the period leading up to the overwhelming electoral victory of the ANC in 1994.[4] The National Party's ideological resistance to television even before it entered the country also marks the South African experience as unusual when compared to almost every other industrialized nation, where television services were usually instituted as soon as they became financially feasible. Thus the social history of South African television and the political history of late apartheid feed off each other in unique ways that anticipate contemporary debates around transnational media and politics.

During the multiple declarations of a "State of Emergency" during the mid- to late 1980s—the high point of repression in a nation already renowned for its state-sponsored cruelty—the most popular television show among all South Africans, including and particularly White South Africans, was *The Cosby Show*. At first glance, this may seem an odd anomaly that represents no more than a strange and ironic disjuncture in a highly racialized setting. However, the intense yet widely divergent reactions to the show, even two decades later, remain striking. For several years, the counterintuitive popularity of the show became a persistent question in my research and, indeed, my social life. I would ask literally everyone I met in any setting in South Africa, whether a gas-station attendant, a fellow partygoer, or the head of the broadcasting regulatory agency, "How do you explain the popularity of *The Cosby Show* among White South Africans in the 1980s?" The responses, though far from a scientific sample, nonetheless displayed noteworthy consistencies. Some White South Africans dismissed *The Cosby Show* as "mere entertainment" or "too American" to have had any impact on their opinions regarding Black South Africans or racialized politics within South Africa. Yet many others claimed that *The Cosby Show* significantly influenced how they and their friends viewed Black South Africans, in essence opening their eyes to the possibility of equality. It was not uncommon for people to go so far as to declare that *"The Cosby Show* did more for race relations in this country than anything else ever has."[5]

Black South Africans, on the other hand, nearly always claimed that *The Cosby Show* held no relevance to political or social life in late-apartheid South Africa. Black South Africans tended to focus on explaining what it was about the fictional Huxtable family that appealed to White South Africans. Most common among these explanations was the opinion that the Huxtables were "safe"—that is, highly educated, upper-middle class, and nonthreatening—a similar interpretation to those critical of *The Cosby Show* in the United States. In the context of Black militancy in South Africa, the Huxtables thus provided White South Africans with an alternative representation that explained the United States' ability to maintain a different form of race relations while reinforcing White South Africans' own views of race relations within their country. In other words, Black South Africans perceive White South Africans as having thought to themselves, in those shockingly yet predictably possessive terms, that "their blacks" (African Americans) are more civilized than "our blacks" (Black South Africans). Though the responses to *The Cosby Show* among White and Black South Africans are in many ways divergent, the show's popularity across these identifications encourages us to look more deeply into the conjunctures of politics and cultural production.

Two paradoxes embodied in these original facts have consistently reappeared throughout the process of writing this book. First, in spite of the fact that the medium of television was from the very beginning firmly under the control of the apartheid state, television nonetheless played a far more complicated and at times contradictory role in the political life of South Africa. The contradictions embodied by apartheid-era television undercut many of the presuppositions of both media studies and democratic theory originating in North America and Western Europe, which provides an opportunity to contribute to *De-Westernizing Media Studies*, as called for by James Curran and Myung-Jin Park in their edited volume of the same name. A second paradox, hinted at in the title of the book (*Starring Mandela and*

Cosby), involves absence and visibility in political and public life. While Black resistance leaders such as Nelson Mandela were removed from public life through various forms of state repression such as the ban, Black entertainment figures like Bill Cosby were not only visible but even beloved by White South Africa. This book seeks to explore these two paradoxes in detail, from the time of television's introduction in 1976 through the establishment of democratic elections in 1994. While late-apartheid South Africa remains the setting for this story, the themes of the telling—visibility and absence, the maintenance and subversion of hegemony—travel well to other times and places.

The Claims

Each paradox mentioned above highlights one of the two central claims of the book. First, television made possible a transformation in the subjectivities and identifications of White South Africans, and this transformation in turn altered the nature of politics in late-apartheid South Africa and continues to reverberate through current efforts toward democratic consolidation. Second, television served as an initial site of negotiation in which the absence of Black South Africans in public life was first dismantled, thus allowing for White South Africans to imagine themselves as part of the same polity with Black South Africans long before the formal inclusion of Black South Africans in institutional political life. Underlying each of these claims is a more fundamental (and counterintuitive) theoretical implication regarding mass media, political action, and ideology: that even a mass medium fully controlled by a hegemonic body (be it a nation-state, a network of corporations, or some other entity) can *potentially* subvert that body's ideology. As such, this narrative sets itself apart from more instrumentalist accounts of media in politics, whether from the perspectives of political economy, framing theory, or representational discourses, as well as theorists who imbue media technology with intrinsic values or affects.

Before exploring each of these claims in more detail, let me also state three important limits to my claims. Fist, I am not claiming that only White South Africans' identifications were impacted by the introduction of television; the medium transformed the subjectivities—though in very different ways—of both Black and White South Africans, particularly in relation to each other and the rest of the world. Second, I am not claiming that the introduction of television was sufficient, or even necessary, to bring about the end of apartheid. And third, I am *not* claiming that the shifts in White identifications were the driving force behind the specific form

South Africa's democracy has taken. Each of these points calls for further explanation.

This study focuses on White South Africans for three reasons, one of which I discuss in the next section and two that I will examine here: a greater ability to analytically isolate the interactions between television and identifications among White South Africans and, more important, the profound differences in the stories of these interactions as experienced by White and Black South Africans. These "shifting selves" in relation to television are in turn more identifiable among White South Africans due to at least two significant factors:[6] White South Africans had far greater access to the medium of television, particularly in the first decade of its presence in South Africa, than did Black South Africans; and White South Africans faced fewer competing ideologies vying for legitimacy during the period under question than did Black South Africans. In one of the most economically disparate nations in the world (both in 1976 and today), White South Africans could afford television sets—which were prohibitively expensive at the time—much more easily than could Black South Africans. The vast majority of Black South Africans did not purchase sets for personal use until the mid-1980s at the earliest, when many townships were placed on the electrical grid, and most waited much longer than that.[7] Even as late as 1986 approximately three-quarters of television viewers were White South Africans.[8]

At the same time, Black South African life was highly politicized during this time period. Political competition between pan-Africanists, the Black Consciousness Movement, so-called charterists (the nonracialists of the ANC and related groups), communists, and others created a highly charged and explicitly political landscape, particularly for those Black South Africans in townships surrounding urban areas. Most White South Africans, on the other hand, considered a far narrower and more mainstream selection of political allegiances, with the vast majority of White South Africans supporting one of the two major political parties, neither of which represented a significant break from the status quo.[9] This is in no way meant to infer that White South Africans' processes of identification were more stable, but that the specific role of television in opening up potential new subject positions can be more clearly focused upon among White South Africans, who experienced the political imperatives of possible revolution in a less direct manner in their daily lives.

The second reason to focus on shifts in White South African identifications develops out of this substantial difference in the imagined ideological landscapes—or what Arjun Appadurai would describe as ideoscapes—of

White and Black South Africans.[10] As a result of these differences, the story of how television impacted Black South Africans' identifications and politics is a significantly different story—though related—than that of how it impacted their White compatriots. This book chooses to focus on what Michael Omi and Howard Winant might describe as the "racial project" of late-apartheid media and social control as driven by the apartheid regime and responded to by White South Africans.[11] It is not a study of the explicit resistance to the regime, but instead of the cracks and fissures in the White supremacist project of apartheid.

The second caveat—that the introduction of television was not sufficient, or perhaps even necessary, to bring about the end of apartheid—is an empirical one. Such a strong, unilinear causal claim is simply unsustainable given the complexity of social life and the number of vectors intersecting in this, or any, political or social situation. Such a claim is both unprovable and unnecessary. The relevance of media and their impact on processes of democratization should not have to rely on claims of singular causality to assert their significance. As Manuel Castells points out, technological determinism as it has been constructed is "probably a false problem" that fails to recognize the long-standing intertwined nature of technology and society.[12] While this book makes a historically contingent argument regarding the demise of apartheid and the specific form of the democratic transition that resulted, it does not argue that this was the only path to democracy that could have—or indeed should have—been taken.

Relatedly, the evidence simply does not support a claim that the transformation of White South African subjectivities was more important to the end of apartheid than were actions taken by activists in the United Democratic Front (UDF), the Congress of South African Trade Unions (COSATU), the Mass Democratic Movement (MDM), or any of the other organs of resistance politics. Make no mistake about it: a complex array of social, political, and economic factors, both within the country and abroad, played a role in ending apartheid, but the driving force behind apartheid's downfall was the willingness of Black South Africans (and some White South Africans as well) to take life-threatening risks in resisting it. For these reasons, my focus on White South Africans should not be understood as minimizing—either intentionally or accidentally—the nature or worth of the sacrifices made by so many South Africans to defeat apartheid. Regardless of the many structural transformations that may have made the end of apartheid *possible*, that possibility would never have been realized without the courage and little-known losses of a multitude of Black South Africans and others in resisting the regime. My focus on White South Africans, then, is not intended to diminish those efforts, but instead to supplement our understanding of them with concomitant insights into the shifting and contradictory practices of White supremacy during the same time.

In this limited sense, television mattered. Television had an impact—through its influence on processes of identification—on forms of political mobilization and demobilization at the end of apartheid. As such, television was one of many factors that came together in a particular way at a particular point in time. Instead of reducing the importance of understanding this unique conjuncture, this particularity draws us closer to the intricacies and nuances involved in interactions among media, processes of identification, and democratization in South Africa and elsewhere, and their implications for large-scale social change.

White Supremacy and the Unit of Analysis

My focus on White South Africans in this book also needs to be understood in terms of my own positionality vis-à-vis the project. As feminist and postcolonial scholarship have demonstrated, an account of how any given author arrives at a research project should be central to the project itself. This necessity is not (or at least should not be) driven by a narcissistic desire for the project to be about the author. Indeed, a bedrock principle of this book is that authorial intent in fact counts for little in how an audience makes meaning from cultural products, particularly products disseminated via mass media, just as the policy intentions of apartheid apparatchiks often yielded failed or even opposite results. Rather, I offer this account of my own trajectory into this project in the interests of articulating the motivations that drive the questions I am asking, particularly surrounding the unit of analysis, as well as the absence of the inquiries I am not pursuing.

My attraction to South Africa was first driven by my friendship with an orphan of the struggle while I was still in high school in a small, rural town in northern Indiana. When I was in college, the two issues that radicalized me politically were the anti-apartheid and Central American solidarity movements. This activism followed me after college into ongoing political activism, which included organizing a speaking tour and raising money for the ANC Youth League in the run-up to the 1994 elections. So this project comes out of a longstanding interest in and care for South Africa. But this is categorically not a heroic narrative—my activism on behalf of the anti-apartheid struggle was never of an impressive order. I was one of many bit players in the U.S.-based support of the anti-apartheid movements, sincere but undoubtedly driven as much by my own desires for identification as a radical antiracist activist as by any comprehension of the impact my actions may or may not have had in South Africa itself.

My anti-apartheid activism therefore grew out of my own ambivalence around my subject position regarding White supremacy in the United States as the beneficiary of interlocking forms of white, male, straight-perceived privilege. Thus my interest in White supremacy in South Africa, and the changing processes of identification among White South Africans, comes not from a sense of superiority or condemnation toward White South Africans themselves, but rather from a deep concern with the ambiguity and pervasiveness of the racial project of White supremacy that extends across South Africa, the United States, and, indeed, around the globe.

To this end, the unit of analysis for this book is that of White South Africans as a whole. It is not a claim that race is *a priori* the most important possible unit of analysis in all cases, but only for this particular study of White supremacy. The losses in defining the unit of analysis as such are significant: beyond the obvious historical cleavage between Afrikaners and English-speaking White South Africans, countless other levels of differentiation exist within this category—gendered, generational, class-based, political, sexual, regional, educational, urban/rural—the permutations are as extensive as White South Africans themselves. And as mentioned earlier, many White South Africans actively resisted apartheid in big and small ways. To the extent possible, then, I mark these intersectionalities as they arise. However, because the object of study is White supremacy itself, a racial project that defined all these categories of differentiation under the racially defined marker of "White," shifting subjectivities within this group as a (mis)perceived whole remain the focus of the book.

As an example, let me briefly examine the distinction between Afrikaner and English-speaking White South Africans. These two groups share different and at times violently colliding historical trajectories, as evidenced by the South African War and the atrocities that took place during that war at the turn of the twentieth century. The choice to not give primacy to the distinction between the two groups of White South Africans is a choice to name the project of White supremacy—and the fissures within that project—as shared between Afrikaners and English-speakers alike. This runs counter to many narratives that place Afrikaners at the heart of the apartheid project and English-speaking White South Africans as unwilling co-travelers along that road. Yet while Afrikaners and English-speakers were indeed positioned differently in relation to the state under apartheid, the narrative of English-speaking marginalization under apartheid overstates the claims of difference (and implied resistance) and understates the shared experience of and acquiescence to being "White" in South Africa. To the extent that White South Africans *as a group* acquiesced to the racial project of apartheid—just as White residents of the United States as a group have continued to acquiesce to and benefit from various racial projects of domination—then marking that social category as a materially relevant unit of analysis becomes not only reasonable but, in fact, necessary. The efforts of those White South Africans and White Americans who resist White supremacy in big or small ways do not account for a dismissal of the category as a whole. To do so would be to dismiss the power of the racial project itself to define, both materially and discursively, the positionality and practices of individuals across societies through the categories of race.

The Fence Posts

This book, then, seeks to consider the ways in which White South Africans were able to reimagine their own possible subject positions in relation to their Black counterparts and in the context of an increasingly globalized world, in part through the shared communicative space of television. In order to do this, I have identified what I call "fence posts"—moments in the history of South Africa that highlight shifts in both the televisual and the political landscapes, or what Appadurai has described as the mediascapes and ideoscapes of the time.[13] The fence posts metaphor is intended to evoke the historical continuity between each specific moment examined, just as a fence continues through many posts, while also calling to mind significant events that bring to the foreground certain phenomena, just as a fence post provides both an anchor for the fence in its surrounding context and a moment of possible change in direction. Fence posts also provide the material grounding for methods of demarking ownership, literally segregating the land into separate spheres of control in the same way that apartheid demarcated racialized categories of people. Recognizing that the metaphor of fence posts is an act of historical imagination that gives shape to the book's narrative, I have chosen them according to their significance for *both* television and politics, rather than one or the other. The result is a narrative that weaves a social history of television in South Africa together with an account of the major political shifts in the late-apartheid era, always with an eye to transnational media flows and global political imaginaries.

The fence post metaphor is not intended to give causal force to the events examined, but instead to invoke a moment in which earlier developments become evident in the reality of that moment and future directions become plausible but not determined. In other words, each fence post provides evidence of changes since the previous post rather than being the cause of things to come. This approach reflects a conceptualization of historical developments that understands history as the conjunctural writing of the present, that shapes the conditions and possibilities of the future rather than predicting it. Likewise, while a fence may decay and fall away, the fence posts tend to remain as reminders of the previous shape and direction of the fence.

To clarify, let me use the fence post contained most obviously in the title of the book—the popularity of *The Cosby Show* among White South Africans. As a fence post, *The Cosby Show*'s popularity does not indicate a singular claim that the show itself caused greater visibility or inclusion of Black South Africans in cultural and political life in the years following its popularity. Rather, that popularity reflects earlier changes in White South Africans' conceptualizations of themselves in relation to Black South Africans, which in turn influence future developments. As such, the question of *The Cosby Show*'s representation of African American life takes a back seat to what its popularity indicates about transformations that had already occurred and were continuing among White South African identifications at the time. Thus the popularity of *The Cosby Show* does not stand alone in this process, but is part of a larger continuity, the third of the four fence posts through which I trace changing White South African subjectivities.

The four fence posts are:

1. Television's arrival and the Soweto Uprising (1976);
2. SABC TV2/3 and constitutional reforms (1983–84);
3. *The Cosby Show* and the States of Emergency (1986–88); and
4. Television and the democratic transition (1990–94).

The rest of this section will outline why I have chosen these particular moments to serve as fence posts while briefly summarizing the chapters to come.

Chapter 1, "Structured Absences and Communicative Spaces," explores the theoretical and methodological underpinnings of the research while situating the book in the context of contemporary debates around transnational media flows, globalization, and democratization in order to ground this project in the specific context of South Africa without reducing it to a national case study. In particular, this chapter looks at the ways in which television as a medium is uniquely able to provide a shared communicative space across various social divisions, thereby becoming a site in which the structured absence of Black South Africans from the social and political life of the nation was first reimagined. This chapter also outlines the methodological approach of the book, utilizing more than 100 ethnographic interviews conducted over several years while triangulating evidence from those interviews with archival and market-driven ratings research.

Chapter 2, "In the Absence of Television," predates the first fence post of the argument. It maps South Africa's mediascape, as well as the political conflicts surrounding television's absence, prior to the introduction of the medium in 1976. By examining the positions of political parties and the resistance movements regarding television, I show how Afrikaner political identifications imbued television with qualities that enforced its structured absence and perpetuated a separation of nearly all aspects of life between Black and White South Africans. While this absence was an explicit attempt on the part of the apartheid regime to resist transnational media flows— particularly representations of the civil rights movement in the United States—the denial of television exacerbated many White South Africans' (particularly English-speakers') sense of exclusion from the international community. This chapter also includes an overview of other forms of media in South Africa at the time and an analysis of why the apartheid regime finally allowed television to enter the country.

Chapter 3, "'They Stayed 'til the Flag Streamed,'" examines the first fence post: television's introduction to South Africa in 1976. In spite of the political contention around television before it arrived, the medium quickly became a popular and important part of the mediascape of South Africa. From the very beginning, television remained under the strict control of the ruling party and its allies; nonetheless, White South Africans began to form a new communicative space through television and, most important, shared that space with the world beyond South Africa through transnational media flows. And even though the South African Broadcasting Corporation (SABC) initially excluded Black South Africans from both television and its conceptualization of its own audiences, Black South Africans also began to participate in this newly forming communicative space of television. Thus television's initial presence in the context of South Africa immediately began complicating the tightly controlled mediascape of apartheid, with transnational media flows crossing both national and racial borders. These flows were further complicated by language, expense, and international pressure, with a combination of British cultural boycotts and the cost of domestic television production shifting the bulk of English-language entertainment programming toward sources produced in the United States and the bulk of domestic entertainment production toward Afrikaans-language programming.

In June of 1976 the SABC faced the first of what would be many challenges in controlling coverage of contentious politics on television with the explosion of the Soweto Uprising. Although the SABC quickly clamped down on any portrayal of the protestors as anything other than criminals, the presence of television played a role in the spread of the Uprising from Soweto to other townships across the nation: even with the government's voiceover, Black South Africans were able to immediately identify the contours of power in the conflict, with some joining the fray as a result. The Soweto Uprising thus marked the difficulties ahead in controlling coverage of mass resistance in a totalitarian setting.

Chapter 4, "Surfing into Zulu," investigates the next fence post: the apartheid regime's introduction of "Black television" in the form of two new channels aimed exclusively at the growing Black middle class in 1983. The introduction of these channels, known as TV 2/3, was part of a larger attempt to develop legitimacy for the apartheid regime in the face of growing international pressure through constitutional reforms establishing a tricameral parliament with a limited franchise for Asian and Coloured South Africans. Instead, massive resistance to the tricameral parliament among all those disenfranchised by apartheid gave birth to the United Democratic Front (UDF), the mass movement that would lead the resistance to apartheid in the final decade.

Paralleling the failed attempt of the regime to win legitimacy through constitutional reform, the SABC also failed to win legitimacy through TV 2/3. In spite of apartheid's ideology, which believed that only White South Africans would be interested in the "White channels" and only Black South Africans would watch the "Black channels," my interviews indicate a large amount of what I call "surfing into Zulu," that is, channel surfing by White South Africans onto so-called Black television and vice versa. Thus the nature of television as a medium proved impossible to control for the apartheid regime, with both transnational and intranational media flows leading to a prototypical form of the cultural miscegenation so feared by apartheid's bureaucrats prior to television's introduction. Although White South Africans often reported disturbingly distorted views of Black South Africans gained through TV 2/3, the channels nonetheless played a role in breaking down the structured absence of Black South Africans in their White counterparts' conceptualization of the nation.

Chapter 5, "Living with the Huxtables in a State of Emergency," considers the role of television in further breaking down the absence of Black

South Africans under the States of Emergency in the mid- and late 1980s, paying particular attention to my third fence post: the overwhelming popularity of *The Cosby Show* among White South Africans. My ethnographic research shows that the SABC's version of current events during the States of Emergency was widely understood to be untrustworthy by Black and White South Africans alike. While Black South Africans lived the States of Emergency—essentially martial law selectively applied to Black townships—in an immediate and visceral way, White South Africans turned away from television news to make sense of their world. One of the places they turned, in extremely large numbers, was *The Cosby Show*.

Through transnational media flows in general and particularly *The Cosby Show*, White South Africans were able to appropriate the language and attitude of "racial tolerance" in the United States while simultaneously conceptualizing a profound difference between Black Americans and Black South Africans. While this often led to apartheid apologetics, the shift from a biological to a cultural foundation for racial domination made formal apartheid increasingly difficult to maintain. Coupled with increasing international pressure, also communicated primarily through transnational media flows, this shift in the ideological foundations of racial domination opened up the possibility for White South Africans to support the end of formal apartheid while simultaneously seeking mechanisms for the maintenance of racialized economic and political privilege in a post-apartheid South Africa.

Chapter 6, "I May Not Be a Freedom Fighter, but I Play One on TV," extends this analysis into the period of political negotiations, bookended by the release (in 1990) and the inauguration (in 1994) of Mandela, both major international media events in and of themselves. As the moment when the structured absence of Black South Africans from political life is overturned and political contestation over maintaining privilege becomes explicit, this fence post represents a crucial turning point in the overall analysis. Contestation around television, particularly control of the SABC, comes to the fore, with a massive increase in both transnational media flows and innovative domestic programming arising simultaneously with an increase in both the scope and magnitude of political violence. Many assumptions of South African social life suddenly opened up for negotiation at the same time that the nation was being reintegrating into international politics and global economies. This period marks both the demise and the reinvention of apartheid in the contexts of democratization and globalization.

The conclusion, "Television and the Afterlife of Apartheid," ends my study by summarizing the major findings and the theoretical themes of this work. Through an analysis of attempts to deal with television's apartheid past—including the transformation of broadcasting, the Truth and Reconciliation Commission of South Africa's hearings on mass media in 1997, and the South African Human Rights Commission's inquiry into racism in the media in 2000—I assess some of apartheid's historical continuities and discontinuities, while also considering their implications for the current and future relationships among globalization, transnational media flows, and processes of democratization.

Culture and the Negotiated Transition

While emphasizing different elements of the framework outlined above, each of the following chapters pursues a coherent narrative of the overall themes of structured absence, communicative space, and shifting processes of identification. These themes assert themselves as essential, interlocking pieces to the puzzle of mediated public life in South Africa at the end of apartheid and during the transition to formally democratic rule. Without taking account of the complicated role of television and transnational media flows in shaping the forms of public life during this period, other treatments of the surprisingly peaceful transition in South Africa tend to overemphasize the role of political leaders and their negotiations. Although these negotiations laid the groundwork for avoiding the full-fledged civil race war that so many predicted, the negotiations themselves would not have taken the shape they had were it not for previous shifts in South Africans' perceptions of themselves, Black and White alike, and their place within both the nation and the world. White South Africans' growing disenchantment with their exclusion from the international community, coupled with a new ability to conceive of themselves as part of the same nation as Black South Africans, led to the support of White South Africans for the negotiations and a relatively peaceful transition to democratic elections. This support, in turn, paved the way for the "new" South Africa— with all its successes and failures in breaking with the apartheid past.

CHAPTER ONE

Structured Absences and Communicative Spaces

The central lesson of Gramsci's *Prison Notebooks*, [Stuart] Hall suggests, is precisely the importance of attending, with all the "pessimism of the intellect" at your command, to the specificity of a historical (and, one should add, geographical) conjuncture—namely, how diverse forces come together in particular ways to create a new political terrain.

—Gillian Hart, *Disabling Globalization*

Each of the fence posts explored in this book—the introduction of television and the Soweto Uprising, the creation of "Black" channels and constitutional reform, the popularity of *The Cosby Show* and the States of Emergency, and the democratic transition of the SABC and the South African government—demonstrate key conjunctures at which the social history of television and the political history of South Africa intersect. However, observing moments of intersection and understanding the dynamics of those interactions are entirely different orders of analysis. To comprehend how television, and media more generally, helped shape the politics of late-apartheid South Africa, we need to develop a richer theoretical and methodological framework within which to work. This requirement becomes even more pressing if we want to comprehend the history narrated in this book not as a discreet case study of media and politics from the past, but as an instance of confluence shaping the present in which transnational media flows and processes of democracy converge within a globalizing world. This chapter examines the theoretical and methodological underpinnings of this project through three concepts that will recur throughout the book: hegemony, structured absence, and communicative space.

By arguing that television is best understood through the shared, transnational cultural space that the unique nature of the medium itself makes possible, though not inevitable, this work considers the relevance of not only critical-rational discourse within the so-called democratic (or democratizing) public sphere, but also the more emotive and less explicit implications of television, both in South Africa and elsewhere.[1] Only by considering the shared space of communication formed by television can we identify the ways in which the medium facilitated the unexpected willingness of White South Africans to participate with Black South Africans in institutional politics and culture, thus smoothing the way for a political transition to formal democracy that was both surprisingly peaceful and predictably incomplete. South Africa provides a particularly rich lens through which to view transnational media flows, given the comparatively late introduction of television (in 1976, the 130th nation to introduce the medium) and the complex set of state-imposed restrictions and internationally imposed boycotts—both unevenly applied—that gave a unique shape to the apartheid mediascape. This work thereby engages with South Africa in order to challenge received notions of mass media in authoritarian or (post)colonial settings while simultaneously confronting crucial questions of globalization and democratization.

Hegemony and the End(s) of Apartheid

During the height of apartheid's repression in the mid-1980s, the key theoretical rubric through which many scholars of South Africa viewed the conflict was that of hegemony as articulated by the Italian revolutionary Antonio Gramsci in his *Prison Notebooks*, written during his incarceration by Mussolini's fascist regime. While the concept of hegemony became influential across global academic circles during this time, its appeal in the context of apartheid was particularly strong: here was a theorist/activist battling against a fascist state, trying to understand the ways in which the dominant ideology of the day had come to be understood as "common sense" by such a large number of his fellow countrymen and -women. Following the end of formal apartheid, however, hegemony has come to be rethought in South African scholarship—at times discarded, but at other times reworked into a more complex conceptualization that refocuses our attention on the nuances of Gramsci's thought.

As Kate Crehan and Gillian Hart have argued, Gramsci's concept of hegemony should be understood less as a question of varying degrees of strength and weakness in exercising social control—as something one does or does not have, or has a greater or lesser amount of—but rather as a set of *problematics* or *processes*.[2] This approach emphasizes the inability of hegemony ever to become a fully closed, static circuit of power or cultural production; it will always contain weaknesses and contradictions that must be reconstructed. As Hart puts it, "Hegemony in this sense does not refer to ideological domination, manipulation, or indoctrination. Rather, it is most usefully understood as a contested political process . . . understood in this way, hegemony is inherently fragile, and must be constantly renewed, re-created, defended, and modified. While by definition dominant, it is never total or exclusive."[3]

This approach to the concept of hegemony allows the narrative to take on a significantly more complex project. My task in this book is not to prove that the medium of television did or did not challenge the hegemony of the South African regime or the racial project of apartheid, or even the degree to which it did or did not do so, but instead to examine the ways in which the communicative space of television helped shape the processes of hegemonic maintenance *and* decay within the racial project of the apartheid state. To reformulate the quote at the beginning of this chapter, how did the many diverse forces—televisual space, transnational media flows, state policy, processes of identification—come together in particular ways in late-apartheid South Africa to create a new political terrain that allowed for South Africa to end formal apartheid in the particular way that it did? This approach further allows a crucial follow-up question: in what ways does the crisis of the apartheid state and the transition to formal democracy constitute, simultaneously, both a *challenge to* and a *reinscription of* the racial project of the South African state? In other words, conceptualizing hegemony as a process, rather than a quality of power to be possessed, opens up the very real possibility—perhaps even likelihood—of simultaneous, contradictory (re)formations of White supremacy within our historical narratives, and of multiple historical trajectories (and multiple endings, or lack thereof) for apartheid itself.

Beyond Representation:
Visibility, Invisibility and Structured Absence

Rather than seeking a strict causal chain from television through culture and identifications to politics, this study explores the layered interactions of these elements through an understanding of television as both cultural content and technological form in the period between its introduction and the inauguration of Mandela, the first democratically elected president of South Africa. At the center of these interactions are the two paradoxes highlighted in the previous chapter: the profound yet never complete control over the medium of television by the apartheid regime; and the structured absences of Black South Africans in the apartheid-era political and social lives of White South Africans.

In *Freaks Talk Back*, Joshua Gamson convincingly displays the paradox of visibility and social power in his portrayal of sexual nonconformists in the world of television talk shows.[4] As he demonstrates, visibility within the medium of television often operates as a double-edged sword for marginalized groups, offering the only outlet for visibility and expression, yet doing so in a context largely beyond their control. Although the presence of Black South Africans on South African television took a very different form than that of sexual nonconformists in the United States, Gamson nonetheless provides us with crucial insights for understanding the dual nature of visibility and representation on television.

Gamson offers us a problematic within which to work: what are the implications of the (re)presentation of marginalized groups in a setting not of their own making? He shows the many layers of rhetoric and politics that intersect with the process of cultural production within a particular genre— the talk show—to create profoundly ambivalent and at times contradictory results. By identifying some of the repercussions of visibility—whether through positive, negative, or somewhere in-between images—Gamson points the way toward an analysis that moves beyond representation without dismissing it.

Similar kinds of analyses have been brought to an understanding of portrayals of African Americans on television in the United States, most notably in a newfound appreciation for early pioneers on television shows, even if the characters to which they gave life were gross caricatures of African American life. For instance Donald Bogle, the author of *Primetime Blues*, claims that:

> Black viewers might reject the nonsense of the scripts for some episodes of "Sanford and Son" or "The Jeffersons" or "Martin." Or the evasions of an otherwise moving series like "I'll Fly Away." But they never really rejected a Redd Foxx or a Sherman Hemsley or Martin Lawrence or Regina Taylor's Lily. What remained consistent throughout television history was that a group of dynamic or complicated or intriguing personalities managed to send personal messages to the viewers.[5]

As one journalistic examination of this history points out: "When television began, official racial segregation was sanctioned in many states, and having a black actress play a maid on TV was considered, among African-Americans, *both* an insult *and* a coup" (emphasis added).[6]

Recognizing the importance of representation while simultaneously realizing that it fails to tell us the whole story proves crucial for understanding television under apartheid. While state censors and members of the Broederbond went to almost comical lengths at times to control the visible content on television, they had little understanding of the deeper implications of television as a technological and social form.[7] Widening the scope of research in this way allows me to develop a different kind of analysis than those most often provided by both earlier work on mass media under apartheid and various studies from around the world that translate progressive political stances into a primary concern with representation of marginalized groups.[8]

In order to fully appreciate how visibility functions, some comprehension of the opposite state of being—invisibility—is also necessary. Here, Louis Althusser's notion of "structured absence" is particularly useful, and I adapt it with an eye to how other South African media scholars have done so in the past.[9] Structured absence, as I use it, results from the *active* exclusion of an individual, group, or object from a given setting, or what Althusser described as "internal shadows of exclusion."[10] As such, power is central to the concept, for only through power of one over another can absence be enforced, that is, structured, through the exercise of that power in ways that appear naturalized on the surface. Structured absence thus requires a certain level of power and discipline (in Foucault's sense of the term), as contrasted to a pure absence.[11] Unlike structured absence, pure absence is simply a lack of presence and/or existence and implies no further enforcement or discipline on the part of either the excluded or the present.

Structured absence is never complete and rarely stable. In much the same way that Gramsci conceptualizes hegemony as a powerful yet always-contested problematic, structured absences are controversial, partial, and full of contradiction. Breaches in the power of structured absences are inherent to any attempt to forcibly exclude, rather than an exception to the rule. Consequently, the concept of structured absence indicates an acknowledgment that these absences were hotly disputed and, in fact, provide indications of larger power struggles taking place under the surface both within and outside of the media. In other words, conflicts around structured absences can serve as coded arguments about other issues and can, at times, tell us more about the operation of power than we can learn from immediately visible dynamics.

Much of the history of television in South Africa is a tale of changing relationships among power, visibility, and structured absences. Prior to 1976 television itself constituted a structured absence in South African social life, excluded by the apartheid regime on the basis of its perceived danger to Afrikaner identity. The structured absence of television paralleled, in a sense, the far more serious structured absence of Black South Africans in the political and social life of White South Africans. Yet in spite of its structured absence within the country, television nonetheless became a site of contestation between competing identities—particularly between Afrikaners and English-speaking White South Africans—even prior to its introduction.

Following 1976 television was no longer absent from South Africa, but Black South Africans continued to constitute a structured absence in political and most of social life, in spite of what Sarah Nuttall has aptly termed the "entanglement" of Black and White South African existence.[12] The following fourteen years saw the slow erosion of Black South Africans' absence on and through television, even as the attempt to enforce their absence from shared institutional political life was escalated through new, more extreme levels of repression and/or cooptation into apartheid ideology. Television thus became one of the first and most important spaces within which South Africans began to imagine themselves as equal players inside the same nation.[13] This trend finally culminated in the unbanning of the resistance organizations and the release of the most prominent political prisoners in 1990. Television then developed into a significant site for introducing former resistance leaders as legitimate political actors in a reformulated South African nation prior to the elections of 1994. The elections themselves mark the formal end of Black South Africans' exclusion from the political arena, bringing the parallel structured absences of both television and Black South Africans to their conclusion. Yet structured absences continue to mark South African life after 1994, as does the double-edged nature of media visibility for Black South Africans, both of which I discuss in the conclusion.

Television as a Communicative Space

In order to understand the role of televisual technology in this process, it is essential to conceptualize television in a manner that includes spatial and temporal dimensions. It has become a truism that television and other electronic media collapse time and distance; indeed, this has become a central tenet, and for many the most significant driving force, of those theorizing globalization as an acceleration or intensification of global interconnectedness.[14] However, while the ability of various communications media to *collapse* or *compress* time and space—for example, through satellite telecommunications or the speed of the Internet—is oft-invoked, it is somewhat less common to conceptualize television as a *constitutive* space in which people meet, gather, and interact. Precisely this kind of constitutive space is inferred by the concept of "cyberspace" and expanded in more recent understandings of Web 2.0, but television as a medium is rarely understood fully in the same terms. Rather than imagining television to be solely a conduit of cultural production, an empty space through which to transmit competing representations, television can be better understood as a collection of places within which various social groups coexist and reimagine themselves in relationship to each other.

As viewers of *The Cosby Show* we do not simply watch the Huxtables, but we inhabit their personal living space with them. We are invited into their living room, their bedrooms, and occasionally even the parents' bed. Yet it is not only the representations of Cliff and Clair Huxtables' bedroom that makes television a communicative space. More important, the shared knowledge of their bedroom, coupled with an awareness that such knowledge is shared, brings together viewers in a common communicative space, whether that space is actively invoked or not. Appadurai's conceptualization of "mediascapes" captures elements of this well, with his emphasis on the role of imagination in constructing this landscape of transnational media flows.[15]

My approach to understanding the spatial aspects of television borrows in part from the work of Joshua Meyrowitz in *No Sense of Place*.[16] Meyrowitz has produced important concepts regarding the ways in which the medium of television has impacted social space and interaction. He focuses on the ability of television to broadcast information both simultaneously and instantaneously, and on the ease with which televisual communication can be deciphered across linguistic, educational, class, and age barriers.[17] This point is of particular importance in a society of such linguistic diversity and high illiteracy as South Africa. Television thereby breaks down social divisions that are maintained by print. Whether one considers the impact of electronic media on society as "good, bad, or neutral," Meyrowitz tells us, "the reprocessing of our physical and social environment is revolutionary."[18] Although I take into consideration Meyrowitz's assumption of North American and Western European contexts, his treatment of both television's ability to simultaneously transmit its content to millions of locations and the greater accessibility of televisual over print media allows us to understand South African television's role in increasing access to existing communicative spaces, as well as creating new ones.[19] Thus we might appropriate the title of Meyrowitz's book, *No Sense of Place*, and reformulate it into "New Senses of Place."

In their Televisuality website, the Televisuality Collective directed by Paolo Carpignano (hereafter Carpignano et al.) has synthesized the work of Meyrowitz, Samuel Weber, and many other media theorists into a coherent understanding of televisual space with critical implications for this book.[20] Carpignano et al. argue that televisual space is fundamentally social and must be understood as such:

> We should be able to establish, from the outset, that the space of television can only be analyzed as a cultural construct, as a space that can only be understood in terms of social relations of communication, and defined by the sense of place of its inhabitants. . . . This is what is meant here by *medium*, not merely a technology of transmission of information but an amalgamation of social relations of communication, ultimately a place of mediation.[21] (emphasis in original)

Carpignano et al. make a crucial distinction here between a determinist view of technology and their own, which incorporates television's technological abilities without reducing it to those abilities.

This conceptualization of television allows us to examine the communicative space created by television in South Africa, in spite of the apartheid regime's control of television's production. Carpignano et al.'s formulation displaces the producers of television from their usual position of exclusive control, while also displacing the audience from its position outside the construction of televisual space. In other words, television breaks down the false barrier between performer (or producer) and audience, instead forcing audiences to inhabit a shared social, though not physical, space. In order to reflect this reality, Carpignano et al. follow Weber in emphasizing the concept of monitoring rather than viewing television. Monitoring, they say, "is a type of access to a space or an event that we become capable of observing at a distance, without literally being there."[22] Thus:

> If television watching has to be understood as a monitoring of a situation, it follows that what is established in the process is not a relationship between a viewing subject and a visible object, but more properly, the inhabiting of a new spatial arrangement to which the viewer has access. In monitoring, the viewer is not a disembodied observer of a representation, but the full bodied inhabitant of a place that he/she helped to generate.[23]

This understanding of television, in which audiences inhabit a shared space, strikes at the heart of communicative space in South Africa. Whereas the shared nature of televisual space is important in many contexts—including the North American and Western European contexts within which much media studies theory is constructed—under apartheid it was revolutionary. In a context in which sharing physical space was not only discouraged but in many cases outlawed, the existence of a space that could be accessed without requiring one's physical presence allowed for one of the first truly shared spaces of any kind:

> The vision *of* the other is also a vision *with* the other. Again, what is significant for television is not what is seen but the collective occurrence of watching. A place that is split and separated, and yet simultaneous, is a composite place, shaped by the collective experience of its dwellers. It is a place that is defined not by the extension of individual bodies, but by the dialogical engagement of a social body.[24] (emphasis added)

Television thus became one of the first locations in which the "social body" of South Africa was not *automatically* divided according to racialized subject positions.

By choosing the term *communicative space*, I am drawing on the work of Meyrowitz and Carpignano et al., as well as the work of Eiko Ikegami and other scholars of communicative networks, network analysis, and identity.[25] In *Poetry and Protest*, Ikegami demonstrates that the opening up of new communicative networks can present an opportunity for the reshaping of identities, even before the invention of modern mass-communication systems, based on shifting social contexts within the so-called public sphere(s). Benedict Anderson has made famously similar observations regarding the manner in which print media paved the way for nationalist identities in *Imagined Communities*.[26]

Communicative space thereby integrates understandings of communicative networks, televisual space, processes of identification, and theories of civil society and the public sphere(s), but resists the *a priori* privileging of any of these schools of thought. Communicative space becomes not a metaphor or a virtual reality, but the actual location of interaction between otherwise segregated South African bodies. A spatial conceptualization of television allows us to recognize the potential for both Habermas's critical-rational discourse and more emotive, less proceduralist forms—including those occurring below the surface of daily life—of communication and identity formation.[27]

Communicative Space and Transnational Media Flows

In order to understand this communicative space opened by television, it is crucial to develop an understanding of television both as a global medium *and* within the specific history and context of South Africa. As such, my research suggests that sweeping generalizations about the social impact of television as a medium ignore the drastic variations in the previous social contexts into which television is introduced. Whether the claim is for the inherently positive, democratizing effect of television, or for the intrinsically negative, spectacularizing effect of the medium, these approaches almost always take the North American or Western European experiences of the medium (its technological form, the conditions under which it is consumed, the level of its penetration into society, and so on) as a given or, at best, an eventual developmental inevitability.[28] Refusing these assumptions, this work grounds its analysis of television in the very specific historical circumstances of late-apartheid South Africa.

Taking the South African context seriously does not mean, however, that transnational media flows take a back seat to an analysis of the nation-state as a case study. Indeed, this error is a common one in what Gillian Hart refers to as "impact" models of globalization, which view the accelerated processes of contact as emanating from a "Western" or "Developed" core and impacting "non-Western" or "developing" peripheries. In this model, South African television in the late-apartheid era could only be impacted by transnational media flows into the country, rather than absorbing *and* creating those flows in an uneven but still constitutive way both within South Africa and beyond. As Hart describes, "So-called 'non-Western' historical geographies, cultural formations and forms of accumulation need to be understood not simply as the effects of accelerating global flows and connections, but as actively formative of them." In *Disabling Globalization: Places of Power in Post-Apartheid South Africa*, Hart further develops the work of Doreen Massey, and Henri Lefebvre before her, in criticizing the use of spatial metaphors in the work of theorists such as Althusser "in abstraction from social practice," claiming instead "a relational understanding of space as actively produced through everyday practices that are simultaneously material and metaphorical."[29] While this work signifies an unorthodox version of Hart's method of "relational comparison"—focusing instead on a single location rather than a comparative project—it nonetheless embraces Hart's insistence on multiple historical trajectories and geographies, understanding television as a communicative space in both material and metaphorical ways. This approach understands place as "always formed through relations

and connections with dynamics at play in other places, and in wider regional, national, and transnational arenas," rather than as a case study (singular or comparative) of a single place understood as a bounded unit and
measured against a universal yardstick.[30] Jan Nederveen Pieterse describes
this theoretical orientation as "translocal culture" (as opposed to "territorial culture"), noting that "translocal culture is not without place (there is
no culture without place), but it involves an *outward looking* sense of place"
(emphasis in the original).[31] Pieterse invokes Massey's famous phrase—"a
global sense of place"—to further explicate his understanding of translocal
culture as co-constitutive across specific contexts.

Such a spatial analysis of television helps identify how the introduction of the medium opened a particular place within which new national
imaginaries could form among White South Africans in two distinct but interrelated ways, one in relation to the world outside South Africa, and the
other in relation to Black South Africans. First, television more thoroughly
included South Africans into a globalizing culture industry and thereby
made White South Africans more aware of their ostracization from the international community. Second, television provided the place within which
Black and White South Africans could begin to conceptualize themselves
within a single national polity.

As they engaged with transnational media flows, South Africans watched
as the Olympics and the World Cup—the two largest sporting events in the
world—went on without them every four years. They became obsessed with
who shot J.R. on *Dallas* and absorbed the *Lifestyles of the Rich and Famous*.
And they watched American liberals and conservatives fight it out on shows
such as *Maude* and *Archie Bunker's Place*.[32] All these experiences heightened
White South Africans' awareness of their exclusion from the international
community while simultaneously increasing their interest in being a part
of that community. In other words, South Africans' inability to engage mu-
tually in the formation of transnational media flows highlighted the *structured* absence of White South Africans from transnational media flows, even
as White South Africans structured the absence of Black South Africans on
domestic television. Indeed, the outside world's preference for Black South
African cultural products (such as the music of Ladysmith Black Mambazo
or Mahlathini and the Mahotella Queens) over White South African cultural exports added to this sense of insult via transnational media flows.

Even more important, the experience of monitoring television was increasingly shared by White and African and Coloured and Indian, by
people across the class spectrum, and by literate and illiterate alike. In spite
of the replication of some of apartheid's power dynamics, the communi-

cative space of television in South Africa nevertheless became the first social space created and shared by all South Africans. Television introduced a
situation where people excluded from the social and political life of the nation through structured absences became visible in new and different ways
by participating—at least indirectly—in the creation of this new communicative space. The experience of this shared space altered individuals' understandings of their own place—both actual and potential—in the social
structure of apartheid and the new political dispensation that followed.

South African Processes of Identification in Flux

My understanding of processes of identification follows the work of many
current scholars by refusing to conceptualize identity as an intrinsic, stable,
discreet entity or attribute that operates on a single level, but rather as a
multiplicity of fluid and shifting processes that overlap and operate simultaneously on political, social, cultural, economic, and legal levels. Identities
take shape only in relation to both individual and collective interactions in
a variety of settings. While recognizing the "pitfalls of identity" as an ana-
lytic concept, Paul Gilroy and Stuart Hall have both written of the necessity
for retaining it, with Gilroy emphasizing the "social workings" of identity
in his phrase "patterns of identification."[33] I have adapted this phrasing to
further emphasize the ongoing *processes of identification,* or what I call *identifications* for short, as a given. Thus the question for scholars becomes how
and why processes of identification shift in certain ways at certain times.
This intrinsic contingency is a particularly important observation for this
project, for I am engaging with racialized identities that were reified and
given attributes for the purpose of political control by the apartheid state.
Indeed, the structured absence of Black South Africans depended on the
false concretization of racialized identities in order to function.

Many scholars have attempted to break down the concept of identity
into various constituent parts, such as political, class, gender, and sexual.
The problem with this approach lies in the very fluidity mentioned above,
not only with an individual's identification with any given label, but also
when those labels cross the boundaries of politics, culture, economics, and
so on. To limit identifications to a single realm of life is to reify the boundaries between these realms and deny the fluidity of both different identifications and their various engagements with social life. As Gilroy has pointed
out, identity "is a junction or hinge concept that can help to maintain the
connective tissue that articulates political and cultural concerns." Gilroy
points out the constitutive relationships among nationality, national iden-

tity, ethnicity, and local and regional identities: "The changing resonance of nationality and the intermittent allure of subnational and supranational identities demand that we note how theorizing identity as sameness unfolds in turn into *a concern with identifications and the technologies that mediate and circulate them*" (emphasis added).[34] Television is, of course, one of the central technologies that mediate and circulate such identifications. So while I am most interested in those moments when identifications intersect with politics, and thus with what many would describe as "political identities," I nevertheless use the more generic term of *identifications* without the adjective *political* in order to indicate recognition of this fluidity. I then use the more precise term *political identifications* only when a given identity is being invoked in an overtly political way.

My approach also acknowledges the observation of many political scientists and social movement theorists, which emphasizes that the mobilization (and I would add *demobilization*) of a given identification is crucial to understanding the political dynamics of any situation. In other words, just because a group may share grievances against another group—be it the state, a business or corporation, an ethnic group—does not mean political action will be taken, or even that the shared grievances will be recognized as such. Indeed, much of social movement theory has focused on what circumstances will make action more or less likely to be taken, just as activists of all ilks have almost always been concerned with the concept of "consciousness raising" and similar constructs for recruiting comrades into struggle.

Here I make a similar claim, but from a decidedly different angle, following the work of Jonathan Hyslop and others: changes in White South African identifications facilitated by television led to the *demobilization* of violent resistance to majority rule.[35] During the decades leading up to the introduction of television and the Soweto Uprising, White South African political identifications were at times splintered into Afrikaner and English-speaking identities and corresponded to support for either the National or United Party, respectively. The political salience of these ethnic identities varied over time, and depended in large part on the issues at hand. For instance, the conflicting identifications between these two language groups shaped the debate around whether television should be introduced. However, Courtney Jung has shown in *Then I Was Black* that over the late-apartheid era a significant shift toward a depoliticization of the split between Afrikaner and English-speaking identities led to a more common political identification of "White" (with subsequent splits in ideology, primarily along "conservative, moderate, or liberal" lines) in relation to the international community and to Black South Africans.[36] This does not mean that White identity was not a salient one prior to the late-apartheid era, but rather that it took on different meanings vis-à-vis both Black South Africans and Afrikaner or English-speaking identifications.[37]

This shift tempered the more extreme elements of previous Afrikaner identifications, particularly the perception of Afrikanerdom as the last outpost of civilization on the Dark Continent, which required segregation for the survival of not only the Afrikaners as a people, but of White Christian civilization as a whole. As a result, the right wing of the Afrikaner community—represented by leaders like Constand Viljoen of the Vryheidsfront (VF-FF, or "Freedom Front") and Eugene Terreblanche of the Afrikaner Weerstandsbeweging (AWB, or "Afrikaner Resistance Movement")—was marginalized in its calls for armed resistance to the democratic changes of the early 1990s. As I will discuss in the sixth chapter, this split reached its apex in the so-called Battle of Bophuthatswana, with the convincing military defeat of the AWB taking place in dramatic fashion on live television, and the resulting decision of Viljoen to participate in the democratic elections.

Unlike some interpretations in the popular press, however, I view the failure of the AWB (and subsequent descriptions of that failure among White South Africans at the time) as reflecting a previously established unwillingness among White South Africans to take up arms—in large part a result of the changes in identifications named above—rather than the cause of that unwillingness. Regardless of whether White South Africans were actually in favor of completely democratic elections, nearly all were averse to the calls for armed resistance from the AWB and the VF-FF by the early 1990s.

Methodology

This book is positioned, in many ways, between the fields of humanities and social sciences through an unusual set of circumstances surrounding historical timing. Most studies that explore processes of identification approach their work primarily in either a historical or contemporary manner, with significant implications for the methodology employed. If one is studying a time period that few of those still living can recall, one is expected to rely heavily on the evidence of archives and other historical methods. Similarly, if one is dealing with contemporary shifts in identifications, one would most likely rely on ethnographic approaches for in-depth analysis or "large-N" surveys and public opinion polling for larger-scale projects.

In this book, however, I examine processes of identification during a time frame that begins several decades back and continues through the present. As a result, many of those who experienced these shifts are still very much alive, yet they are looking back on a time period that has been heavily influenced by the memories of the intervening years. The revision of memories is a particularly challenging conundrum for this study, with the presence of a significant historical rupture—the end of formal apartheid—standing between the beginning of the time period under consideration and the present. As Shula Marks and Stanley Trapido observed just two years after the elections of 1994, it has become exceedingly difficult to find anyone who admits to having supported the National Party, in spite of the fact that they won every national election between 1948 and 1990. Comedian Pieter-Dirk Uys has performed a skit where his alter-ego, Evita Bezuidenhout, travels across the country, desperately trying to find someone, anyone, who supported apartheid; he is, of course, unsuccessful.[38] Ironically, then, the changing processes of identification that I am trying to distinguish are actually masked by those very changes themselves. This work cannot identify such shifts in either purely historical or purely contemporary terms, but must rely on a cross-referencing combination of the two. My research therefore relies on both historical and ethnographic methodologies in the form of extensive interviews and archival work, as well as use of the statistical data of the All Media Product Survey (AMPS).

Interviews have proven to be the method most capable of exploring shifting processes of identification. Research assistants and I conducted more than 100 interviews between August 1999 and July 2006, including a number of instances wherein the same individuals were interviewed multiple times, creating a longitudinal record.[39] Given the focus of this study on White South Africans, all but a handful of these interviews were with people who identified as such. Respondents are therefore identified by their first language (e.g., Afrikaans-speaking or English-speaking) throughout the book if they identify themselves as White, while those who identify as Coloured or African or Asian are identified as such.[40] All names appearing in the text are pseudonyms assigned to interviewees in order to protect their own anonymity and allow them to speak as freely as possible. Where interviewees identify others who are not public figures, such as neighbors or friends, these names have also been changed to pseudonyms. Interviews conducted with Afrikaans-speaking individuals were conducted in the language of their choice; all other interviews were conducted in English.[41] All of the interviews included a set of consistent questions exploring two points in particular: the individuals' and groups' own experiences with television during the period in question, and their impressions of what impact, if any, these experiences may have had on their identifications or world views. These interviews were conducted in a semistructured manner, allowing the interviewee to move the conversation in many different directions while maintaining a consistent set of data gathered across all of the interviews.

Most interviewees were initially identified through the snowball sampling method, wherein one interviewee identifies the name of another possible interviewee, who then identifies a third, and so forth.[42] Care was taken to identify roughly proportional numbers of Afrikaans- and English-speakers, men and women, and representation across multiple generations (categorized as those who were adults at the time of television's introduction in 1976; those who came of age around the time of 1976; and those who grew up with television from their earliest memories).[43] This methodology expressly does not provide a *random* sampling and should not be taken as such. The sample of interviewees was, however, broad enough to identify general trends without using them in isolation to make universal claims. Further, my interviewees were gathered almost exclusively from in and around towns and cities within South Africa due to the greater exposure of these groups to television in the early years, prior to the availability of terrestrial broadcast signals and later satellite television in the more rural areas.[44] One exception that proves this rule is Colin, a fifty-five-year-old English-speaker, who described acquiring an aerial that reached 150 feet into the air in a (mostly unsuccessful) attempt to receive a broadcast signal in a rural area in 1976. This distinction is crucial to understanding the analysis that follows throughout the book: the shifting processes of identification recognized through this research were predominantly a nonrural experience and had a far more profound impact on those White South Africans located in cities and towns, reaching those living in rural areas much more slowly.

Age has proven to be a particularly crucial variable of the research. Those born around or after 1976 described significantly different experiences with television compared to those born before 1976, with the latter group experiencing television quite differently depending on whether they were adults or children at the time of its introduction. Generational differences also proved significant regarding the strength of various racialized identifications; in approaching the elections of 1994, for instance, those who had lived under apartheid for decades consistently reported experiencing the political changes with considerably more trepidation and insecurity.[45] As a result, I have chosen to indicate the age of each of my respondents throughout the text. In order to assist the reader in putting this age in context, I have standardized this identifier to their age in 2004. For reference, then, each respondent's age as it appears in the text is ten years older than he or she would have been at the time of the 1994 elections and twenty-eight years older than at the time of television's introduction in 1976.

In spite of the richness of these ethnographic interviews, they can yield only contemporary views of historical processes; thus other methods have also been necessary to complete the picture. I therefore rely heavily on archival research as well. My work in the SABC's archives focused on documenting the decisions of the television programmers and the degree to which the changing demographics or perceived identifications of different groups were considered in these decisions, as well as records of past programming. Furthermore, the extensive clippings file at the SABC contains thousands of articles on television in South Africa from newspapers, magazines, and other sources. Two additional archives, the National Archives of South Africa in Pretoria and the historical papers collection at the University of the Witwatersrand, contain many documents regarding both private and public controversies surrounding the introduction and early reaction to television within South Africa. I also explored the visual archives located at the Mayibuye Center at the University of the Western Cape.

Finally, I have taken advantage of data from the All Media Product Survey (AMPS) to round out the picture. AMPS is an extremely innovative marketing tool, which was created in the early 1970s to compare mass media exposure to the population across media. In this sense, AMPS is similar to American television's Nielsen ratings, but it measured newspapers, magazines, radio, television, and site-specific media (such as billboards) on a common scale from before the time of television. Because the data in AMPS began to be collected prior to the introduction of television, it has been a particularly fruitful site for before-and-after comparisons, both quantitative and qualitative, as well as comparisons between television and pre-existing media. These historical methods have allowed me to check the retrospective memories that came out of the interviews against information from the time period under examination. Because this work seeks to give as much voice as possible to those interviewed, the other methods involved in my research often play a more silent role in the presentation of that research; these other methods played a central role, however, in forming the analysis explicated here.

Interpreting a Messy World

As Ien Ang, one of the pioneers in the research of transnational televisual flows and the ways in which varied audiences make meaning from those flows, has pointed out, "Viewers' statements about their relation to television cannot be regarded as self-evident facts. Nor are they immediate, transparent reflections of those viewers' 'lived realities' that can speak for themselves."[46] What, then, is the role of the researcher in this process? Ang's insights are worth quoting at length in this regard:

> What is of critical importance, therefore, is the way in which those statements are made sense of, that is, interpreted. Here lies the ultimate political responsibility of the researcher. The comfortable assumption that it is the reliability and accuracy of the methodologies being used that will ascertain the validity of the outcomes of research, thereby reducing the researchers' responsibility to a technical matter, is rejected. In short . . . audience research is undertaken because the relation between television and viewers is an empirical *question*. But the empirical is not the privileged domain where the *answers* should be sought. Answers—partial ones, to be sure, that is, both provisional and committed—are to be constructed, in the form of interpretations.[47] (emphasis in the original)

The theoretical and methodological perspectives outlined in this chapter provide the basis for moving forward with an analysis of media, democratization, and the end(s) of apartheid. My creation and interpretation of this research need to be understood as at best partial answers to complex questions of social change and transnational media flows, made with a deep commitment to the ethical and political responsibilities such interpretations entail. In her argument in favor of ethnographic approaches to audience research, Ang acknowledges the "inherent symbolic violence of any kind of research" but reminds us that retreating from such research as a result only encourages the "dangerous illusion" that we are exempt from such realities "as if it were possible to keep our hands clean in a fundamentally dirty world."[48] It is in this spirit of active engagement with the messiness of reality that *Starring Mandela and Cosby* is written.

CHAPTER TWO

In the Absence of Television

More than 130 nations preceded South Africa in establishing a television service. Unlike nearly every other country without television at the time, South Africa resisted television as a concept long after it had attained both the financial and technological resources to make either commercial or state-owned television broadcasting a reality. South Africa's lack of television prior to 1976 was neither a quirky oversight nor evidence of an unsophisticated Ludditism. Rather, the absence of television was the result of the ruling National Party's ideology of cultural purity combined with the appropriation of cultural imperialism discourses from leftist critiques originating in North America and Western Europe.

The absence of the actual medium of television within the country does not mean that television played no role in the social or political life of South Africa before its introduction. On the contrary, South Africans were very aware of the transnational media flows of television to which they did not have access; television was a structured absence in relation to which political identifications were reflected. Its absence was constitutive rather than pure. Debates around television became a forum in which the growing isolation of the South African nation could be safely discussed by White South Africans without delving into the more important issues of apartheid policies. The structured absence of the medium was constituted by a conceptual understanding of television, which bore only loose resemblance to the medium itself, and came to represent much larger issues within the terrain of South African processes of identification.

The comparatively petty structured absence of television was mirrored by the far more consequential and complex structured absence of Black South Africans in conventional politics in profound ways, both before and after television's introduction. Not unlike the situation with television prior to 1976, Black South Africans were prevented from active participation in conventional politics, yet their distorted presence in the form of a White-constructed understanding of them—the *swart gevaar*, or "Black peril"—dominated politics and public policy.

This chapter briefly sketches the mediascape of South Africa prior to the first fence post—television's introduction—through the debates surrounding television at the time, borrowing heavily from and extending the work of Rob Nixon, in order to explore the National Party's social engineering that perpetuated both apartheid and the banning of television.[1] This chapter also addresses the question of what changed, allowing television to be introduced in 1976. Although my primary concern is the impact of television following its introduction, an understanding of the context within which television was at first prevented—and later introduced—is essential if we are to comprehend the form it took and the results it created after 1976. Subsequent chapters will show the continuing parallels between television and the structured absence of Black South Africans in conventional politics, and the implications of these interactions for White South African identifications leading up to and continuing through South Africa's democratic transition.

Verkrampte Fear and the Banning of Television

The primary constraint on the development of broadcast television infrastructures is most often economic, since the technology itself requires a much larger amount of capital to initiate than other forms of mass media such as radio and print.[2] However, South Africa had established itself as a highly industrialized economic power since the turn of the twentieth century, due largely to massive natural resources of gold, diamonds, and other minerals mined through the exploitation and social engineering first of segregation and then of apartheid.[3] Though the cost of initiating a national television service was certainly formidable, South Africa had adequate resources and infrastructure to create such a service.[4] The lack of television prior to 1976 was instead a direct result of the divisions within South African society as expressed through the state's media policy and the power of the verkrampte (the conservative wing of the National Party).[5]

In *Homelands, Harlem and Hollywood*, Rob Nixon demonstrates that the established political camps of South Africa positioned themselves in the debate surrounding television into three primary categories: the ruling National Party (referred to as the Nationalists or the NP in South Africa), the relatively less conservative United Party (UP), and the variety of social movement organizations in opposition to apartheid.[6] Those readers familiar with South Africa will immediately recognize these three political camps as drawing their overwhelming support from corresponding racial and ethnic categories within South Africa: Afrikaners, English-speaking White South Africans, and Black South Africans, respectively.

Nixon reconstructs an insightful glimpse into the discourse with which the Nationalists rationalized barring the medium, while Carin Bevan has examined the resulting policy debates themselves in particular detail.[7] This discourse was based on an opposition to an unusual combination of ideological foes, with a heavy dose of what might today be called "family values" thrown in. According to Nixon, the Nationalists' opposition to TV was a part of their

> struggle against national "dilution" in all its varieties—through liberal individualism, racial mixing, communism, imperialism, monopoly capitalism, commercialism, and the cosmopolitanism of English-speaking South Africans and the Jewish and Indian diasporas.[8]

It's a dizzying and incongruous set of enemies unless one is familiar with the historical trajectory of Afrikaners within the nation and as represented by the Nationalists. Although this history is far too long and full of interesting turns to do it justice here, it should be noted that the Afrikaners struggled for many years against the British for control of South Africa, leaving the British Cape Colony along the southeastern coast to form the Orange Free State and the South African Republic (ZAR) of the interior in the mid-nineteenth century.[9] After gold and diamonds were discovered in the ZAR, England claimed the ZAR and the Free State for its own, culminating in the South African War at the turn of the century.[10] Hence the Afrikaners have, almost from the beginning, resisted English control with some success and a good deal of failure. Not until the National Party won the 1948 elections did Afrikaner ethnic nationalism succeed in gaining political control over all of South Africa, although economic control still lay largely in the hands of English-speaking South Africans.

This domestic history, combined with the Soviet support of the armed resistance to the South African state, left the Nationalists heavily invested in a siege mentality. The struggle against television became a struggle to retain a pure national identity against both capitalism and communism, the United Kingdom (and the United States by association) and the Soviet Union, individualism and internationalism. Given the power of Cold War international divisions, the Nationalists' insistence on viewing both sides as suspect—combined with their rejection by the nonaligned states because of apartheid—left South Africa a largely isolated political entity.[11]

The effort to maintain the "purity" of the Afrikaner was imagined to face an internal threat as well: racial miscegenation. The fear of miscegenation was linked to television, as given evidence by a particularly interesting fable told to Parliament by Albert Hertzog, the Nationalist Minister of Post and Telecommunications and son of a former prime minister:

> It is afternoon and the Bantu house-boy is in the living room cleaning the carpet. Someone has left the television set on. The house-boy looks up at the screen, sees a chorus line of white girls in scanty costumes. Suddenly, seized by lust, he runs upstairs and rapes the madam.[12]

The fable exposes many layers of racialized fears, from the terror of miscegenation to the myth of Black hypersexuality to an implied inability of indigenous people to view television with a critical eye. But the cautionary tale above becomes more than just a warning to White madams when inserted into parliamentary debate; it reveals the apartheid regime's construction of national identity and the government's resulting need to restrict television in order to protect that construction. The story also shows the extent to which White South Africans, in spite of the nearly ubiquitous physical presence of Black South Africans in their lives as so-called house boys, maids, gardeners, and other kinds of manual workers, viewed Black South Africans as a mostly unfamiliar, "seen but not heard" entity.[13] Black South Africans were viewed in the context of a structured absence.

The fear of miscegenation and the destruction of racial, gender, and economic hierarchies through the power of television was transformed into a particularly powerful trope when extended to international relations, further reifying White South African identifications as one and the same with national identity. Thus television became the great racial and cultural miscegenator via capitalist-communist international imperialism, destined to destroy the White man and his moral superiority as given its purest incarnation in the Afrikaner people. At least one parliamentarian, J. C. Otto, made the argument explicit:

> Liberalists, communists and leftists all use TV to influence people. In many programmes the white man is presented as a bad person, as the suppresser and exploiter of the black man. The white man is depicted as the person causing misery and frustration for the black man. . . . The overseas money

magnates have used television as a deadly weapon to undermine the moral and spiritual resilience of the white man.[14]

For the guardians of apartheid, the coverage of the American civil rights movement on television became proof positive of the medium's evil. Nixon rightly points out that editorialists on both sides of the Atlantic claimed a significant role for television in the civil rights movement's success, regardless of their opinion regarding the positive or negative nature of that success. For example, conservative writer James Burnham wrote a 1966 editorial for the *National Review* that claimed:

> The absence of a native liberation movement in South Africa is equivalent, very nearly, to the enforced absence of television. . . . What is "the civil rights movement," what could it be, apart from the media? The Montgomery bus strike that began its history, the march on Selma that brought it top billing, would have been nothing but a local bus strike and a local marching if it were not for the media; nothing would have constituted them part of a "movement" of historical significance.[15]

Such claims created a good deal of anxiety for the proponents of apartheid, complicated by the already rising ideological interactions between the Black Consciousness movement in South Africa—of which Bantu Steve Biko was the best-known spokesman—and the Black Power movement in the United States.[16]

All of these discursive elements fused to become a massive specter on the Nationalists' horizon. Hertzog himself told Parliament that "inside the pill [of TV] there is the bitter poison which will ultimately mean the downfall of civilizations."[17] Thus the Nationalists fought the battle over television not as a side skirmish, but as central to their very understanding of Afrikaner identity. The structured absences of both television and Black South Africans made space for a phantasmagoric construction of both the medium and the people, as well as of the interactions between the two.

Verligte Defending the Homelands: Separate but Equal

Not all opponents of television utilized such a basic cause-and-effect approach to the medium, however.[18] One of the more interesting strategies Nixon identifies was to co-opt the role of defender of non-White sovereignty. This paternalistic argument used the literal translation of apartheid—apartness—to claim an ideal of separate but equal. In this line of reasoning, television was not a threat to the universal White man or to a more specific Afrikaner identity, but rather to the supposedly fragile yet honorable cultural traditions of the indigenous African peoples themselves, portrayed here as classic noble savages.

These arguments gained strength in the 1960s as the bantustan system gained momentum with the ruling Nationalists. Concepts such as Marshall McLuhan's "global village" reinforced these fears.[19] Nixon quotes journalist Beaumont Schoeman's description of television as a despised "powerful medium of integration":

> TV doesn't respect differences and stresses uniformity. It breaks and loosens up cultures, it sweeps aside borders and eats away at the values of communities. The propagandists call it a powerful agent of democratization which is a sweet-sounding equivalent of calling it an agent of homogenization. . . . Nor is there a more effective instrument for the furtherance of integration.[20]

Then Nixon follows with the words of McLuhan:

> As electrically contracted, the globe is no more than a village. It is this implosive factor that alters the position of the Negro, the teen-ager, and some other groups. They can no longer be *contained*, in the political sense of limited association. They are now *involved* in our lives, as we in theirs, thanks to the electric media.[21] (emphasis in original)

Nationalist leaders were thereby able to justify opposition to television as a threat to indigenous African cultures. The inherent contradictions between the race-war scenario and the protection-of-vulnerable-native-cultures scenario ran throughout the National Party and the apartheid state. The arguments surrounding television also reflected these contradictions and foreshadowed the shifts in both media policy and racialized identities that led to the arrival of television and, eventually, the transition from apartheid. Even before international media products themselves were available inside South Africa, transnational media flows were shaping the political debates within the nation.

The International Status Symbol

Not all White South Africans favored the ban on television. The Nationalists' struggle to keep the medium out of the country was significant in that it was, indeed, a struggle; as always, the hegemony of the ruling discourse was neither complete nor unchallenged. The SABC's *Annual Report* of 1945 indicated that postwar plans included introducing television, but these plans were scuttled after the Nationalists won the 1948 election.[22] The supporters of television remained outspoken and persistent, first requesting its introduction in 1953 and frequently afterwards until they were successful in 1976. Television remained a constant and contentious issue. Its supporters were primarily identified with the United Party (UP), the majority of whose supporters were English-speaking White South Africans.

The role of English-speaking White South Africans in apartheid-era politics has been a consistent source of controversy and remains so today. This group has been viewed by some as consistently opposing the nationalist and isolationist rhetoric of the National Party outlined above, while advocating for a more cosmopolitan and liberal approach to race relations. Critics claim that the UP was provided the easy escape hatch of self-righteousness by the extremism of the Nationalists, while continuing to benefit from the economic and racial policies of apartheid. Both of these claims were evident in the debate concerning television.

The English-speaking press consistently defined the absence of television in South Africa as embarrassing evidence of South Africa's isolated, backwater status. This group of South Africans had always maintained much greater ties to Europe in general and the United Kingdom in particular, often attending British universities or spending some time in the Commonwealth, resulting in both greater sensitivity to international opinion and less affinity to the Afrikaner nationalism of the ruling party. Thus the absence of television came to represent all that was isolated and internationally embarrassing; television was the international status symbol of modernization and civilization that was denied.

Yet this approach was far from free of its own racialized perspective. As Nixon argues, the clamor for television allowed the members of the UP to portray themselves as "outriders of progress and rationality" based on the equating of both Afrikaner and African cultures as "mired in irrationality."[23] This type of argument becomes particularly loaded in the context of African colonial history, with yet another group of White people claiming to carry the flame of civilization into the Dark Continent. What was not mentioned in this argument was the very real possibility that an economically powerful yet politically weakened English-speaking South African community would benefit from, perhaps even control, commercial television if it were introduced.[24]

Perhaps most ironic is the importance which the UP and its supporters placed upon television at a time of fierce state repression against the anti-apartheid movements.[25] The extent to which the UP continued to support the linchpins of apartheid while claiming a progressive role in the struggle for television and, by inference, race relations has been pointed out by several scholars.[26] Nixon goes so far as to call this "displaced shame," citing an ironic statement by the UP:

> The United Party believes that the policies of the Nationalist Government over the years in regard to television have placed South Africa in a humiliating and indefensible position in regard to other countries, and we reject the intolerance, bias and falseness of such policies.[27]

Nixon also cites a 1969 editorial which said "this deprivation has been deliberately imposed on the people of this country. . . . The extent of the stultification to which South Africans have thus been subjected is practically incalculable." These statements are nothing short of ludicrous coming from a party that consistently rejected attempts at real reform of the apartheid system, the source of international condemnation of the South African state. Yet the extremism of the National Party and the "safe technological terrain of TV enabled a group [the UP] that benefited from and (in all important spheres) advocated apartheid, to portray itself as the standard-bearer of a progressive modernity."[28]

Contesting the Airwaves through South African Radio

As we have seen, the major political parties of White South Africa viewed the struggle over television as essential to their understandings of the world and their position within it, as well as tying television to ideas of progressive or conservative politics. However, in spite of the raging controversy surrounding television in South Africa, nearly 85 percent of the population—Black South Africans—remained essentially disinterested in these debates.

Only 1.5 percent of Black homes even had electricity in the mid-1960s. As a result, the introduction of television would most likely have created yet another disparity between White and Black life. More important, the Black communities of South Africa faced minimal wages, disruption of home life due to enforced migrant labor and long commutes, abominable housing conditions, fierce police brutality, and the complete lack of formal political channels to challenge these circumstances, all due to the system of apartheid. It can hardly be surprising that the anti-apartheid movements of South Africa never took up the cry for television as even a remotely high priority.

For Black South Africans, television came much closer to being a pure rather than structured absence. The lack of financial resources to engage in television production, coupled with the Nationalist government's control over broadcasting facilities, left little reason for the anti-apartheid movements to hope that the introduction of television would result in any substantial gains for their cause. Instead, the anti-apartheid movements turned their media attention toward radio, which became a site of contestation between the movements and the apartheid state.

Radio began in South Africa in several places as a scattered, experimental, private medium. Not until the arrival in South Africa of Sir John Reith, the British Broadcasting Corporation's (BBC) founding visionary, on a state-sponsored trip in 1934 were efforts made to organize radio broadcasting in a consistent manner. Reith brought with him the guiding philosophy and model of public service broadcasting on which the BBC was based, and the government followed Reith's suggestions in the founding of the SABC in 1936.[29] The SABC was designed to serve the public interest and to build a national identity, although both this public and this nation excluded Black South Africans. The SABC was also expected to play a role in uplifting the culture of this public; in other words, the SABC was not intended simply to entertain and inform White South Africans, but also to educate them in an effort to "improve" their tastes and preferences.

The result of this English-derived mandate, when applied to South Africa in the period between the South African War and the rise of the National Party, was a broadcasting policy that seemed innocuous and neutral to most English-speaking South Africans. Afrikaners, on the other hand, viewed much of the SABC's programming as an elitist, external assault on their culture. The limited use of Afrikaans on the early SABC and the elevating of European cultural products over local interests exacerbated the sense that the SABC was serving the needs and interests of the English-speaking elite rather than those of the Afrikaners.

With the National Party's rise to power in 1948, the SABC became an early target for the appropriation of the means of cultural production.[30] The degree to which the National Party directly controlled the SABC—as opposed to indirect control through appointments to the board and other means—in the ensuing decades remains an issue of some contention. But regardless of the exact extent of direct party control, there is little dispute that the SABC became a much more unequivocal mouthpiece for the government under the Nationalists, particularly in the 1960s under Meyer's leadership.[31] Given that all radio originating within South Africa was affiliated with the SABC, this new role for the SABC was significant.

Prior to the 1960s, SABC radio was broadcast almost entirely in English and Afrikaans, with a small smattering of the more widely spoken African languages. Yet radio held the potential to reach by far the largest percentage of the population. In a mediascape without television, and within which a sizable portion of the population is not literate (approaching 50 percent in many areas of the country), radio was the most easily—and most commonly—consumed form of mass media by the vast majority of the South African population.

Given this history, the anti-apartheid movements therefore did not view television as a method of engagement in the struggle, favoring instead the cheaper and more accessible medium of radio. Beginning in the 1950s, radio became the medium of choice for forces both inside and outside South Africa hoping to influence the political situation. By 1952 South Africans could receive transmissions from Radio Moscow, and within ten years the country was receiving radio broadcasts in opposition to apartheid from at least eight decolonized African countries, as well as Moscow and Beijing.[32] The introduction of Radio Freedom, broadcast by the ANC in exile over Tanzanian frequencies, caused even greater alarm in the ruling party.

When television was again requested by the UP in 1961, the government insisted instead that funds would be better used to initiate Radio Bantu, which became the government's largest propaganda weapon aimed at the Black population. On Radio Bantu, most of the African languages had their own stations, or at least their own programs. This structure of separate channels for each language fit nicely with apartheid's ideology of separate development, which attempted to subvert African nationalism by claiming that the ethnolinguistic divisions between various groups of Black South Africans (e.g., Zulu, Xhosa, Sotho) were more significant than their similarities.[33] There was no room in Radio Bantu for the fact that many if not most South Africans actually speak a mixture of two or more languages during the course of their day, and often during the course of a single sentence in urban areas.

In a stroke of technological brilliance, the government broadcast Radio Bantu on high frequencies that could be heard on extremely inexpensive FM radios that were far more accessible to the Black population. This meant that for a relatively affordable sum of money the average Black South African could purchase his or her personal radio and tune in to Radio Bantu. This same radio could not, however, pick up transmissions from Radio Freedom or other foreign broadcasts, which needed to use shortwave technology in order to travel the distances required by their locations beyond South Africa's borders. Shortwave radios, unlike their transistor counterparts, were often beyond the financial means of individual Black South Africans.

The structured absence of Black South Africans on SABC radio during this period parallels their structured absence on television in the years following its introduction. First, they were excluded entirely from the conceptualization of the listening audience and, by inference, the nation itself. Later, with the introduction of Radio Bantu, they were included in the audience and as radio personalities as well; however, this inclusion in the listening audience was an explicit exclusion from public life and the nation as a whole through the separate channels of SABC radio. Rather than creating programming for SABC radio that would be shared by Black and White audiences alike, the SABC segregated Radio Bantu onto separate channels, according to its bantustan ideology. The newfound presence of Black South Africans on Radio Bantu as social beings—consumers of music, soap operas, the news, and so on—was predicated on the continuation of the structured absence of Black South Africans as political beings who might take a hand in shaping the news itself. Yet this absence on SABC radio was continually challenged through Radio Freedom and its counterparts.

The dominance of radio as the medium of the so-called masses was so firmly established in the 1950s and 1960s that Hayman and Tomaselli would still claim as late as 1987 that "[i]n modern urban society within a large nation-state, the radio is clearly the medium through which many people experience the world beyond the geographical limits of their daily life."[34] Although this statement is debatable, the authors' claim points to the much larger influence maintained by radio in South Africa even after the introduction of television than elsewhere in the industrialized world. This should not lead us to minimize the impact of television on South Africa, but rather to recognize the importance of understanding the South African mediascape as a whole and radio's role within that mediascape.

Influencing the Elite through Print Media

While radio reached the largest number of South Africans, print media was arguably the most influential among the well-educated elite, both White and Black. The use of print media as a tool of mass communication in South Africa stretches back to broadsheets under colonial rule in the Cape. The influence of modern newspapers in English took hold during the expansion of the British empire to the north and east of the Cape in the latter half of the nineteenth century, and the South African War that resulted from that expansion. Newspapers printed in Afrikaans gained prominence

in the first part of the twentieth century, growing largely out of the Afrikaner nationalist movement that sought to establish Afrikaans as a modern
language tied to Afrikaner identity, rather than a mere dialect or "kitchen-
Dutch" that developed from communication with and among slaves.[35] By
the mid-twentieth century, four companies controlled the vast majority of
print media—both newspapers and magazines—in the nation: the Argus
Group, the South African Association of Newspapers (SAAN), Perskor, and
Nasionale Pers (Afrikaans for "National Press," but more commonly referred to as Naspers).[36] The first two companies published in English and
came to be known as the English press; likewise, the latter two companies
published in Afrikaans and were known as the Afrikaans press.

Although all four companies were members of the National Press
Union and other national press corps bodies, the divisions between the English and Afrikaans press were striking. The Afrikaans press earned a reputation as the more conservative of the two, often playing the role of government envoy, whereas the English press adopted a more liberal stance as the
"fourth estate," often challenging the government though almost always
avoiding too forceful a conflict. In the words of Robert Horwitz, "The English language press in particular operated as an adversarial press mostly
within, but sometimes beyond, the confines of the English-Afrikaner nationalist accommodation . . . and practiced a distinct brand of conservative
liberalism."[37] Both the Afrikaans and English presses had very little overlap in their readership, and as a result the two companies in each grouping
competed primarily against each other, rather than across language barriers.

In addition to the English and Afrikaans presses, a third category of
printed media came to be known as the "African" or "Black" press. The African press traced its roots to the newspapers and newsletters connected to
missionaries in the nineteenth century. These were followed by a small resistance press, which took shape around the turn of the twentieth century
and into the 1930s and took a much more explicitly political view in line
with the petit-bourgeois leadership of groups like the ANC (at that time).
African newspapers reached their peak in 1930, with nineteen papers officially recognized by the government. This number dropped to only seven
in the following quarter century due to increased state repression and economic depression. More significantly, the seven periodicals that survived
were all owned by White South Africans, unlike the earlier heyday of the
African press.[38]

The most famous of these seven periodicals, the monthly magazine
Drum, tentatively sought to engage Black politics along with its cutting-edge
features on writing and music, but remained a more significant part of the

cultural rather than the explicitly political realm for Black South Africans. Likewise the tabloid *Golden City Post*, owned by the Argus Group from 1964, dabbled in politics only occasionally. With the alternative press—associated with the rise of the Black Consciousness movement and post–Soweto Uprising resistance politics—yet to emerge, the African press tended to minimize issues that its ownership might deem too controversial.[39] Thus the structured absence of Black South Africans in conventional politics remained intact, at times enforced from the outside and at times maintained through fear of reprisal.

Print media did offer South Africans, Black and White alike, the widest diversity of content and perspectives to be found among the various media. Yet South Africa's high rates of illiteracy and lack of a "reading culture" meant that most print media was (and still is) unable to reach a majority of the South African population. In addition, because of the ways in which print media maintains social divisions through the exclusions of language, age-specific content, and physical production, for example, coupled with the extremely limited circulation of titles that reached beyond the safe confines of the major printing houses, print media never had the same ability to expand the outlook of the general populace afforded by other forms of media. Like radio, print media formed an important part of the South African mediascape prior to television's introduction in 1976, but it was unable to provide the larger transformations in the social fabric to which television contributed.

The Explicit Structuring of Absence through "the Ban"

More than 100 laws were passed between 1950 and 1990 restricting the operation of South African mass media, which significantly altered the mediascape of the time.[40] These laws ranged from outlawing publications to active censorship of the news to requiring journalists to reveal their sources. With regard to broadcast media, legislation also demanded that the SABC "shall broadcast nothing which may inflame public opinion or may directly or indirectly lead to any contravention of the law or may threaten the security of the state."[41] Media law in apartheid South Africa was extensive and contentious, and deserves a great deal of attention, but for the purposes of this work I will deal only with the most infamous of these legal restraints, known as "the ban."

When imposed on an individual, the ban made it illegal for that person's face or words to be printed or broadcast, or for that person to be present in any gathering of more than three people. The ban made any dissident placed under it (and many were) a *persona non grata*. She or he literally disappeared from public life during the course of the ban. When imposed on a publication, it became illegal for that publication to be possessed, distributed, or reproduced. Even the structured absence of the ban was not absolutely effective; individuals often broke (or attempted to break) banning orders, just as underground pamphlets, posters, and even videotapes were often produced.[42] Perhaps most ironically, a publication could not be banned until after it had been published, thus allowing periodicals and other texts to be published and distributed to their readers, even if they were sure to be banned at a later point in time. Similarly, banned individuals and organizations often found ways to fly under the radar of the apartheid state and continue to organize within Black communities.

Nonetheless, the ban became a powerful tool for enforcing the structured absence of Black South Africans in the political life of apartheid South Africa. Only through the ban could Nelson Mandela, long after achieving the highest profile of any political prisoner in the world, walk through the streets and malls of the Western Cape unrecognized in the months preceding his release.[43] The ban more often than not prevented Black South African political leaders not only from fully participating in conventional politics on a level playing field, but also from even entering the pitch at all. Although Black political leaders may have been able to maintain a presence within their own communities, they were effectively removed from the political world of the nation as a whole, controlled as it was by the institutions and elites of White South Africa. Ironically, the banning of nearly all Black South African political leaders created a kind of vacuum in White perceptions of Black life, a vacuum that would be filled, in part, by television.

The Third Technological Revolution

The SABC appointed a commission in 1969 to explore the viability of television in South Africa. Dr. Piet Meyer, the head of the SABC and one of the leading ideological opponents of television throughout the 1950s and 1960s, headed the commission stacked with members of the Broederbond.[44] The commission concluded its work in 1971 and released a report recommending the introduction of television, though it would be another five years before the service was unveiled.[45] What led Meyer and the Broederbond to reverse their decision regarding television?

The answer most often given is a classic example of elite divisions as theorized by the political process model.[46] The National Party had been experiencing increasing tensions between the verkrampte and the verligte and, in 1969, South Africa underwent a shift in elite political alignments. Prime Minister B. J. Vorster (one of the verligte who rose to party leadership following the assassination of Hendrik Verwoerd in 1966) expelled Hertzog from the cabinet; in response, Hertzog and other conservatives formed the Herstigte Nasionale Party (HNP). The Broederbond itself was split, but eventually landed on the side of the verligte, reducing Hertzog's new party to a peripheral force. Suddenly, Meyer and the Broederbond were no longer disparaging the poison of television, but instead advocating for its use in maintaining social control. According to this narrative, the split in the National Party allowed an increasing number of successful Afrikaner capitalists to join in the call for the international status symbol of television, thus paving the way for its introduction.

Although elite splits undoubtedly impacted the introduction of television and its timing, other factors were also at work—factors that problematize a simple political process model reading of the situation. As one group of scholars pointed out:

> It is commonly thought that the eventual introduction of television so many years after its appearance in the rest of the world was largely because that arch-recalcitrant, Albert Hertzog, who had opposed television, was banished to the political wilderness by the National Party. In fact, many more complex processes were at work and would have overshadowed Hertzog even if he had remained in the Cabinet.[47]

These scholars highlight what they term the "third technological revolution" (borrowed from Ernest Mandel), particularly the development of satellite technology, which was made operational in 1969. With this technology any South African who could afford to purchase a satellite dish and television set would soon have access to the wonders and debauchery of television, regardless of "whether or not South Africa was formally locked into the world television grid."[48]

Even worse from the government's perspective, television would be produced not by White South Africans for White South Africans, but by foreign sources. All of the Nationalists' worst fears of television's impact now lay outside the control of the party due to a material technological development beyond their political jurisdiction. This fear was made explicit by the Meyer Commission in its report advising the introduction of television:

> In a world rapidly approaching a stage where direct reception of television transmissions from overseas sources via satellites will become a reality, South

Africa must have its own television service in order to nurture and strengthen its own spiritual roots, to foster respect and love for its own spiritual heritage and to protect and project the South African way of life as it has developed here in its historical context.[49]

The material development of satellite technology forced the Nationalists' political hand, giving them the choice of producing their own television or having it inflicted upon them by foreigners. The risk of uncontrolled transnational media flows suddenly overshadowed the dangers of television itself.

Media Events and International Inclusion

In addition to the third technological revolution and elite divisions in the National Party, Nixon introduces another element that calls into question both of these explanations as the impetus for introducing television: the desire on the part of South Africans to be included in simultaneously broadcast international media events.[50] Nixon rightly focuses on the Apollo moon walk as the defining moment that left an increasingly internationally minded South African elite—Afrikaners included—"reduced to twiddling the dials on their wirelesses" while 800 million people around the world watched Neil Armstrong:

> More dramatically than any prior event, the moon landing impressed upon people TV's power to produce the sensation of simultaneous, "global" community. . . . In that act, a moment of audiovisual idealism—TV at the zenith of its powers—fused with a moment of transcendental incorporation, the "family of man" seeing itself observed from a divine angle of vision.[51]

Yet South Africans were left out of this global event, an exclusion that meant a great deal more in 1969 to an increasingly cosmopolitan Afrikaner as well as English-speaking community than it might have twenty years earlier. This exclusion had the effect of threatening "both their technological self-assurance and their sense of racial superiority."[52] The structured absence of transnational media flows became, in a media event instant, exceptionally visible.

Although Nixon uses this example to highlight the importance of international exclusion, his illustration also points toward the role of changing identifications in paving the way for television. White South Africans' concern for inclusion in the international community of nations stemmed from a shift away from the isolationist identifications of the past and toward a process that was increasingly defined vis-à-vis the rest of the world. The choice to institute television came in part from the National Party verligte's attempt to claim and give shape to a wider shift in political identifications, one in which the old isolationism was being supplanted by an updated Afrikaner identification that was more comfortable in the wider world, albeit within a conservative nationalist understanding of that world.

Thus we see, on the eve of television's introduction, the beginning of a change in White South African processes of identification that were later shaped and accelerated by television itself. The third technological revolution and South Africa's exclusion from media events indicate a role for material and cultural factors leading to the introduction of television, in addition to the role played by changing political alignments among the elite. More important, the combination of these cultural, political, and technological factors provide a first intimation of the changes in White South African identifications to come.

Did Television Enhance or Subvert the Hegemony of Apartheid?

Throughout the debates preceding television's introduction into South Africa, outside observers were often surprised by the state's reluctance to embrace the medium's potential for propaganda, a stance that persists in some historical accounts. For instance, Bevan states as recently as 2008 that "[i]f the NP government were able to control the existing media, surely the material broadcast over South African television could be censored as well, and the effect of foreign ideologies could be curtailed."[53] This perspective views technological advances in communication as strengthening the state's ability to disseminate and control images of nationhood and itself, thus buttressing the state's power.[54] Indeed, this approach was adopted by the ruling party after—but only after—it became clear that they could not completely prevent television from entering South Africa through satellite technology.

The claim that the Nationalists' hands were tied by satellite technology, and that they had no choice but to institute television, explains just part of the story. The National Party's policy shift can only be fully explained by also taking into account the beginnings of the realignment in White South African identifications described above. As White South Africans became increasingly concerned with their standing in the rest of the world, processes of identification began to modify; the introduction of television is thus best understood as a partial effect of these changing identifications, as well as a precipitating cause of future changes. The structured absence of television in South Africa gave way in 1976, but the structured absence of Black South Africans in conventional politics persisted. It would take many years to chip away at the more insidious exclusion of Black South Africans from political life. Through each of the upcoming fence posts, I show the role of television in continuing the transformation of these identifications and their relationships to politics in a process that was full of contradictions and contingencies, but that nevertheless cleared the way for the particular form of political transition that South Africa experienced.

South Africa's television history is unique in that opposition to the medium largely exhausted itself before television's introduction; in most of the rest of the world, arguments against television arose only after it had been established. As a result, few scholars have paid much attention to television after it came to South Africa. Did television's introduction fulfill the earlier fears of the Nationalists, destroying social hierarchies and mixing the races? Or was the apartheid state successful in using television to further consolidate state power and hegemony as many outsiders feared it would?

CHAPTER THREE

"They Stayed 'til the Flag Streamed"

On January 1, 1976, the South African Broadcasting Corporation began airing television on a single channel, SABC Television One (TV1), evenly split between Afrikaans and English for five hours each evening. The fierce political competition prior to television's introduction led to an ironic silence following that very introduction. Apart from a handful of negative letters to the editors of various newspapers and the occasional op-ed piece, the printed press carried very little opposition to television as a medium. The voices in opposition to television rang with a hollow sort of old-fashioned rhetoric that could easily be dismissed as behind the times and almost humorous in its lack of relevance, fighting a battle that had already been lost. In addition, the lag time between the Meyer Commission's decision to introduce television in 1971 and its actual implementation—due to the insistence of the SABC to wait for the technology to create a nation-wide, color system—created a sense of inevitability around television for most South Africans.[1] The fight over television's social role was, in effect, long past by the time the medium itself arrived. The speed with which television gained acceptance among the general populace of South Africa is remarkable given the political resistance prior to its inception.

Television generated a great deal of excitement initially, causing the focus of debate to shift quickly away from whether the medium of television was inherently bad for South African culture and identity and toward questions of content. This shift was ideal for the apartheid regime, for it cleared the way for control of televisual content—through censorship, appointments to the SABC and its board of directors, and similar methods—in the name of apartheid ideology. Although the regime continued to give lip service to issues such as free speech and other democratic freedoms, the stage was set for increasing control of media content, particularly on television, by the apartheid state.

For the typical viewer, the primary concern regarding television's arrival dealt less with political ideology or issues of free speech, but rather the level of entertainment value it provided. With the exception of some excellent children's programming, one sentiment regarding early television in South Africa appears to be nearly unanimous: the quality of the programming itself was less than stellar. This impression was exacerbated by the fondness of the SABC for dubbing American programming such as *The Waltons, Starsky and Hutch,* and *The Love Boat* into Afrikaans. In the same way that American audiences laughed at—but continued to watch—the slightly mis-synchronized speech of Japanese actors in the Godzilla movies that were once ubiquitous on American television, South African audiences (including Afrikaans-speakers) tended to find the dubbing of American television and film characters simultaneously distracting and compelling. In spite of the fact that the production values of domestically produced television were nowhere near the level of programming imported from outside the country, both domestic and imported television nonetheless quickly captured the imaginations of South Africans; the tap of transnational televisual flows had been turned on.

Marketing statistics for the time period show that television sets were purchased at a surprisingly rapid rate by White South Africans given their exorbitant cost (the equivalent of nearly US$1,000) created by the government's insistence that sets be produced domestically, even if under the name of a foreign company, in order to boost local industry. The cost of a set remained far above what many if not most White South Africans could afford, and completely out of the reach of almost every Black South African.[2] Rather than preventing South Africans from viewing television, however, the high cost of the equipment led to a much more communal experience of watching television—somewhat similar to the very early years of the medium in the United States. Nearly all the White South Africans interviewed reported that their first experience with television was with large groups of friends or relatives in the home of the only family with television "on the block" or "in the neighborhood." Likewise, many Black South Africans first watched television in *shebeens* or on street corners, often powered by a car battery since most townships were not yet electrified.[3]

Test Patterns and Shop Windows

Many South Africans recall their excitement not only when programming began, but even at watching the test patterns, those once-familiar vertical color stripes from the days when television stations were not broadcasting twenty-four hours a day. Whether the televisions were in shop windows or in homes, observing the test patterns for some length of time—a remarkably consistent experience for interviewees—marked a profound sense of anticipation around the medium itself, irrespective of the quality or type of content eventually broadcast through television. This excitement comes out clearly in both the language used and the stories told by respondents when describing their first experiences with television.

Steven, a forty-year-old English-speaker, recalled that his family received a television set in 1975 because of his father's work with Barclay's Bank, which financed one of the local producers of sets. At that time the SABC had begun broadcasting the test pattern. According to Steven, "We got one of the first [sets], and certainly one of the first locally; people used to come to dinner parties to watch five minutes of test broadcast." Jean, a thirty-eight-year-old English-speaker, described herself as "very excited" about television:

> We were one of the first families to get one and it was "Wow." . . . The engineer came to install it and my mum told me he was just trying it out and it wasn't going to stay. How cruel parents are! I watched the test pattern for about an hour.

Susanna, a forty-two-year-old Afrikaans-speaker, recalled her own jealousy toward people like Jean and Steven who had television sets in their homes, but still had similar experiences with the test patterns in public places: "I saw a TV in a shop window. It had the test panel . . . on—I stared at it for a long time."

After the SABC began broadcasting content beyond the test patterns, the sense of wonderment continued for nearly all of those interviewed, and the precedent of watching through shop windows and during gatherings in homes continued. Marike, a sixty-four-year-old Afrikaans-speaker, said:

> I remember very well that everyone went to the shops where the television sets were switched on the whole night, so that they could see what was going on, because many people of course didn't have television at all for a long time. But then they stood at the furniture shops with the TV set on in the shop and they all watched through the window. . . . I think there was amazement. Absolute amazement. We couldn't believe it. . . . Everyone was there. Everyone who lived there. Everyone. All colours. You just couldn't walk past. You stopped when there was a TV set on in the window.

Whether on the street or in homes, television monitoring almost always took place with fairly large groups of people. Margaret, a forty-year-old English-speaker, said, "Everyone on the street watched in our home." Harry, a twenty-eight-year-old English-speaker, remembered that "all our friends from the neighborhood would go to the Coetzees' house to watch TV, often fifteen kids or more. Most houses in the 'hood still did not have TV, even though it was thoroughly middle class." Marelize, a thirty-one-year-old Afrikaans-speaker, also recalled childhood memories of television with friends:

> Our neighbors got TV before we did, and we were only allowed at night, after dinner and after we had taken a bath, to go, in your pajamas and night gowns, to the neighbors to watch *Heidi*. . . . It was magic, seeing the pictures on a screen like that.

Monitoring television at others' homes was so common, in fact, that it was the subject of a wordplay—"seeing TV by the pal system"—which plays off the acronym for South Africa's broadcasting technology, Phase Alternate Line, or PAL.[4]

Many other elements from the early days of SABC television became entrenched in the memories of interviewees, such as the on-screen clock that would count down the final minutes to the evening broadcast, leading to great anticipation particularly among children, or the opening of each broadcast with scripture readings and/or a prayer, most often by a conservative *dominee* or pastor.[5] But it remains the social aspect of early television monitoring that South Africans recalled most clearly. These two facets—the ritualized ingredients of each broadcast and the social viewing patterns— are combined in a common phrase to describe when guests have stayed late that refers to the closing shot of each night's broadcast: an image of the South African flag waving in the breeze while the national anthem, "Die Stem," played in the background. According to Marike:

> We still have the proverb to this day, when people come to visit and stay late, then you say they "stayed 'til the flag streamed." They don't go home until the last amen and "God Save the Queen" is played. You know what I mean— "Die Stem," not "God Save the Queen."

Though both the excitement around its introduction and the tendency to view it within large groups of people wore off over time, particularly as television sets themselves became more common, the early years of television in South Africa nonetheless pose two significant challenges to common assumptions involving television and social life. First, the highly social context in which television was viewed during this time undercuts the common claim in media studies that television as a medium fractures us into residential units as we watch in our individualized living rooms. While this may be a more common practice in today's South Africa than in 1976, it remains far less so than in North America. These observations point to the fact that monitoring television is not intrinsically an individualistic activity, any more so than other media or performance art. As the experiences related above show, television can be a profoundly social experience in some contexts. Second, the excitement around television as a medium—to the point of dinner parties arranged around watching a test pattern, or contemporary equivalents like viewing parties around major sports events or reality television finales—indicates an awareness of television's social character that goes beyond merely another method of conveying content. White South Africans had a sense early on in their experiences with television that it would expand the scope of their lives and their place in the world, even if they remained unsure what direction it would take.

Monitoring television in groups complicates any attempt to control the transmission of an ideology or hegemonic discourse through the medium. If that discourse resonates with the audience receiving the message, then the audience members may reinforce each other's perceptions of the accuracy or preferability of that discourse in conversations during and after the actual viewing of the program. However, if some members of the collective audience take issue with the dominant discourse and share that disagreement with each other, then the collective nature of the monitoring experience can actually disseminate counterdiscourses through social networks and speed the creation of shared dissonance in relation to the intended message.

The Soweto Uprising on Television

Less than six months after it went on the air, SABC television was faced with the first of countless political conundrums to come in the ensuing decades: how to cover political protest and violence. On June 16, 1976, schoolchildren gathered in the township of Soweto outside of Johannesburg to protest the imposition of Afrikaans as the language of instruction in schools.[6] After assembling in various parts of the township, separate groups of students converged to become a single mass, at which point the police confronted them. By all accounts, the police fired live ammunition at the children unprovoked. The township exploded in violence that quickly spread to other regions of the country and lasted several months, costing hundreds of lives. This violence came to be known as the Soweto Uprising. What started as a peaceful local protest rapidly came to signify the end of apartheid's relatively unchallenged status within the nation—a moment now commemorated every year on June 16 as a national holiday called Youth Day.

This confluence of the new medium of television and the unanticipated increase in overt resistance to apartheid policies marks our first fence post. In the hours and days following the start of the Uprising, the SABC found itself unprepared to handle such a situation. Their initial response was to show footage from the scene, including images of police shooting at schoolchildren, with a voiceover that emphasized the threat supposedly posed by the unarmed youth. The SABC, however, had little experience with the power of images and failed to take into account the possibility that their voiceover might not have the effect they intended. Longtime ANC activist Father Michael Lapsley recalls watching the initial news coverage of the Soweto Uprising at the University of Natal in Durban with a group of students, several of whom were so moved by the images that they immediately set off for Soweto, several hundred kilometers away.[7]

While there is no evidence that this reaction was widespread, it demonstrates that viewers construct their own interpretations from images, in conjunction with but not determined by narration, conversations with fellow audience members, and their own experiences and knowledge of the issues at hand. After coming to this same realization, the SABC became far more selective in its choice of images as the Uprising continued. The news coverage became more and more sanitized and the documentary department was denied permission to produce a series on the unrest, with the SABC justifying its stance as avoiding "falling into the trap—as has happened so often in other parts of the world—of [television] being an instrument for promoting unrest and panic."[8] As a result, very few of the respondents in this study recalled direct impressions from coverage of the Soweto Uprising unless they were already highly attuned to politics. Instead, broader, more conceptual memories came to the fore. For instance Steven, who was eleven years old at the time, said that the Soweto Uprising was the first time he learned that Black South Africans were a majority in the country.[9] A group of geographers at the University of the Witwatersrand later described the Uprising as a wake-up call regarding how little they knew of township life, prompting questions such as "How did those angry people on our television screens make a living?"[10]

The nearly simultaneous introduction of television and occurrence of the Soweto Uprising—a coincidence that helped inspire this book—appear to have little direct relationship (such as television coverage inspiring the Uprising or significantly stoking ongoing protests after it began) but profound long-term consequences. White South Africans' reactions to both television and the Uprising give us some indication of the direction future interactions between television and politics would take. The SABC's fumbled handling of the first couple of hours of the Uprising, combined with a widespread acceptance of television as a medium, led to a shift toward greater political attention to controlling the content of television. Meanwhile, White South Africans' views of their country, their world, and themselves were beginning to take into account a broader context—including the lives of Black South Africans and transnational media flows, albeit in limited ways—through the medium of television.

"South Africa is not a mixed society and we shouldn't pretend to show it as such."

Television One was explicitly and unequivocally intended for White South Africans only. As a result, "the portrayal of blacks on television was initially excluded completely," according to Keyan Tomaselli and Ruth Tomaselli, "the rationale being that they would have their 'own' channel at a later date." Later on, TV1 would occasionally show Black South Africans, but only if "they fulfilled their accepted roles in the division of labour; for example, as domestic servants, labourers or mine workers, and the occasional affluent individual."[11] In the words of one former "Organiser," a middle-management position instituted by the SABC to run interference between television producers and upper-level administration, "[The Head of English TV] was always adamant in his belief that South Africa is not a mixed society and said that we shouldn't pretend to show it as such."[12] In this sense the structured absence of Black South Africans on TV1 was nearly absolute.

The mechanisms by which South African television's content was controlled, as well as the loopholes in that system, have been dealt with thoroughly and compellingly elsewhere.[13] Of most significance for this book is the presumption of Black South Africans' absence from televisual content. Because this absence needed to be actively structured, a large number of topics and genres were immediately off-limits to producers. Coupled with residual Nationalist ideological fears of television's impact, the result was a schedule that relied heavily on news (covering parliamentary politics and events that primarily impacted White South Africans), cultural, religious, and educational programming. Educational shows are remembered remarkably warmly, especially those in Afrikaans (perhaps because they were locally produced), by both those who grew up with them and those who were already adults at the time. One program in particular, *Haas Das se Nuuskas*, an Afrikaans show featuring a rabbit presenting the news, was mentioned by nearly every interviewee, regardless of race or first language.

The voice of Haas Das was performed by an icon of early South African television, Riaan Cruywagen. Cruywagen was also the news reader at the time and continues to serve in that role on occasion today, following a popular outcry over the planned termination of his contract in 2003. Like *Haas Das se Nuuskas* and *Wielie Walie* (the educational program within which *Haas Das se Nuuskas* appeared), Cruywagen was mentioned by nearly every respondent as part of their memories of that time; Cruywagen, however, received more mixed reviews than his long-eared alter ego. Jessica, a thirty-five-year-old English-speaker, reported that she and her family would watch television at the neighbors, but "all I remember watching was a man with a very red face reading the news." Marelize, an Afrikaans-speaker, also remembered Cruywagen distinctly: "the news was dominated by a strong White male who reminded me of our pastor in church." She continued by adding a gender analysis of her memories of Cruywagen:

> So I suppose, now reflecting on it, that it influenced the amount of "power" and authority that White men had in my culture—in fact, I am still more likely to have my say in English than in Afrikaans, and I do feel more in control in a work environment if I speak in English. It's almost as if me being successful at work and speaking Afrikaans (if I did) would clash in my mind.

Marelize later added a more humorous twist to Cruywagen's iconic status, warning that "if one watches TV you end up mesmerized by Riaan Cruywagen's wig and that's no way to live."

Cruywagen came to represent White male power and privilege to Black as well as White South Africans. Musa, a thirty-one-year-old African, said, "I remember the six o'clock news with Riaan Cruywagen and the entire street congregating in our tiny living room. Initially [watching television] was a social event with the entire street packed in our living room." Musa's quote reveals that, not surprisingly, Black South Africans also tuned in to the SABC signal, even if it was not intended for them. Indeed, although TV1 refused to recognize their Black viewership, Black South Africans watched the channel from the beginning. This development may not have had a profound impact on Black South Africans' views of their White counterparts; they had, after all, been working in the homes and businesses of White South Africans for decades, and thereby been forced to accommodate some awareness of White South Africans' ways of life. However, the Black viewership of TV1 does point toward the limits of controlling who consumes a broadcast signal, an issue that becomes crucial later in this analysis. Likewise, the shared iconic status of Cruywagen, *Haas Das se Nuuskas*, *Wielie Walie*, and other early South African programming also exposes the limited and contingent nature of structured absences. Try though they may, the apartheid regime was never able to completely exclude Black South Africans from participating in the social life of the nation.

"We were forced to realize that the rest of the world did not behave as we did."

Although it would take some time for the monitoring of television across racialized groups to impact South African identifications, another influence of television was far more immediate—the broadening of White South Africans' worldviews. This influence was in part symbolic, as a result of the previous political positioning of television as a cosmopolitan international status symbol, but those interviewed also described television as a major stimulus in their understanding of South Africa in an international context through transnational media flows. This context did not need to be explicitly political for White South Africans to realize the degree to which they had been insulated and isolated from the wider world prior to 1976, or to recognize South Africa's pariah status. For example, the televised Olympics were not explicitly politicized programming, yet the absence of a South African team—particularly in a nation as sports-minded as South Africa—was instantly apparent.

South Africa's rejection by the international community was also highlighted through television by the British actors' union, Equity, and its interdiction preventing the BBC and Independent Television (ITV) from exporting programs to South Africa that included Equity members.[14] Since the United Kingdom was the nation with which many White South Africans, particularly English-speakers, had the closest ties, the denial of the bulk of British programming was a significant slap in the face to many South Africans.[15] In addition, the interdiction took place in 1975, just in time for the advent of South African television, thus effectively limiting the SABC's imported English-language programming almost entirely to shows produced in the United States.[16] Because television shows are much cheaper to import than to produce, large amounts of American programming were purchased in order to reserve the bulk of the SABC's production budget for programs in Afrikaans—which could not be imported because the language is not dominant in any nation outside of southern Africa.[17] Thus transnational media flows related to television began to circulate through the country with the introduction of television, but those flows were contingent and still shaped by nationally defined media policies and practices.

Programming from the United States marked another, less explicitly political difference between White South Africans as they observed the more consumerist, liberal lifestyles portrayed on their television sets. As described by Jonathan Hyslop, "Television programmes reflecting the relatively liberal ethos of the 1970s in America were dramatically out of kilter with prevailing white South African representations of race, gender and sexuality."[18] This disjuncture forced White South Africans to reconcile their own understandings of the world with those being presented on television; they could no longer take for granted the received notions of their own worldview.

A growing awareness of the world outside South Africa and differences between the lifestyles of South Africans and others, as well as the nation's pariah status, were shared across generations, much more so than some of the other influences of television identified here. For instance, consider Marike's description of her experience of television:

> I suppose I got more of the feeling that I'm just a speck of dust. The world is so large. I still think about TV—did then and still do now—that TV allows me to see things that I would never be able to see for myself. . . . Definitely a wonderful thing. . . . Yes, you realise how large the world really is. Not just this country—the whole world, because you see and hear so much more. You realize that you're just a small cog in the machine.

Compare her experience with that of Jessica, more than twenty-five years younger than Marike, who said, "[Television] opened up a whole new world to me. . . . I lived through my television set, I loved it . . . it is part of the reason I became a scientist." Steven also said that television "made me aware of many other world events," while William, a thirty-eight-year-old English-speaker, said, "[Television] helped reduce the sense of isolation from the rest of the world, and it changed family and community life. I think it also created desires for experiences and possessions that we hadn't known about before." This reduction of isolation concurrent with new desires connected to a larger world view provided the seeds for a fundamental realignment of White South African identifications, one much more concerned with the views of others outside of South Africa.

Television not only opened new worlds to White South Africans, but also brought with it a sense of South Africa's difference in relation to those other realities. Pieter, a sixty-six-year-old who was raised fully bilingual (one parent Afrikaans-speaking, one English-speaking), remembered a sense of inadequacy "as our family who could travel overseas came back and told us how interesting and informative TV was and how backward we were in SA."[19] Even after television arrived in South Africa, Pieter still sensed that "the developed world was some twenty years ahead of us in the introduction and development of TV." Jean, more than twenty-five years younger than Pieter, shared this sense of difference through television but tied it specifically to racialized identities: "I think [television] did [have an impact] because we were forced to realize that the rest of the world did not behave as we did, with apartheid, servants, garden boys, racial terror and the 'normal' events of our lives." Susanna also connected television to a newfound sense of South Africa's unusualness around race, concluding that television "certainly broadened my horizons from growing up in a narrow minded, sheltered community."

Being conscious of your own difference does not and should not automatically lead to a realignment of your own identifications or behavior to remove that difference. Nonetheless, the role of television—both as a technological form and as the source of transnational media flows—in making White South Africans more aware of the dissimilarity between their lives and the lives of many others across the globe provided a critical step toward rethinking their own identifications. What once was merely a vague understanding that South Africa faced disapproval abroad suddenly became a much deeper and more visceral rejection experienced through, and in some cases on, television. As Hyslop describes it,

> white South Africans, whether they sought to embrace or resist change, had to create new narratives of the self. Especially (but not exclusively) amongst NP supporters and "reformist" whites, this re-narrativization of personal history took place in a manner which suggested that a global audience was being addressed.[20]

Whether individuals chose to accept or reject the criticism coming from outside the country, television's heightening of that criticism's role in the nation's social life forced White South Africans to consider their choices more directly.

The Ambivalence of Television's Advent in South Africa

The introduction of television did not shatter either apartheid ideology or the apartheid state overnight. Nor did it become a tool for the National Party to seal the seams of its hegemony, making resistance permanently futile. Instead, this first fence post began a slow process of restructuring White South Africans' social spaces, in turn altering their views of themselves in relation to other South Africans and the rest of the world. Coverage of the Soweto Uprising confirmed the state's ability to manage broadcasts to their liking, but the Uprising still reached White South Africans as a qualitatively different experience than previous unrest because of the nature of televisuality. More important, White South Africans enthusiastically gathered together to experience the new medium and thereby participated in the social construction of a new communicative space made possible by television's technological abilities. White South Africans were particularly aware of sharing this space with people around the world, thereby significantly broadening their frames of reference and providing the catalyst for a reshaping of their own identifications. Although Black South Africans were denied an *overt* presence in this communicative space, they also participated, inhabiting perhaps the only social space shared by all South Africans. Black South Africans monitoring "White television" foreshadowed the phenomenon yet to come of White South Africans channel surfing into "Black television," thus further expanding their perception of the communicative space of television.

CHAPTER FOUR

Surfing into Zulu

Although the Soweto Uprising was eventually squelched through fierce state repression, its aftershocks have been felt throughout the following decades. The aftermath of the Uprising resulted in a groundswell of support for the anti-apartheid movements within the country and the rapid escalation of various kinds of sanctions against the apartheid regime from the international community. Massive numbers of young Black South Africans left the country to join the armed wings of the resistance (most notably Umkhonto we Sizwe [MK], the armed wing of the ANC, and the Azanian Peoples' Liberation Army [APLA], the armed wing of the PAC), often located in the recently liberated Frontline States, which were themselves hostile to the apartheid regime.[1] Many others—particularly those who could afford to or had arranged sponsorship through an international church or aid organization—emigrated in order to pursue a quality education, which had become nearly impossible for Black South Africans within the apartheid system of "Bantu Education." These young students in turn became powerful sources of information and influence among students in North America and Western Europe. The pressure on the apartheid government was mounting on all sides. Although it was by no means clear at the time, the Soweto Uprising is now recognized as the beginning of the end of apartheid.

This revolution, however, was not to be televised—at least in South Africa itself. In the midst of this tension, television offered a sanitized version of South African life to the White audiences at which it was aimed. As discussed earlier, television established itself as a popular medium that maintained essentially the same structure it held at the time of its genesis and in the years following its introduction. Although both the number of broadcast hours and the variety of programming increased, TV1 continued to alternate between Afrikaans and English, with news and religious programming of a conservative bent, and both domestically produced and imported entertainment. Television continued to be aimed solely at White audiences, with very few Black people, particularly Black South Africans, appearing outside of occasional news reports or in subservient roles. Not only was news largely sourced from international events or carefully neutralized domestic issues, but much of the entertainment was either imported from outside the country (often dubbed into Afrikaans) or cautiously erased Black South Africans' presence in any significant role.[2] Thus the early years of television did little to alter the structured absence of Black Africans in either political or social life.

By the early 1980s things started to change. The National Party began to view some sort of appeasement and reform as necessary for the continued survival of apartheid ideology. This need was exacerbated by the rise of the manufacturing sector during the previous decades, which required and created a more stable and skilled workforce than the migrant labor of the mines or the rural agricultural sector. Thus the government, under the leadership of P. W. Botha (who became prime minister in 1978), began implementing efforts to co-opt the growing urban Black middle class that made up this skilled workforce. Taken as a whole, these efforts became known as the campaign to "Win Hearts and Minds," with the unfortunate though apropos acronym WHAM, which has been used in many other locations as well.[3] New legal structures created political representation for both Coloured and Asian South Africans in a tricameral parliament formed by a new constitution, while maintaining all effective control for White South Africans. Along with new forms of representation for indigenous Africans through local metropolitan councils in the townships, these constitutional reforms served as the centerpiece of the government's attempt to reestablish legitimacy for the apartheid state.

WHAM was implemented on the cultural as well as the explicitly political fronts. As part of the attempt to co-opt the growing urban Black middle class, the SABC instituted two new television channels aimed at this population—Television Two and Television Three (TV2/3)—in the early 1980s. This chapter continues to weave together the histories of television and apartheid-era politics through an examination of TV2/3, the significance of these channels as the first television programming aimed specifically at Black audiences in South Africa, and the impact of these channels on White South Africans who found themselves watching TV2/3 through channel surfing, or what I call "surfing into Zulu." This second fence post is best understood within the context of the intertwined attempts to win legitimacy for apartheid in the eyes of the urban Black middle class through both the SABC and institutional politics.

Not only did both of these attempts at legitimization fail, but their ramifications went far beyond their intended consequences, introducing a generation of White South Africans to their Black counterparts on television through the new channels and in politics through the birth of the United Democratic Front (UDF). Thus the first major cracks in the structured absence of Black South Africans on television, like the introduction of television itself discussed earlier, occurred simultaneously with major events in the political life of the nation. Yet unlike the (mostly) coincidental parallel of the introduction of television and the Soweto Uprising in the first fence post, the simultaneity of TV 2/3 and the formation of the UDF both stemmed from the same attempt to reform apartheid and thus carried with it profound implications for the future of South Africa.

WHAMming the People

The introduction of TV2/3 and the SABC's attempt to win legitimacy for apartheid through the new channels was one part of much larger developments in the arena of national politics, and needs to be understood as part and parcel of those developments.[4] As South Africa entered the early 1980s, the ostracization of South Africa was gaining momentum and Botha was searching for ways to reincorporate the nation back into the international community, lift sanctions, and win the allegiance of certain segments of the Black population, particularly Asian, Coloured, and urban-based indigenous South Africans. Meanwhile, White South Africans were increasingly able to access some but not all transnational media flows. This uneven access continued to frustrate their aspirations to international status and acceptance.

In addition to the introduction of TV2/3, Botha's efforts resulted in three broad initiatives grouped under the rubric of WHAM. Indeed, this acronym captures well the essence of this period of reforms and Botha's leadership as a whole.[5] Although constantly speaking in the name of reform, the Botha era saw by far the fiercest, most militarized repression of the entire apartheid period, with frequent detention, torture, and murder of activists and suspected activists. The three initiatives consisted of forming the National Security Management System (NSMS), implementing a "total strategy" to confront the so-called total onslaught, and pushing forward a new constitution and mechanisms for localized autonomy in the townships.

The most notorious element of this process was the establishment of the

NSMS. At the time, the NSMS was portrayed simply as a rationalization of the security apparatus of the state. However, information that has come to light in subsequent years has shown that the NSMS—which consisted of local Joint Management Centers (JMCs, also known as security councils) that reported up a chain of command and ultimately to the State Security Council (SSC)—operated as a quasi-independent shadow government.[6] The SSC "usurped many of the cabinet's executive functions" and reported directly to the Office of the State President, while often tasking local security councils with carrying out the dirty work of the apartheid regime without directly implicating the government or party officials.[7]

The security councils became a key element of the "total strategy," which was a rhetorical twist that brought together the harshest forms of state-sponsored violence and repression together with reforms in order to convince Black and White South Africans alike that a "total onslaught" from communist revolutionaries was bent on destroying the nation. Claiming the peril of total onslaught allowed the apartheid regime to justify nearly any and all means to reach the end of maintaining its power through total strategy. Total strategy thereby merged the military and political focus of the apartheid security state with matching "counteroffensives on the political, diplomatic, religious, psychological, cultural, economic, and social fronts."[8] In spite of the National Party's overt amalgamation of political, military, and cultural defenses for apartheid, most analysts have overlooked the crucial cultural aspects of total strategy, much less their intersection with institutional politics or state security.

The most visible of WHAM reforms was the infamous 1983 constitution, one of many through which South Africa cycled in the 20th century, and the closely related Koornhof Bills. Because of the increasing power of the manufacturing sector within the South African economy and its concomitant needs for a more skilled labor force located in relatively close proximity to the cities, one of the key components of apartheid ideology had broken down: the idea that indigenous Africans were only passing through urban areas and that all of their primary affiliations, whether political, social, or familial, remained in a government-designated bantustan. Although generations of Africans had been born and raised in the urban areas by the 1970s, much of earlier apartheid legislation, most notably the Group Areas Act of 1950 and the Bantu Authorities Act of 1951, was designed to deny this presence and even—through forced removals—structure the absence of a permanent, urban-based African population.

The new constitution attempted to build off the work of the 1982 Black Local Authorities Act, commonly known as the Koornhof Bills, which established urban councils that were given some limited control over local issues in the townships of indigenous Africans. These councils simultaneously recognized the permanence of the townships as more than a dormitory for migrant workers and attempted to co-opt the wealthier, more educated sectors of the Black population through offers of political patronage and local power. Through the town councils, the government intended to quell the international community's calls for democracy by arguing that Africans were being given democratic representation in their bantustans and through these local councils.

As part of the same effort to co-opt the growing middle class among other Black South Africans, the 1983 constitution established a tricameral parliament with each of three separate houses elected by White, Coloured, and Asian South Africans respectively. Numerical superiority and legislative power, however, remained centered in the House of Assembly elected by White South Africans. The new constitution was passed by an all-White referendum in 1983 and placed into effect later that same year.

The first elections for the new parliament and local councils thereby became a major showdown for the legitimacy not only of the new structures of representation, but also for the bantustan system and apartheid as a whole. In response to the government's claims of newfound democratic legitimacy, opponents of apartheid formed the United Democratic Front (UDF), a coalition of various political, civil, labor, and community-based organizations.[9] The UDF's work was focused on the defeat of the new constitution and the Koornhof Bills through a boycott of the elections to fill the legislative positions they created. In a resounding success for the UDF, the vast majority of Black South Africans refused to exercise their new franchise, casting instead a clear vote of illegitimacy for the entire system.[10] In the process, the UDF—ideologically aligned with the ANC but nonetheless a separate organization—became the locus of resistance in the 1980s until the unbanning of the ANC in 1990. Just as the Soweto Uprising marks the beginning of a new generation of resistance, the formation of the UDF and the moral defeat of the 1983 constitution arguably denote the initial moves of the opposition in the end game of apartheid and the struggle against it.

Radio Bantu with Pictures?

In the midst of the political struggles around the new constitution and the Koornhof Bills, the SABC participated in the total strategy of WHAM by introducing a television channel aimed at the growing urban-based African middle class. By instituting TV2/3, the SABC joined the government in recognizing not only Africans' permanent place within urban areas, but also their potential role as consumers. This shift in apartheid policy carried significant implications for everyday township life in addition to the political changes mentioned above. Rather than denying their presence and occasionally bulldozing their homes, the government was forced to consider ways in which to integrate urban Africans into both apartheid policies and political strategies. Another element of the WHAM campaign became the development of some basic levels of infrastructure in the townships. This infrastructure was limited to the so-called middle class of Black South Africans, whose standard of living, it should be emphasized, remained far below that of White South Africans who would be described as middle class. Improvements in infrastructure included the electrification of many townships for the first time, paving the way for television to target township dwellers as a new audience. The result was what six scholars from Rhodes University (hereafter Tomaselli et al.), in a study on TV2/3 in the late 1980s, called "Permanent Urbanization and the Strategy of Co-optation."[11]

With the townships placed on the electrical grid and an increasingly media-minded Black middle class forming, the introduction of TV2/3 was designed to reach this new and increasingly influential group of Black South Africans who were not served by the old-fashioned apartheid ideology carried by Radio Bantu. Whereas Radio Bantu was designed to reach primarily those Black South Africans located in rural areas or in homelands, and carried with it a traditionalist ideology of the invented kind, television transmitters based in the major urban areas—and requiring an expensive item like a television set to receive the signals—were ideally suited to reach this urbanized and educated population.[12] As Tomaselli et al. put it:

> Whereas Radio Bantu aims its messages of traditionalism at the lower-income, less urbanized and rural dwellers in an attempt to draw them into the economy on a migrant basis, TV2/3 focuses on the growing but numerically limited black middle classes domiciled in the "white" urban areas.[13]

At the time of TV2/3's introduction, however, the experiences of the Black middle class with Radio Bantu led them to be highly suspicious of the proposed television channel aimed at Black South Africans. Marketing research at the time showed that the intended audience, young urban Black consumers, believed that "Black TV will be run exactly as Radio Bantu—to keep a black permanently down" and that "only illiterates, children, and old people would watch."[14]

In spite of the hostility among its intended audience, SABC TV2 was introduced in 1982 and split a year later into TV2 and TV3. Although both TV2 and TV3 were broadcast on the same channel, the SABC described them as two separate channels in order to buttress apartheid's divide-and-conquer strategy, with one broadcasting in the Nguni family of languages and the other in the Sotho family of languages.[15] Thus TV1, split between English and Afrikaans, remained a single "White" channel while TV2/3's parallel split was deemed by the SABC to reflect further ethnic and linguistic divisions requiring separate "channels."[16]

Writing in the late 1980s, Tomaselli et al. identified four major themes in the content of TV2/3:

1. A careful differentiation of classes via a split between urban and rural Black South Africans;
2. An emphasis on education as the route to individual success and communal progress, defined as production and consumption;[17]
3. Recognition of an extended market through the rising urban Black consumer, particularly for electronic goods, including television sets; and
4. An emphasis on manufacturing consent for apartheid among this group.[18]

In addition to these four thematic observations, the content of TV2/3 displayed significantly lower production values than programming on TV1 and an even more noticeable deficit when compared to the content of overseas stations. Tomaselli et al. rightly attribute this differential to two significant, interrelated issues: first, the lack of sufficient funding for producers at TV2/3, limiting both their creativity and their resources for filming and editing; and second, the belief among the mostly White production staff that "black viewers will not understand time-worn conventions that signify time and space."[19] This belief resulted in a "muddle of codes" in programming on TV2/3.[20]

Thus TV2/3 was "not simply a 'radio bantu with pictures,'" but rather deserves a more detailed and subtle reading.[21] Tomaselli et al.'s claim that both the introduction of TV2/3 and its content were closely tied to class structures and the growing Black middle class is convincing. Most important, they insist on a complex and intertextual reading of the channels:

> Our broader analysis has shown that even programmes "written, produced and directed mainly by Whites"[22] are often confusing and counter-productive as far as the dominant ideology is concerned. Scholars who believe in the monolithic nature of TV2/3 as a means of manufacturing a mass culture are clearly unaware of the contradictions operating within the medium and of

the fact that even the people involved in the "manufacturing" are themselves, at times, undermining the process of negotiating consent because of a lack of knowledge about the textual codifications that govern the medium.[23]

This analysis reflects both the interest in Gramscian understandings of manufacturing consent common among South African scholars of the time as well as the beginnings of an account that recognizes such hegemony as partial and contradictory. Two decades later, a fresh look at TV2/3 shifts the question more explicitly from the ways in which the channels attempted to communicate apartheid ideology toward how TV2/3 *failed* to manufacture consent for apartheid, not only among Black South Africans, who already viewed the SABC with an extremely suspicious eye, but also among White South Africans. To understand the impact of TV2/3 in the 1980s, we need to explore how it was viewed not only—or even primarily—among its target audience, but also among those who the administration of the SABC most likely never imagined would be watching: White South Africans.

Crossing the Social Divide through Television

Joshua Meyrowitz provides a helpful entry point into understanding how television as a medium can reach and influence audiences for which the programming on television was never intended. One of Meyrowitz's central arguments in *No Sense of Place* is that the relationship of individuals to the medium of television is fundamentally different from that of print. I will highlight two ways that this difference directly impacted the way in which White South Africans interacted with TV2/3 and the result of these interactions. First, Meyrowitz emphasizes that the ways in which televisual codes work in cultural production are much easier to decipher across linguistic, age, gender, and other social barriers. Second, the ephemeral quality of television as a commodity requires a different level of personal identification with the product than does printed media.

The first of these issues, the comprehension of televisual content, is encapsulated in Meyrowitz's conceptualization of "media access codes." Because print media relies much more heavily on written language while television relies more heavily on images, it is self-evident that one is able to understand more of a television show being broadcast in a language one cannot comprehend than one can understand of a book written (or a radio show broadcast) in that same language. "Communication through writing and books is 'automatically' restricted to those who know the required access code," Meyrowitz tells us, whereas "television viewing involves an access code that is barely a code at all."[24] Though Meyrowitz overstates his case, ignoring the many levels of complexity around encoding and decoding explored by Stuart Hall among many others, his point regarding the greater level of initial access to television vis-à-vis print in an unfamiliar language remains both insightful and crucial to understanding TV2/3 in a nation like South Africa, with eleven official languages and high rates of illiteracy.[25] Even if we recognize the complexity of televisual codes, we can still acknowledge that televisual programming consists of content more presentational in nature (i.e., closer in appearance to the "real life" it hopes to portray) than is the written language on which most print media depend.[26] As a result, Meyrowitz points out:

> Once you know how to watch and listen to one television program, you essentially know how to watch and listen to any television program. You may not understand all that you see and hear—just as you may not understand all that people say and do in a real-life situation—but you need not penetrate a complex superimposed filter of printed symbols to "enter" the communication situation.[27]

Thus television was accessible to anyone able to receive a television signal (thereby excluding most rural parts of the country) and view a television set. While these observations have become far more commonplace with satellite television, Web 2.0, and similar trends since Meyrowitz's original formulation, the significance of the televisual medium remains crucial to understanding how these later technologies operate. This particular characteristic of television had at least as much of an impact on White South Africans viewing TV2/3, since they were less likely to speak an indigenous African language, than it did on Black South Africans viewing TV1, who were likely to have at least a working knowledge of either Afrikaans or English, if not both. In spite of the attempt to replicate apartheid's ideological segregation on SABC TV by separating the channels aimed at one or another racial group, televisuality's ability to cross over linguistic boundaries, combined with its relative inability to prevent unintended audiences from viewing its content, created the possibility for South Africans to view programming intended for the other. With the introduction of TV2/3, the first cracks in the structured absence of Black South Africans from South African social life begin to appear.

The possibility of transgressing these social divisions lends itself to the functioning of power through television in a significantly different way than through print as well. Whereas one can write for a fairly specific audience and encode one's written language to ensure the audience is thus circumscribed, it is much more difficult to limit the audience of any given broadcast in ways other than those who can receive the signal:

> Unlike print, television offers its content to all members of the population. Television, therefore, does not readily support an information elite that completely controls interpretation of the culture's stock of knowledge, *nor does it lend itself to segregated systems of discourse.* The content of television can still be manipulated and controlled by powerful economic and political forces, but controlling television is not the same as controlling print. While different people read different books, whatever is on television tends to be accessible to anyone who can make sense of it. Unlike books, television cannot readily be used by elites to communicate only among and about themselves.[28] (emphasis added)

"Segregated systems of discourse" were, of course, the very basis of apartheid policy, particularly those cultural policies designed to manufacture consent for the regime. Note that Meyrowitz is not claiming that television does not operate within relations of power, but rather that it changes the nature of those relationships, with particular attention to the difficulty of maintaining separate, closed systems of information. Although this may be only one small part of the ways in which power functions within television, the implications for apartheid ideology were profound. In a situation where relative status was defined to a great extent by skin color, the inability of apartheid's architects to preserve exclusive methods of information sharing posed an acute threat to the segregation on which apartheid was based and maintained.

In addition to television's implications for breaking down the social barriers maintained by print, crucial differences in personal identification with the products of mass media created by print as compared to television also exist. These differences turn on the role of the printed material itself, which serves as an object of identification in a way that television, with its ephemeral quality, does not. The consumption of printed material requires acquiring the object, usually in a public setting like a bookstore or a library, and often involves a purchase price as well. The object itself is then carried with the consumer and frequently placed in the home partially as ornamentation on a bookshelf or coffee table. Even taboo printed material runs the risk of being discovered "under the mattress" as it were, whereas viewing taboo material on television could only be discovered if the viewer was caught in the act. Each of these steps requires a level of commitment on the part of the consumer which free-to-air television does not.[29]

This commitment on the part of the consumer toward a specific object of printed media requires a greater level of identification with that object and what it represents. Meyrowitz calls this phenomenon the "association factor."[30] What makes the association factor significant, however, is not only the differing level of personal identification with a given media product, but the willingness of individuals to consume media products through television that the association factor would prevent them from consuming in the form of print, often due to the specific targeting of the product to the supposed other. For example:

> Many people who would be uncomfortable going into a bookstore and buying a magazine on transvestites would have no qualms about watching a program about transvestites on television. Talk show hosts . . . have built their careers on this dual response to the same content in different media.[31]

The impact of the association factor is twofold: first, broadcast media consumers are exposed to a wider variety of content than they would choose to associate with in print media; and second, the content itself may be altered as the producers become aware that even specialized programming may be reaching audiences outside their intended target. The first of these effects is somewhat counterintuitive, since the long-time complaint with broadcasting in general and television in particular (especially under commercial models) is that it requires mass appeal in order to succeed, which limits the diversity of voices—particularly regarding news and current events—that print media is more capable of sustaining. While this is undoubtedly true, the association factor highlights the self-selection of print media consumers, which tends to gravitate toward one's own opinion or interests. Thus the greater diversity of perspectives and topics in print media is mitigated by the lesser likelihood of consumers acquiring print media products with views or interests widely divergent from their own.[32] Although the representation of transvestites on talk shows tends toward the sensationalized, television remains the rare medium in which transvestites speak—at times even in their own voice—to large segments of the rest of the population.[33]

The second effect, wherein creators of television programs alter the content of their shows in recognition of a much broader audience than those specifically targeted, strikes at the very heart of controversies surrounding television. Because a broadcaster cannot guarantee who will be viewing his or her product, the content of that product has the potential for much greater controversy than do printed materials, which can restrict distribution much more carefully. Meyrowitz utilizes two gendered examples to explain this affect. Whereas *Sports Illustrated* serves an almost entirely male audience, ESPN's audience is more than one-third women. Likewise, *Playboy* magazine's overwhelmingly male readership translates into a mere 60 percent of the Playboy Channel's audience, with women watching alone making up 20 percent of its viewers, and another 20 percent comprised of women watching with men.[34] According to Meyrowitz, the result of this shift is that "the producers of the Playboy Channel are now trying to modify the programs to appeal more to women without simultaneously losing the men."[35]

The example of the Playboy Channel exposes the source of many controversies around television, not because women may be watching along with men, but because of parental fears that children also have access to the Playboy Channel (or less explicit portrayals of sexuality and violence that are nonetheless intended for adults rather than children). Similar to the current debates raging around the Internet, television's lack of discrimination regarding who can view its content fuels much of the controversy surrounding it. "When looked at as a whole," Meyrowitz tells us, "it becomes clear that much of the controversy surrounding television programming is not rooted in television content per se, but in the problems inherent in a system that communicates everything to everybody at the same time."[36]

Whereas print media creates an object—a book or a magazine—that we carry with us from place to place, or into the intimate space of our home, the only concrete object required for television is the television set itself. Because the set is essentially neutral in terms of content, meaning that any kind of televisual content could (theoretically) pass through the set, most television viewers do not view the ownership of a television set as a moral or ideological position in and of itself.[37]

Some South Africans took exception to this view of television as neutral, particularly in the years prior to its introduction. Most of those who attributed moral meaning to television ownership at that time were positioned on opposite sides of the South African political spectrum—the verkrampte on one side and apartheid dissenters on the other. As described in chapter 2, the verkrampte claimed television was evil and should therefore be avoided, using a discursive approach similar to that of some conservative religious groups in the United States. On the opposite side of the political spectrum, the left wing rightly feared the National Party's control over the SABC. Several of my interviewees reported that their family or someone they knew refused to purchase a set because they believed it would broadcast only apartheid misinformation. For instance Steven, a forty-year-old English-speaker, recalled that "by 1977 almost all my friends had TVs—except the Smiths, who didn't want government propaganda." But in spite of these abstentions, the vast majority of citizens in South Africa, not unlike the United States, would avoid such a strong moral statement on the ownership of television, both in the late 1970s or early 1980s and today.

Meyrowitz's arguments regarding television and its ability to break down social barriers—through both less stringent access codes and a reduced association factor with (particularly controversial or prurient) content—is persuasive. However, Meyrowitz joins other optimistic treatments of electronic media's impact on politics by focusing on the democratizing affects of gained access for marginalized groups.[38] In these accounts, electronic media open the political playing field by providing access to those formerly excluded—women, people of color, sexual nonconformists—from information-sharing systems. Conversely, the introduction of TV2/3 in South Africa provides an example of the flip side of that particular coin. Rather than providing Black South Africans with a window into the culture, politics, and information shared by White South Africans, TV2/3 provided glimpses of the excluded to those doing the excluding. It was primarily White South Africans who had new worlds opened up to them, rather than the other way around, thus further eroding the structured absence of Black South Africans in the political and social life of the nation.

Surfing into Zulu: White South Africans Monitoring TV2/3

By reversing the direction of the democratizing implications of television as conceptualized by Meyrowitz, the fundamental questions surrounding television and politics shift away from who controls the political economy of the medium toward questions of communicative spaces, processes of identification, and social imagination. In a move that appears to have been completely unanticipated by both the producers and advertisers at the time, perhaps due to their own belief in apartheid ideology itself, White South Africans included TV2/3 in their own viewing habits—albeit to varying degrees and with equally varying results.[39] Through the ability to channel surf—one of the medium's most distinct features—many White South Africans found themselves surfing into Zulu.

The vast majority of White South Africans interviewed for this project reported that they did indeed watch TV2/3 on occasion. The motivations for tuning in were wide-ranging, including interest in learning an indigenous language, watching sports that were conceived to be "Black" (especially soccer), and music programming. Although none of the interviewees reported watching primarily TV2/3 as opposed to TV1, the implications of this boundary crossing remain significant. White South African's monitoring of TV2/3 can be imagined as a kind of televisual tourism, leading to a limited and partial engagement with an exotic other, yet always concluding with a return "home" to TV1.[40]

Many of the White South Africans interviewed reported a hope that they would be able to learn the languages they were watching, a strategy that is often recommended to language students in the United States as well. William, a thirty-eight-year-old English-speaker, said, "We were excited [about TV2/3] because we hoped we'd be able to learn an African language from watching TV, but it didn't work." Likewise Margaret, a forty-year-old English-speaker, reported that "for some time I tried to learn Zulu by watching TV. I gave up and went to classes in Yeoville [a neighborhood in Johannesburg]." Harry, a twenty-eight-year-old English-speaker, remembered, "As a kid my siblings and I would try to mimic the African languages, especially Xhosa with all the clicks. It was a bit farcical and probably a bit racist, too." Although no one reported that they were successful in their attempts to learn an indigenous language through TV2/3, engaging instead in what social linguists Jaworski et al. have described as "linguascaping," the number of people who attempted to do so is striking.[41]

The other common motivation for White South Africans to tune in to TV2/3 was to watch sports that were not covered on TV1. The most frequent among these was soccer (a phenomenon familiar to American soccer fans without cable or satellite television who can receive Univision or Telemundo over free-to-air broadcast signals), though boxing and other sports were often broadcast on TV2/3 as well. Sports were also a common reason given by Black South Africans for tuning in to TV1.

Yet in addition to individuals who specifically sought out TV2/3 in order to learn a language or watch a specific sporting event, even more interviewees described happening upon something on TV2/3 while channel surfing. This initially accidental viewing of TV2/3 by White South Africans—the far more significant phenomenon in terms of both quantity and importance—appears to have been completely unanticipated by those who produced it. As media scholars have often observed in the past, individuals often choose a block of *time* for watching television (say after returning home from work, or as they prepare dinner) rather than specific programs. If the content on TV1 happened to be of little interest during that block of time, it was not uncommon for White South African viewers to switch over to TV2/3 at least briefly, and from time to time something would catch their eye. Respondents often described watching music shows in this manner. A thirty-five-year-old English-speaker named Jessica, for example, echoed the thoughts of many White South Africans, saying she remembers "watching some of the music shows on TV2/3 and enjoying the rhythm of the people." Jessica also pointed out that she and others happened upon TV2/3 by actually being drawn into the unknown, again evoking a kind of exotic tourism: "I used to occasionally watch TV2/3," Jessica said, "more out of interest since I could not understand them."

The impressions of Black South Africans that TV2/3 left with White South Africans were often very problematic, as evidenced by highly racialized stereotypes of musicians with good rhythm and the supposed dumb jocks of the athletic world. Like the double-edged sword of visibility and representation in U.S.-based talk shows, TV2/3 was the first channel designed to appeal to Black South Africans by featuring topics and shows of relevance to them, while simultaneously creating representations of Black South African life that were often stereotypical. Harry recalled the novelty of bare-chested women on both drama series and music programs on TV2/3, which led to a kind of othering similar to the common critiques of *National Geographic*. "I guess it made me think of African music and tradition as backward and somewhat silly—I was young!"

In spite of the ways in which TV2/3 may have reinforced White South African interpretations of Black South African life during this fence post, my research makes it clear that it had a critical mass of White South Africans occasionally watching. Many respondents reported that, although they now look upon much of how life was portrayed on the SABC (both TV1 and TV2/3) as skewed, TV2/3 nonetheless made them view Black South Africans in a different light at the time. Most notably, watching TV2/3 was often the first space within which White South Africans came to appreciate even small elements of African culture or to realize that Black South Africans had a sense of self or agency.

Jean, a thirty-eight-year-old English-speaker, recalls that watching TV2/3 in the 1980s

> was [the] first time I realized that black people had a sense of humor. There were lots of "slapstick" comedy programs that were extremely amusing and very satirical. As a White South African in the '70s and '80s, I was never fully aware that black people had their own identities.

Even if Jean and others like her received misinformation regarding the content of Black South Africans' identifications through TV2/3, their recognition of the other's humanity was no small step within the polarized context of apartheid. And unlike print media or TV1, TV2/3's desire to gain legitimacy among Black South Africans mitigated the extremes of misinformation propagated by the apartheid regime. Although the content of TV2/3 was influenced by apartheid ideology in much the same way as other broadcasting, programming aimed at Black South Africans was nonetheless forced to afford greater dignity toward them in its attempt for popularity and legitimacy. This depiction of dignity was neither necessary nor common in mass media aimed at White South African audiences, so when young White South Africans tuned in to TV2/3, they might very well have been surprised by what they found—portrayals, however stereotypical, of humanity.

Unanticipated Audiences:
White South African Reactions to TV2/3

Ironically, the SABC's attempts at covering up racial conflict further exacerbated this undercutting of apartheid ideology in at least two ways: the portrayal of Black South Africans as having access to the accouterments of White middle-class life, and the almost complete exclusion of White South Africans from programming on TV2/3. Each of these tendencies further shaped White South African monitoring of TV2/3 and the inferences they drew from the channels.

The depiction of Black South Africans as consumers with resources to spend was clearly imbued with hopes for co-opting the growing Black middle class into a life of leisure. As they discuss programs like *We Can All Be Beautiful*, Tomaselli et al. claim that "while the programme can be criticized at the level of appearance for presenting an idealized view of sophisticated recreational facilities that are unattainable to the majority of (even urban) blacks, symbolically it is a glorification of a leisured lifestyle." While they focus on the portrayal of "the capitalist myth par excellence," the more pressing concern of the apartheid government may well have been to divert this class from the growing militancy of the townships at the time.[42] The content of TV2/3 seems to have been at least as intent on convincing the new middle class that they had more to lose than gain from political upheaval as it was on developing a new group of consumers—though both dynamics are clearly related.

Regardless of the more specific motivations for these portrayals, there can be no doubt that the goal was to influence support among Black South Africans for the status quo. What has not been considered previously, however, is how these portrayals impacted White South Africans. Again, the results of these representations operated as a double-edged sword. On the one hand, the unrealistic portrayal of Black South Africans as having access to financial and other resources similar to that of White South Africans served to absolve White South African viewers of guilt. TV2/3 certainly did not focus on the depravations of township life, and when it did portray such hardships (sometimes in films made for the big screen decades earlier by front companies for the Department of Information, then recycled on TV2/3), the blame was placed at the feet of Black South African social life, not the systemic oppression of apartheid.[43]

On the other hand, TV2/3 actually narrowed the perceptual gap among White South Africans between themselves and their Black counterparts. Although the portrayal of middle-class luxuries available to Black South Africans was often inaccurate and actually delegitimized TV2/3 among its intended audience, it nonetheless gave White South Africans the impression that they shared the same values and desires. This newfound identification with Black South Africans marks the beginning of a shift in the construction of White South African identifications vis-à-vis Black South Africans, moving toward a recognition of similarity rather than difference for the first time.

White South Africans' reactions to their own role on TV2/3 contributed to this shift. Because TV2/3 was aimed at Black audiences with the intention of gaining legitimacy, the portrayal of White South Africans posed a very difficult problem: if White South Africans were portrayed on TV2/3 in the roles they usually played in Black South Africans' lives—bosses, madams, and other authority figures—how could employee/worker tensions, which often took on profoundly racial overtones, be avoided? The answer, according to Tomaselli et al., was simply to remove White South Africans from any kind of portrayal whatsoever: "While exceptions do occur, the most obvious absence on TV2/3 during the study period were the subjects of the dominant classes—whites. . . . Inclusion of whites into the texts of series, serials and plays would have the effect of pinpointing the source of ideological tension."[44] Thus favor was given to the strict segregation of apartheid ideology built on the myth that White and Black South Africans led completely separate lives. It is indicative of life under apartheid that, even in a production system controlled by White South Africans, the SABC deemed the positive portrayal of White employer/Black employee relations less plausible than the complete removal of contact between the two. While this may have been conceivable for some rural Black South Africans, whose contact with White South Africans often came in more systemic and less direct ways, the omission of employer/employee contact was glaring to the growing Black middle class of the urban areas at which TV2/3 was aimed.

The unanticipated viewing of TV2/3 by White South Africans resulted in another unintended outcome of this absence. White South Africans saw portrayals of Black South African life that were completely separate from themselves and in which they played no part. Though this, of course, buttressed the separate development theme of apartheid ideology, it also gave life to an abstraction that most White South Africans had never fully considered, nor had reason to—that Black South African life could carry on quite nicely without them. Though this portrayal erased the systemic oppression of apartheid, it also placed White South Africans in a position to which they were unaccustomed—outside the social life of the nation.

Though respondents had difficulty articulating this experience, the overall affect comes through clearly. Their own exclusion from the portrayal of life on TV2/3 furthered the idea mentioned earlier that Black South Africans had a greater level of autonomy and individual dignity than White South African viewers, particularly younger viewers, had previously recognized. Along with this recognition came a more dire realization—that they as White South Africans could, in fact, be completely displaced from their position in the South African nation. Although these realizations were only tentative and initial at the time, they nonetheless provided the beginnings of a reconceptualization of relationships with Black South Africans, based on a more equal footing and with a greater urgency from fear of displacement than previously imagined possible.

The Impact of TV2/3

As a result of the inaccurate or incomplete portrayals of Black South African life on TV2/3, the new channel never did win the legitimacy sought by the SABC among its target audience. Even more than the programming mentioned above, the news on TV2/3 (like TV1) also maintained the National Party line, making it nearly impossible for Black South Africans to accept the new channels. As Mandla Langa, the former chairperson of the Independent Communications Authority of South Africa (ICASA) put it, "black people who weren't pale imitations of their masters always took what the press said or didn't say about them with a liberal pinch of salt. And they passed this knowledge on to their children. The skeptical cannot be lied to."[45] Like the tricameral parliament and the Koornhof Bills,

TV2/3's attempt to gain legitimacy among Black South Africans was a spectacular failure. On the other hand, White South Africans were less skeptical of TV2/3 and by watching the new channel came to rethink their assumptions around both Black South Africans' identifications (or perceived lack thereof) and their own.

These dynamics echo scholarship in studies of whiteness and postcolonial theory, which emphasize the co-constitutive nature of identity formation.[46] Rather than focusing solely on how oppression shapes the social and psychological life of the oppressed, these studies have emphasized ways in which those in power have defined themselves over and against the subaltern. Whereas Black South Africans had been forced to understand significant parts of White South African culture and ways of relating, the structured absence of Black South Africans had allowed White South Africans to avoid a similar kind of coming to terms. As the structured absence of Black South Africans began to break down during this period, particularly in the realm of television, many White South Africans were required to both familiarize themselves with Black South African life to a greater degree than before and to rethink their own role within that life. As we shall see, the rethinking of the nation was not far behind.

Not every White South African viewed TV2/3, and many of those who did viewed it for short and comparatively scattered amounts of time. It may therefore seem strange to be making such large claims for the role of TV2/3 in the reshaping of White South Africans' impressions of Black South Africans. Indeed, ways of seeing race in South Africa, as elsewhere, are formed in many contexts and through many outlets.[47] Yet studies of mass media have shown that the impact they have on the social life of even those who do not directly consume the media product itself can be substantial. Often, mass media impacts our lives simply through our awareness that it exists, regardless of whether we actually take advantage of its presence. The metaphor of the ocean is often invoked in order to understand this phenomenon—media becomes the very ocean in which we swim (assuming, that is, that we are fish!).

The trouble with this metaphor lies in its tendency to conceptualize mass media as an inescapable totality without examining the ways in which its influence actually takes place. Consider instead the breaking news "special report." This particular genre of broadcast journalism serves to assure us that we know if anything of the utmost importance is happening in the world. Indeed, it assures us of this awareness when it is not being used even more than when it is: if there is no special report on television or the radio, then we can fairly safely assume there are no world events that have crossed the threshold of "essential" information. Leaving aside the question of who decides what qualifies as "essential" information, the special report helps to illustrate how the ways media operate can affect our lives even when they are not being put into action.

Similarly, White South Africans did not need to watch TV2/3 extensively, or at all for that matter, for the very presence of TV2/3 to shape their understandings of the nation and others within that nation. In the same way that a television viewer in the United States recognizes that there is a substantial Latino population able to sustain national networks in Spanish without actually watching Univision or Telemundo, the presence of TV2/3 on the airwaves helped communicate the growing importance of Black South Africans in social and economic life to White South Africans. Likewise, for those White South Africans who did watch TV2/3, even for a very limited time, these scattered and often stereotypical images gave shape to their social imagination regarding their connection to Black South Africans. Even without consciously expressing these impressions with friends and relatives, their changing views of the nation and its constituents through TV2/3 nonetheless seeped into the general consciousness of White South Africa.

From a War of Position to a War of Movement

Born from the growing pressure against apartheid both at home and throughout the world, the National Party under P. W. Botha attempted to balance a program of reforms with an increasingly militarized stance to neutralize both international opinion and domestic resistance. Almost all the reforms designed to win legitimacy for the apartheid government—including the inception of SABC TV2/3 for the growing Black middle class located in the urban areas—failed to accomplish their purpose.

However, these attempts at legitimacy did not simply fail, leaving the apartheid regime back where it began. Rather, they led to unanticipated outcomes that actually developed new threats to both apartheid ideology and the political structures that supported it. Formed in the crucible of the fight against the new constitution and the Koornhof Bills, the UDF maintained the momentum of its victory and continued to mobilize against the government, becoming the most important and successful resistance organization of apartheid's end game. Likewise, TV2/3 became one of the first significant, nationwide locations within which White South Africans began to reconsider their social relationships with Black South Africans. Understood as part of the same program intended to manufacture consent for apartheid, the otherwise seemingly coincidental creations of the tricameral parliament and TV2/3 were cut from whole cloth.

The parallel developments of the UDF and a profound shift in White South Africans' understandings of themselves and of Black South Africans are also best understood in relation to each other. As the failure of the new constitution increased both internal and external pressure against apartheid, the foundation of the staunchly independent and belligerent stance so often taken by White South Africans in the face of previous criticism—an identification defined by profound antithesis to the Black South Africans around them—began to break down. Along with this shift came a diminished ability as well as desire to continue structuring the absence of Black South Africans from the social life of the nation, even while fiercely maintaining their structured absence from conventional politics.

In *The Prison Notebooks*, Gramsci describes the moment when hegemony breaks down as evident in the shift from a war of position (the ideological and cultural struggle over dominant discourse as naturalized common sense) to a war of movement (or maneuver, as it is sometimes translated), with greater reliance on the use of physical force. The failure of TV2/3 and the new constitution to gain legitimacy for the apartheid regime represented the government's loss of the war of position. Predictably for Gramsci, the apartheid regime responded by escalating the war of movement and increasing its reliance on direct force. The government's shift from the war of position to the war of movement is the connective tissue between the fence post described here and our third fence post: the States of Emergency and the popularity of *The Cosby Show*. As we will see, the reconceptualization of White South African identifications that began in this period was further tested during the States of Emergency of the mid-1980s and led to the increasing distaste of White South Africans for the racial conflict that had come to define their nation. In its attempt to win the hearts and minds of the people in the early 1980s, the apartheid regime in fact mobilized opposition to the injustices it propagated, inadvertently exposed the contradictions within its ideology, and sowed the seeds of its downfall.

CHAPTER FIVE

Living with the Huxtables
in a State of Emergency

The rise of the United Democratic Front and its initial victories in discrediting the reforms of the apartheid state led, in a relatively short time, to an inexorably deepening crisis for the South African regime. Less than three years after the introduction of both the tricameral parliament and TV2/3, the first State of Emergency was declared in July of 1985. By the time it was lifted seven months later, in March of 1986, much of the nation had plunged into violence and chaos—the "ungovernability" called for by the chartist organizations. Fatalities during the seven months of emergency nearly doubled from the previous year of agitation, contributing to a total of more than 1,200 since the initiation of the new constitution.[1] Only three months after the first emergency was lifted, the second and final State of Emergency was initiated, which would last until the unbanning of the ANC and the release of Mandela in 1990. The UDF's secretarial report of February 1986 proved prescient when it stated, "Now, there can be no turning back."[2]

During the mid- to late 1980s, the battle for legitimacy continued to be waged on the political, military (and paramilitary), and cultural fronts. However, this period distinguished itself from the early 1980s in the SABC's return to the seeming disconnection of SABC television from the lived reality of the vast majority of South Africans. Whereas the introduction of TV2/3 showed an attempt on the part of the SABC to embody the political reforms of the National Party in a cultural form, the disintegration of apartheid's legitimacy in the face of the UDF and the States of Emergency led the SABC to retreat to a kind of Pollyanna existence. As Ruth Teer-Tomaselli has convincingly shown, SABC television news recognized the conflict in the most minimal and sanitized way possible.[3] If Nero fiddled while Rome burned, the SABC entertained while more and more Black South Africans died.

The third fence post—the popularity of *The Cosby Show* in the midst of the States of Emergency—raises the question of what part, if any, television played during the States of Emergency in the so-called crisis of will among White South Africans in the mid- and late 1980s. This crisis of will led directly to the acceptance among White South Africans of the negotiation process toward democratic rule, which continued into the early 1990s. However, while formal apartheid faced a crisis of will, that crisis represented not only a dismantling of the status quo but also a reinscription of White privilege. In other words, the crisis of will provided an opportunity for White South Africans to adopt and adapt a more internationally accepted, "civilized" form of White supremacy, shaped in large part by transnational media flows and the understandings they provided of White supremacy in other parts of the world. This process of dismantling and reinscribing power inextricably ties the crisis of will to the concept of hegemony; the crisis of will marks the moment in which hegemony must reinvent itself in order to survive. If consent can no longer be manufactured in the way it has been previously, the rationalizations of power and privilege must be reconstructed along new terms, releasing the forms of power exercised through earlier material practices while attempting to maintain the underlying power of consent and domination. The crisis of will becomes a moment in which both the lasting, flexible power of hegemony and its inability to complete the circuit of power are manifest, and facilitates a conceptualization of hegemony as ongoing contestation instead of static domination.

Rather than claiming it to be a singular cause of the crisis of will, my research locates the massive success of *The Cosby Show*, introduced to South Africans by the SABC in the same year as the first State of Emergency, as an entry point to expose television's role in this dual process of dismantlement and reinscription. *The Cosby Show* enjoyed immense popularity across all racial and language groupings of South Africans, including and especially White South Africans, during arguably the most volatile period of South African history. Although the Huxtables were African American characters, *The Cosby Show* nonetheless marks a significant incursion into the structured absence of Black South Africans in the social life of the nation because of the shared affection for the program among all South Africans. Such broad acceptance in the midst of an extremely polarized context begs explanation.

Claims that the content of *The Cosby Show* had a direct, pedantic impact on White South Africans' views of race tilt perilously close to what Stuart Hall has criticized as the "low-flying behaviouralism" of much scholarship that views television as "a behavioural input, like a tap on the knee cap."[4] Rather, *The Cosby Show* helped expose—and through its popularity, perhaps accelerate—some of the shifts that were already taking place in White South African views of their Black counterparts and therefore their own identifications that had been built in contrast to these perceptions. White South Africans grew increasingly distant from both apartheid ideology and official policy, leading to a disjuncture between apartheid policy and SABC programming (which attempted to toe the National Party line) on the one hand and the day-to-day realities faced by both White and Black South Africans on the other. SABC television's lack of resonance among South Africans during this time helped create a cultural space in which the nation could be both challenged and reimagined, and *The Cosby Show* became a crucial location within which these struggles were both reflected and given shape.

Apartheid's Crisis of Will

In her history of the UDF and its role in the struggle during the 1980s, Ineke van Kessel echoes the commonly held view that a "crisis of will" among Afrikaners opened political opportunities for the opponents of apartheid. "The Afrikaner's own belief in the God-given right of the Afrikaner nation to rule over disenfranchised blacks was unraveling," van Kessel tells us. "It was this crisis of will and the attempted transformation from ideological apartheid to a technocratic, market-related system of preserving white privilege that opened up the space for the opposition to organize and expand, thus in turn exacerbating the political crisis."[5] Van Kessel points to the dual nature of the crisis of will as both challenging the status quo of apartheid and simultaneously reinscribing White supremacy through technocratic, market-related systems. Though academics have debated the relative weight of regime failure and grassroots protest in bringing about the end of formal apartheid, there is broad consensus that Afrikaners (and I would add English-speaking White South Africans) lost their taste for the level of violence required to maintain the apartheid regime during this time period.

But what prompted this crisis of will? Narratives of the 1980s have postulated a wide variety of possible causes for this reduction in commitment on the part of White South Africans to continue to support the more extreme elements of apartheid. The many reasons commonly mentioned include the deployment of conscripted soldiers in the townships, suddenly bringing the war closer to home for White South Africans; an increase in international pressure, which included sanctions that coincided with an economic downturn, creating even more pressure on the South African economy; and the willingness of anti-apartheid activists to raise the stakes of the conflict through less discriminate attacks on White civilians. Each of these elements and many more contributed to both the conflict in South Africa and the change in political direction among White South Africans leading to the negotiated settlement, or what Patrick Bond has called the "elite transition."[6]

Rather than searching for a single cause, the crisis of will among White South Africans should point us in the direction of shifts in political imagination and the ideoscapes of the nation, which became necessary in order to accommodate a negotiated settlement. South Africa's history stands apart from many other conflicts because of its resolution in the absence of a clear victor in military or even political terms. Although one could never claim that White South Africans relinquished power willingly, and minimizing the violence of the apartheid era would do great violence to history, the negotiated settlement represented a much less bloody outcome than many had anticipated. The question, then, is not only what were the many combinations of events that led to the crisis of will, but also what were the shifts in how White South Africans viewed themselves that allowed for negotiations to be seen as an option at all, much less emerge as the best option in enlightened self-interest? Jonathan Hyslop constructs a convincing narrative of these shifts, combining the economic downturn and other external pressures with an increasingly individuated, consumerist, middle-class orientation among White South Africans. Hyslop ties these shifts to Anthony Giddens's analysis of late modernity, as well as some speculative explorations of the role of *The Cosby Show* and other cultural products from the United States in this process.[7] Although developed independently, the analysis that follows parallels much of Hyslop's narrative while delving into the role of televisual cultural production generally, and *The Cosby Show* in particular, in much more depth. Both studies show that a crisis of will like the one experienced by White South Africans in the mid-1980s could only grow out of a rethinking of the racialized political subjectivities that lay at the heart of apartheid; likewise, the solution to such a crisis would require a reidentification process on the part of White South Africans in particular.

In the highly polarized political context of South Africa under the States of Emergency, it should come as little surprise that institutional politics provided few opportunities for White South Africans to experiment with what Sonja Kuftinec has described as "rehearsing and revising new identifications."[8] While the rise of organizations like the End Conscription Campaign (ECC) and other White-identified anti-apartheid groups, along with

the vibrant alternative press of the 1980s, provided an outlet for more radical White South Africans, these groups were nonetheless unsuccessful in
providing new identities with which the majority of White South Africans
were able to identify. One result of this polarization was the shifting of politicized identity struggles toward the more open and fluid realm of cultural
production. Music became a crucial element in reimagining the South African nation.[9] Cultural production also became one of the few areas in which
Black and White South Africans regularly collaborated with each other, as
they did in several theatre companies and musical groups.[10]

The SABC—with its strong alliance to the National Party—may seem an
unlikely location for such struggles over identity, but *The Cosby Show* was,
as we will see, one of the more high-profile terrains on which this reidentification would play out. As my examination of the previous two fence posts
has shown, the introduction of television had already begun to shift some
White South Africans' view of the world and their place within it. After the
initiation of TV1, White South Africans became increasingly aware of the
international community at the same time they were being progressively
more ostracized from that community. With the launch of TV2/3, White
South Africans turned their gaze from the wider world toward their compatriots, recognizing perhaps for the first time the humanity and agency of
Black South Africans.

In the midst of the States of Emergency, television played a role in splitting the object of White South African introspection with a profound re-
consideration of both South Africa's role in the international community
and White South Africans' roles within the nation. Television continued to
make South Africans more aware of their own exclusion from the international community of nations through the live televising of major sporting
events from which South Africans were banned, and through news coverage that, although slanted toward the government's rationale, nonetheless
made White South Africans acutely aware of their pariah status.[11] At the
same time, the extent to which the SABC needed to sanitize its own programming—both news and entertainment—left White and Black South Africans aware (though to varying degrees) of the disjuncture between their
daily lives and the portrayal of those lives on television. In short, rather
than trying to establish legitimacy as the SABC did in the earlier part of
the decade, the broadcaster reverted to light entertainment and highly biased news of the supposed total onslaught. It is within this context—where
news and related programming is firmly and undeniably in the hands of
the state—that the popularity of *The Cosby Show* stands out and requires
explanation.

Intertextuality and Hegemony

Media studies theorists have long contended that intertextuality—the interaction of various texts across cultural spaces—is an essential element to understanding cultural production and the so-called manufacturing of consent. The South African case shows this to be absolutely true, while at the same time undercutting some of the assumptions of these theories. For while any cultural product such as *The Cosby Show* cannot be understood outside of the wider political and cultural context of apartheid South Africa, intertextuality in this situation worked across purposes, exposing tensions rather than continuities within hegemonic discourse.

Although the major theorists of intertextuality have not expressly discounted this possibility, their focus has tended to be on the ways in which various cultural texts actually build upon one another to strengthen an overarching discourse or cultural hegemony. This focus grows out of an attempt on the part of many media theorists to expose the workings of hegemony in nonauthoritarian states such as the liberal democracies of Western Europe and North America. For these authors, it becomes essential to understand the ways in which seemingly disconnected cultural texts build upon each other to support a broader hegemonic discourse. The result in the work of scholars such as Noam Chomsky and Michael Parenti is often a blending of political economy and media theory that tends to emphasize the aspect of domination in the Gramscian notion of hegemony while marginalizing the contradictions and processes within hegemony in which Gramsci himself was particularly interested.

South African television during the States of Emergency, and *The Cosby Show* in particular, turns some of these presumptions on their head. Under the authoritarian state of apartheid, and in an electronic mediascape completely dominated by the parastatal SABC, intertextuality becomes crucial in understanding the fissures within hegemonic discourse as well as the consistencies. Indeed, although South African activists and scholars were themselves often focused on ways in which the apartheid regime managed to manufacture enough consent to retain power in the mid- and late 1980s, this period conforms more closely in retrospect to Gramsci's concept of organic crisis—the breakdown, rather than the maintenance, of hegemony.[12]

In the midst of this breakdown, intertextuality demands that we consider more than just the control and content of television news and other "actuality programming"—the term used in South Africa for news, talk shows, documentaries and current affairs programming, that is, shows that deal with "actual" events or issues. We must also consider how such programming operated within the larger context of SABC broadcasting, including entertainment programming such as *The Cosby Show*. By taking this broader approach, we see that the SABC's well-documented bias during the States of Emergency, though it provided cover for the death squads of Vlakplaas and other forms of state repression and was the source of endless frustration for anti-apartheid activists, failed to manufacture consent in the manner hoped for or intended. Because SABC news was already discredited by nearly every segment of society, particularly those who already disagreed with the National Party, South Africans turned to other forms of cultural production to construct meaning from the volatile political situation of the time.

Even some within the SABC recognized the possibility of using entertainment programming as a strategy for circumventing SABC censors. According to one scriptwriter:

> In the light of my experience, it seems that if you are doing a straight documentary, then you are seen to be asking questions. But if you fictionalize it . . . You see, if they [the SABC] think it's a story, they're a lot happier, they're going to go with it a lot easier. . . . I think they're scared of the format of documentary, they're scared of certain key themes.[13]

According to this scriptwriter, the SABC management was "literal in the extreme" in its attempts to filter information, "and that can't be difficult to get around." Although such intentional subversion of the status quo through subtle coding in cultural production is important, it also faces severe limitations. Most notably, as Tomaselli et al. point out, the more subtle the coding used to pass under the radar of media gatekeepers, the more likely that coding will be lost on the audiences for which it is intended as well.[14] This observation does not infer a lack of sophistication among the intended audiences (though some of the cruder versions of this analysis tend to fall into that trap), but rather questions the control of the author over the text after it leaves his or her hands.

Indeed, this line of questioning was the genesis of the concept of intertextuality. Developed largely within the field of literary criticism, intertextuality became a key weapon in that discipline's attempt to move away from the privileging of an individual author's intention when trying to understand a given text.[15] The relevance of this approach comes into high relief when looking at a phenomenon like *The Cosby Show*: a television show produced for U.S.-based audiences that deals with race in ways specific to the United States and then becomes an internationally successful phenomenon. As Ien Ang has shown in *Watching Dallas*, a given television program that is transported to a wide variety of international contexts comes to be understood and enjoyed within each of those contexts in unique ways.[16] Through the differing texts and contexts with which a series such as *The Cosby Show* comes into contact in this process, the intertextuality of such shows cannot help but part ways with those intended by their creators. In South Africa during the mid-1980s, then, *The Cosby Show* cannot be understood outside of its relationship with SABC actuality programming and the States of Emergency.

Experiencing the States of Emergency on the Nightly News

Although actuality programming was heavily slanted toward the apartheid state, there was a broad awareness among all parts of the population, including Afrikaners, of this bias. Thus the SABC's efforts to sanitize both the news and entertainment aspects of South African life on the air paradoxically contributed to the crisis of legitimacy for both the SABC and apartheid as a whole. My research clearly indicates that news-related programming had little success in fundamentally convincing the regime's opponents of its validity, and even called into question the loyalties of some of its own proponents. For instance, Marike, a sixty-four-year-old Afrikaans-speaker, described the news during this period:

> You never knew everything. What you saw on the news was never the whole story. You always wondered what else, and what is behind that. What is happening that you don't know about? That sort of thing caused lots of stress. . . . One got the feeling that some reporters wanted to say more, but that they weren't allowed to. So if you don't allow someone to say what they want to say or write what they want to write, you wonder what else is happening that you don't know about.

What Marike explains as a sense of generalized stress around what Afrikaners were aware they did not know, many Black South Africans express instead as rage over what they knew but were not being shown on television. Musa, a thirty-one-year-old African, tells of his reaction to news reports during the States of Emergency:

> Anger and disgust. My opinions were already molded by interaction within the community and the death, exiling and persecution of family members.

Television merely fueled my anger towards the apartheid regime and in truth White people in general.

English-speaking White South Africans also described watching the news during the States of Emergency in ways that roughly paralleled their social position vis-à-vis White Afrikaans-speaking and Black South Africans. William, a thirty-eight-year-old English-speaker, recalled watching

> young supposedly former ANC members dismantling and assembling AK47s in record time. I think that even though we knew the news was distorted, it did create the impression that the ANC was a dangerous communist organization. This was backed up by my involvement in church circles, where I heard and learnt that apartheid was wrong, but also learnt to fear the communist ANC alternative.

Steven, a forty-year-old English-speaker, echoed William's perspective, saying, "I was a White liberal—the Emergency was necessary but excessive; [I] thought that the NP were just going to provoke more trouble."

Rather than manufacturing consent from thin air, then, SABC television news tended to reinforce the already-formed opinions of White and Black South Africans alike. In the words of Pieter, a sixty-six-year-old who is fully bilingual, the news "only served to confirm my personal convictions of wrong doing by the powers in charge." If anything, the obviousness of pro-government bias in the SABC news during the States of Emergency exacerbated the already extremely polarized positions of South African politics. A far cry from its attempts to gain legitimacy in the early 1980s, the SABC seemed to abandon any attempt at valid newsgathering in favor of a retreat into denial that accepted the National Party's information and perspective at face value.[17]

Nonetheless, most White South Africans felt a certain abstract distance in relation to the States of Emergency, in contrast to the personalized anger and disgust expressed by Musa and other Black South Africans. Jean, a thirty-eight-year-old English-speaker, recalls that "we didn't see any violence except on TV, and it was a bit unrealistic to me. The main thing I remember was our maid, Betty, was constantly being arrested for gambling or not carrying her pass. . . . The police were totally ridiculous in the 1980s, but it was never reported on TV." Similarly, Marike recalls that "people were worried if they had to travel or wanted to travel. Should they travel or shouldn't they? What would happen if they started a long journey? Just that sort of worried feeling."

Particularly for younger White South Africans, this vague sense of anxiety even became normalized. Andrew, a thirty-four-year-old English-speaker, remembers, "The impression I got was that the declaration of a State of Emergency was not an 'out of the ordinary' occurrence. I have since seen that they are not ordinary in any way." The main exception to these kinds of oddly distanced experiences of the States of Emergency for White South Africans primarily involved those who had family or friends conscripted to serve in the townships. For example Vanessa, a thirty-five-year-old English-speaker, remembered "seeing images of 'chaos' in the townships and being quite afraid at the time because my brother was doing his army [service] and I did not want him to be sent into the townships."

With a strange combination of histrionic fear around the total on-slaught, a somewhat detached day-to-day reality, and an intense awareness of South Africa's exile from the international community, White South Africans were left in a highly volatile situation within which to form work-able identifications. The exceedingly and recognizably biased presentation of news on the SABC, with its reliance on old versions of South African na-tionhood that were appearing less and less sufficient, provided little assis-tance. Entertainment programming on the other hand, with its less explicit political agenda, became a space into which individuals' hopes, fears, and desires for a future South Africa could be projected with a great deal more freedom.

M-Net and TV4: All Entertainment All the Time

The introduction of the Electronic Media Network (known more often as M-Net), the nation's first subscription television service, contributed to the sense of detachment and denial among White South Africans but provided little of the space for experimentation with desire that we find with *The Cosby Show*. Initiated in 1986, M-Net's licensing agreement explicitly pre-vented it from providing actuality programming of any kind, for the obvi-ous reason that the government could not as easily control the news output from a private station as it could from the parastatal SABC. Nearly all my interviewees indicated that they had not been able to afford the service, or if they did it was not until the 1990s. As a result of its expense, most South Africans, White and Black alike, only viewed M-Net during its "open time," usually a couple of hours in length on most days during which the M-Net signal was transmitted unscrambled on the SABC and therefore accessible to anyone who could receive the signal, or in viewing parties at the home of a friend who had access to the network, harkening back to the early days of communal television monitoring. During open time—and the rest of the day for those few who could afford it—South Africans were treated to a steady diet of American situation comedies, light drama, and movies. Because the Equity Ban was solidly in place by the time M-Net arrived, the service was restricted almost completely to imported material from the United States.[18]

The SABC also introduced another service, Television Four (TV4), in March of 1985. Aimed at White South African audiences, TV4 broadcast on the same channel as TV2/3 after it signed off at 9:30 p.m., providing sports and imported entertainment programming. Like M-Net, TV4 was designed as a politically neutral source of light entertainment and leisure with no political agenda—either explicit or implicit—intended. Perhaps not surprisingly, this lack of political agenda combined with escapist programming made TV4 the most popular late-night television channel for the SABC within a year of its introduction.[19] After initially airing on TV1 in 1985, rising to the number one television program in South Africa shortly thereafter, *The Cosby Show* found its home on TV4.[20]

Interpreting *The Cosby Show* in South Africa

South Africans made meaning out of *The Cosby Show* through a wide array of interpretations. The following sections will explore how the program was experienced within South Africa, particularly with regards to race and racism, but they are not concerned with finding a single "correct" interpretation. Rather, understanding the variety of ways in which South Africans constructed meaning from the show points us in a slightly different direction. What was important about *The Cosby Show* in South Africa was not the message of its content but the phenomenon of its popularity. I return to this phenomenon and its relevance for South African politics and identity, but I examine first the various popular interpretations of *The Cosby Show* in South Africa.

That American cultural products are consumed in different ways abroad than they are at home seems obvious, and all the more reason to recognize the author's loss of control over the interpretations of his or her text. This is particularly true of transnational media flows circulating through the highly charged racial atmosphere of mid-1980s South Africa.[21] Yet like Black Nationalism in the first half of the twentieth century, and hip-hop music today, the portability of race, racial discourses, and cultural products between the United States and South Africa proved to be a complicated process. *The Cosby Show* did not travel overseas in a vacuum, but brought with it many of the critiques—both positive and negative—from the United States, along with elements of the racialized political discourses from which those critiques grew.

Some popular understandings of *The Cosby Show* in South Africa closely paralleled those in the United States, while others rejected American interpretations out of hand. Most often, however, American analyses were adapted to fit into the South African context, adding an additional layer to what Stuart Hall describes as a "lack of equivalence" in the processes of encoding and decoding communicative events in mass media.[22] Hall's work describes three possible positions vis-à-vis the interpretation of any cultural text: first, the dominant-hegemonic position, which operates inside the dominant code; second, the negotiated code, which attempts to reconcile inconsistencies within the dominant code or between that code and lived experience; and third, the oppositional code, which attempts to read against the hegemonic "common-sense" interpretation. According to Hall, the most significant moments for politics derive from "when events which are normally signified and decoded in a negotiated way begin to be given an oppositional reading. Here the 'politics of signification'—the struggle in discourse—is joined."[23] Just such a struggle in discourse was engaged, albeit often under the surface, around understandings of *The Cosby Show*.

South African adaptations of popular U.S.-based interpretations of *The Cosby Show* relied on the similarities but more important the differences in the racialized political contexts of the two nations at the time. In the United States, reactions tended toward one of two polarized opposites: the first position—which Hall might describe as the dominant code—held that the show was a groundbreaking effort in positive, antiracist programming, whereas the other stance viewed the series as an unrealistic whitewashed version of African American life that contributed to racism through a false sense of equality and supposed color-blindness, an oppositional reading of the show. Both of these interpretations were adopted more or less completely by some in South Africa. However, many of my respondents reported that they added an extra filter to their interpretation of *The Cosby Show*—always viewing the Huxtables as specifically "American" in a negotiated code—which held profound implications for how they built meaning from the show in relation to South African subject positions.

When *The Cosby Show* was first introduced in the United States, it received immense praise for portraying an African American family different from every other such family that had appeared on American television. The Huxtables were a powerful, well-educated, financially successful, psychologically well-adjusted, tight-knit family. Far from the "standard raucous ghetto family that cracks jokes or sounds off on one another," the Huxtables presented a view of Black families that was far more appealing to the American mainstream.[24] Although this portrayal was originally seen as innovative and positive without qualification, the mainstream appeal of *The Cosby Show* came under significant criticism as the program's popularity skyrocketed.

With *The Cosby Show*'s dominance in the ratings—achieved very quickly—the Huxtables became not just a new and unusual Black family on television but instead the *archetypal* Black family, both on television and in general cultural discourse. Such status was accompanied by intense criticism of the show for being out of touch with the realities of most Black people in the United States. The seeming lack of complication around race in the Huxtables' lives became a liability rather than an asset, and demands that the program deal directly with racism, poverty, and other social issues began to grow. This criticism may have never gained purchase had the show not succeeded to such an exceptional extent, or if there was a wider array of television programming that featured Black characters. Nonetheless, in a mediascape where the Huxtables had little or no Black competition for the attention of viewers, *The Cosby Show* became a key lightning rod for debates around race, class, and popular culture in the Reagan era.

The Cosby Show encountered similar kinds of praise and criticism when it arrived in South Africa, just one year after its debut in the United States. In her highly positive take on the program, *The Cosby Show: Audiences, Impact, and Implications*, Linda Fuller features a brief case study on the show's impact in South Africa. Extending her optimistic argument to South Africa, she borrows from a graduate student's paper—an informal audience research project that involved eight South African participants—to claim that "these Black respondents report that watching *The Cosby Show* encourages them to work hard to attain a higher standard of living. Meanwhile, whites are being educated to another perspective of Blacks than they perhaps would have considered." My own research indicates that the views Fuller found are indeed common, but share consideration with many other perspectives, some of which are far more negative and/or complicated.[25]

For instance, Musa, a thirty-one-year-old African, echoed Fuller's view: "*The Cosby Show* gave me a positive outlook on life that being middle-class was not the preserve of White people, i.e., you can be a doctor like Dr. Huxtable." Likewise Anton, a thirty-six-year-old Coloured South African, found the show "uplifting and it did a lot perhaps for black people's perceptions of themselves," though he adds, "but I did not think it improved race relations." Anton points to an important distinction in interpreting

The Cosby Show, both in the United States and in South Africa, between improving race relations and providing positive role models. In both countries, these two issues—which are often conflated but can be understood better when kept analytically separate—represent the flip sides of the racialized audience coin. For when critics describe the show as providing positive role models, they are more often than not referring to positive, successful role models for Black people, and Black children in particular (the assumption, arguably a false one, being that White people have many positive role models on television or are less likely to identify with Black characters). On the other hand, when critics describe the show as improving race relations, the inference is that the program alters White individuals' views of Black people. These two claims are thus dealing with very different kinds of impact *The Cosby Show* may have had on racially separated audiences. The latter of these two claims—the impact of the show on White South Africans' views of race—is the more important to consider in the context of my research.

When asked about their impressions of *The Cosby Show* and its impact on their views of race relations, White South Africans responded with a wide array of perspectives. Indeed, what is striking in my interviews is less the consistency of a given reading of *The Cosby Show*, but rather the variety of readings offered. Even more important is the strength of the responses I received. *The Cosby Show* was the only show on the SABC between 1976 and 1994 that *every* respondent, regardless of race or age, mentioned as one of the top five shows they recalled watching during this time period. Moreover, the energy with which interviewees responded to questions about *The Cosby Show* was nearly always notably higher than during the rest of the interview, and superlatives were used more often than not to describe their feelings for the series. There can be little doubt that the program was not only popular, but also left extremely strong impressions on South Africans at the time, impressions that remain strong today.

In spite of their variance, White South African interviewees' readings of *The Cosby Show* and its impact on racialized perceptions can be broadly grouped into three categories. First, a dominant reading: many respondents claimed that, in the words of one individual, "*The Cosby Show* did more for race relations in this country than anything else ever has."[26] Second, an oppositional reading: many felt that the Huxtables fed into the apartheid regime's ideology by either (or both) championing a *de facto* racialized capitalist system or the benefits of living separate but equal. Finally, many White South Africans dismissed *The Cosby Show* as meaningless for racialized identities by othering the characters, most profoundly by tagging the characters as specifically "American." In this negotiated code, the Huxtables' American identity proved essential to distancing South Africans from any deeper conclusions regarding race in their own nation, a crucial reidentification process to which I will return.

"The Cosby Show *did more for race relations in this country than anything else ever has"*

This quote most likely strikes the reader as surprisingly simplistic, not to mention shocking in the importance it gives to a single cultural product in the midst of such a highly contentious racialized political context as mid-1980s South Africa. However, apartheid's success at thoroughly separating the lives of White and Black South Africans goes some distance toward explaining the power of a positive portrayal of Black people on television. As one scholar put it, the inclusion of *The Cosby Show* in SABC programming was "a complete reversal of previous broadcast policy," featuring Black characters on so-called White television.[27] The impact of the show thus needs to be understood in its departure from both the lived and televised reality of South African life at the time. In other words, the success of the apartheid regime at structuring the absence of Black South Africans made *The Cosby Show* far more exceptional than it would otherwise have been.

According to Marelize, a thirty-one-year-old Afrikaans-speaker, her family:

> LOVED *The Cosby Show*—we still have them on tape. It was our fav[orite] show ever. My father credits it with the fall of Apartheid. White South Africans saw Black people were just like them. Hell, Theo even had a "Free Mandela" poster in his room!

As if aware that her claims around the show were extremely strong ones, Marelize insisted on returning to the topic at the end of the interview, insisting that "I mean them quite seriously." Vanessa, a thirty-five-year-old English-speaker, echoed Marelize's comments:

> I loved *The Cosby Show* as did my whole family and my friends; we often spoke about the episodes. I think the show had a positive impact on race relations and helped break the stereotype of how people in this country thought about Black people.

William presented a similar but somewhat more complicated reading of the show:

> *The Cosby Show* was a favorite. Everybody liked it. I think my maternal grand-parents hated it as they didn't like to see Black faces on the "White" channel. I really think it made an impact on many White South Africans—to be able to identify with a Black family who lived a middle-class life and made them laugh—and the laughter was one of identifying with many of the issues and situations brought up in the show.

William points toward the role of different generations in the shifts that had already started to occur in White South African identities. For whereas his grandparents could not abide seeing Black characters on channels intended for White viewers, this does not seem to have been an issue for younger viewers like him and his parents. While his grandparents had been raised in the stricter segregation of earlier apartheid—wherein the structured absence of Black South Africans was far more complete—the younger generations were more accustomed to the gradual breakdown of that absence, and thus less shocked by *The Cosby Show* further diminishing it.

These interpretations reflect the role of *The Cosby Show* in leading White South Africans to think differently about what it meant to be Black. In spite of the fact that the Huxtables lived a life inconceivable to many African Americans, and so much more so to Black South Africans, they nonetheless portrayed a kind of family with whom White South Africans felt they could get along, perhaps even as equals. Although *The Cosby Show* may have made no progress toward helping White South Africans gain an authentic understanding of Black South Africans' lives, even exacerbating the misconceptions, the show nevertheless presented an opportunity for White South Africans to rethink their own identifications in relation to people of color. According to this analysis, if they could feel warmth toward the Huxtable family, perhaps they could also feel such warmth for Black South Africans in real life.

"I don't think that The Cosby Show *was in any way subversive of late-apartheid ideology"*

In spite of these optimistic readings of *The Cosby Show* in South Africa, many of my respondents indicated that the program did little to contradict apartheid ideology, and in some cases even provided succor to it. According to these interpretations, classist and segregationist undertones in the show negated any positive portrayals it may have provided. The first of these accusations—that the Huxtables were "safe" Black characters to White viewers because they were wealthy and educated and reflected "family values," that is, the heteronormative ideals of the neoliberal nuclear family—is a common one in critiques of the show in the United States as well. The second accusation, however—that the show can be read as segregationist— is far more persuasive within the South African context than in the United States, and thus provides additional evidence for the importance of understanding cultural products within the context they are consumed.

The claim that the Huxtables' wealth goes beyond a mere character trait into the realm of negative social impact is also the thesis of the other major book-length treatment of the show, Sut Jhally and Justin Lewis's *Enlightened Racism: The Cosby Show, Audiences, and the Myth of the American Dream*. Published earlier in the same year as Fuller's book, Jhally and Lewis arrive at far less positive conclusions. Ironically, Bill Cosby and his wife, Camille, commissioned this book in order to counter the growing criticisms of the show, but put no limitations on the authors or their methods. Although Jhally and Lewis neither take a wholly negative view of the show nor question the good intentions of the Cosbys or the show's other producers and participants, their audience research drew a crucial conclusion: White U.S.-based audiences had determined from *The Cosby Show* that Black Americans could "make it" if they only tried hard enough. In other words, *The Cosby Show* fed into the American Dream that true racial equality had been achieved, and that policy initiatives near and dear to the African American community—antipoverty efforts, education, housing, affirmative action—were no longer necessary, if they ever had been. Hence the "enlightened racism" of their title, in which a liberal-minded color-blindness denies the particular struggles and needs of Black Americans. In light of this argument, Fuller's claim that Black South Africans were encouraged by the show to strive for a higher standard of living becomes more insidious than constructive, indicating the successful traveling of a color-blind ideoscape from the United States to South Africa via transnational media flows.

A similar kind of argument can be found in the responses of some South Africans to the show. For instance, Anton added to his earlier comments:

> In hindsight, I think it would make for an interesting aside to investigate how screening *The Cosby Show* fit in with the state and capital's attempt in late apartheid to spread capitalism to Blacks, since Cosby epitomized success in a capitalist system.

Anton's concern with late-apartheid capitalism is reiterated by Marc, a thirty-four-year-old English-speaker, who also raised the issue of class while incorporating an additional critique that the program supports a segregationist view of life:

> I don't think that The Cosby Show was in any way subversive of late-apartheid ideology. I don't think it made the government of P. W. Botha or the SABC in the least bit uncomfortable. The Cosbys [Huxtables][28]—so charming and approachable, so respectably middle-class, so segregated (very few Whites in the show to my recollection, the Huxtable kids going to black colleges)—sat very well with how White South Africa wanted to see Black people. "If only our Blacks were like 'them'" or "you see, they're not so scary after all." Theo's poster was a small price to pay for these messages.

Marc's criticism also includes an analysis of the way in which many White South African audiences distanced themselves from thinking about the Huxtables in terms of race by strictly dividing race via possessive terms into "our blacks" and "them."

Reading the show as supportive of a segregationist ideology complicates how a single cultural product can be read in significantly different ways in different contexts. In the United States, The Cosby Show highlighted contemporary African American culture in a way that had rarely been done before on television. The Huxtables often entertained well-known African American celebrities such as B. B. King, Stevie Wonder, Lena Horne, Dizzy Gillespie, and Count Basie, and though the show studiously avoided the use of "black language," contemporary African American fashion (albeit acceptably middle-class African American fashion) was carefully integrated into the show. Likewise, the decorations of the home and various story lines carefully highlighted African American themes like Black History and the Negro Leagues of baseball.[29] In the United States, this served as a helpful corrective to television's blind spot to the richness of African American culture.

This centering of African American culture did not go unnoticed in South Africa, as Marc's quote above suggests. Barbara Buntman of the Department of Art History at the University of the Witwatersrand also noted the purposefulness of this approach: "As a person who works with visual images about race and identity, I remember remarking on several of the images that used to feature on the wall in the Cosby [sic] home—clearly always carefully selected to reinforce an aspect of their African-ness and/or African-American identity."[30] Yet in South Africa, this focus on African American culture was often read as evidence for how successful Black people could be without "interference," that is, segregated from White people. For while the Huxtables did occasionally entertain White visitors, the show was not integrated in a profound way. This segregation was continued in spinoffs of the show, such as *A Different World*, in which the character of Denise Huxtable attends a historically Black college that would fit well into apartheid's own racially segregated system of higher education.[31] Ironically, the show's focus on highlighting Black cultural institutions usually marginalized in U.S. media could thus be interpreted as buttressing apartheid ideology in a South African setting.

"Bill Cosby is an American for me, no race involved"

Perhaps the most interesting response of White South Africans to *The Cosby Show* is the complete dismissal of race as a factor at all in their viewing of the show. Such a dismissal would have been almost inconceivable in the United States at the time, except by the most vociferous proponents of a naïve color-blindness. Although the show was alternately accused of "whitewashing" race and praised for breaking down stereotypes, nearly every reading of *The Cosby Show* in the United States recognized the important role played by race. Nonetheless, many White South Africans claim that race was irrelevant, or even unnoticed, in their consumption of the show. This reading most often incorporates some combination of three different methods to distance the issue of race from White South Africans' enjoyment of the program. The first is to use the issue of education and class by declaring the Huxtables "normal," in effect deracializing the characters as if their Blackness was essentially implausible—at least in South Africa—*because* they are well educated and well off. The second uses a tribalization discourse, consistent with apartheid ideology, which focuses on the supposedly primitive nature of Black South Africans to discount any connections between them and the Huxtables. The third, and most commonly mentioned in my interviews that fall into this category, views the Huxtables as uniquely American, essentially trumping their Blackness with their foreign status. These three strategies were rarely employed entirely separately from each other, but rather with a great deal of overlap between them. The effect remained the same: *The Cosby Show* had no meaning regarding race because the Huxtables are too different from "our" Black people in South Africa.

Reactions to race and *The Cosby Show* provide an excellent illustration of how thoroughly White South African identifications were established as the default positionality in television under apartheid. This could take relatively mild forms, like Denise, a twenty-seven-year-old English-speaker who recalled her childhood perspective:

> I remember how my friends and I used to rush home from Brownies on a Wednesday afternoon to watch *The Cosby Show*. I found it very funny, but didn't think of it much in racial terms, except that it was strange that a Black girl had my name.

Similarly, Jean said:

> I don't think *The Cosby Show* ever changed my opinion on race relations because they were a different genre of Black person. I had rarely, in South Africa, personally met a Black doctor or lawyer, living in a huge house. It didn't relate to real life.

Many respondents, however, were more explicit in their equating of "normal" with not being Black. For instance, Pieter described *The Cosby Show* as a

> Very good show and was very popular and true to life. . . . Race was never on my mind when I watched the show as the characters were normal people and it was a typical family day to day situation which we, who had children in the family, experienced to some degree.

Thus race was a nonissue because the Huxtables were "normal," that is, de/racialized. Fuller discovered similar responses in her survey, though her analysis of these responses is more optimistic than my own. For instance, one White South African respondent said:

> I must say when we first watched the show it did seem rather strange to see how "normal" everyone was. It didn't take long before we stopped thinking of the Huxtables as a Black family and began to relate to them as one would to any show about a middle-class family.[32]

Again, it was necessary for this viewer to stop thinking of the characters as Black in order to accept them as normal, essentially de- and re-racializing the characters in a single moment of interpretation.

As with the verligte argument opposing television prior to the 1970s, this perspective could be phrased in ways that claimed to speak on behalf of Black South Africans, rather than in opposition to them. For instance, one of Fuller's White South African respondents claimed:

> The black population is mostly un-educated. . . . Consequently, these people do not find much to be amused about. Furthermore, they do not see any humour in seeing other black people finding it "so easy" and most probably even feel a little resentful.[33]

In fact, we know that *The Cosby Show* enjoyed immense popularity among Black as well as White South Africans. But even if this was not the case, this respondent's reaction tells us more about his own concerns and thoughts on race than that of Black South Africans. The difficulty some White South Africans had recognizing the Huxtables' Blackness is a testament not to color-blindness but to the success of apartheid in so thoroughly structuring the absence of Black South Africans in White South African life. Even into the very last years of apartheid, many White South Africans had great difficulty in seeing any Black person as "normal" or participating in "real life."

Many respondents consciously attributed this difference in standards of normality to an understanding of Black South Africans as rural, primitive, and tribal, particularly when compared to the presumably modernized Black people in the United States. Although a substantial cultural gap undeniably exists between African Americans and Black South Africans, the distinction as it is often made by White South Africans falls back on old-school apartheid—and colonial—ideology, wherein Black South Africans are marginalized as less advanced on some grand evolutionary scale. The ways in which this discourse attempts to glorify the so-called noble savage and the violence done in its name is well documented, both in South Africa and elsewhere.

As with the issue of education and class, this method of removing race from the pleasure of *The Cosby Show* could take weaker or stronger forms. For instance, Susanna, a forty-two-year-old Afrikaans-speaker, states:

> Bill Cosby was so different to the Southern Sotho people we dealt with on an every day basis—it therefore did not really impact on our thoughts of race relations.

This relatively mild distinction stands in contrast to one of Fuller's respondents, who declared:

> *The Cosby Show* is a *cultural* and *not* a *colour* thing. Black South Africans, with
> whom I grew up, do *not* relate with white humour and do *not* relate with
> American Negroes or "people of colour." (emphasis in original)[34]

In spite of the difference in how strongly these two claims are stated, they
nonetheless share two key elements. First, each claims a legitimacy—to
"know" Black South Africans—in an attempt to privilege their own perspective and speak on behalf of their Black counterparts. Second, "tribal"
South Africans are said to be so different from an African American like
Bill Cosby that no parallels can be drawn. Just as Fuller's study removes the
crucial differences in South Africa and the United States from the picture,
these claims ignore the similarities in White supremacy and how it functions in the two nations in an attempt to remove any racial analysis of *The
Cosby Show* that might shed light on South African politics, while also invoking the same kind of desired identification with the "civilized" nations
of North America and Western Europe that had made television a symbolic
stand-in for modern development in the earlier debates around its absence
in the country.

Marelize also drew this distinction while incorporating both the earlier perspective on class and a clearer tie to the Huxtables as specifically
American:

> I wouldn't particularly say that [the show] changed my perceptions about
> race. The people in *The Cosby Show* were firstly Americans to me, before they
> were from a specific race, so I didn't equate their culture with the culture of
> the different rural tribes in SA [South Africa], for example. I think that people
> disregard the effect that economic standing and affluence has on one's per-
> ceptions of class and style, much more so than skin color.

While Marelize may well be correct that the intersections of class and race
are often disregarded, race remained the formal legal determinate of where
you lived, what kind of job you had, and many other elements of everyday
life in late apartheid South Africa. Marelize's comment thus displays the
shifting identifications of White South Africans, moving away from race as
the legal, formal mechanism of segregation toward class as a de facto main-
tainer of cultural boundaries.

Many of my respondents echoed Marelize's statement that the Huxtables
were firstly American, and that their being American completely erased any
possible implications regarding race. For instance Margaret, a forty-year-old
English-speaker, said:

Bill Cosby is an American for me, no race involved. I was never able to equate an African American with a Black South African.

This perspective was by no means limited to White South Africans, either. Phillip, a twenty-eight-year-old English-speaker, reported the following incident:

> I remember once watching the show—I was probably ten or eleven or so, and our domestic worker came in and started watching with me. She remarked that these people were American "Negroes" and that they were different to African Blacks. I remember then thinking that was a bit strange, but I guess I believed it too. I remember her saying that they were like "Europeans"— loaded syntax for SA in those days.

Steven reflects the kinds of conversations that used to go on among friends, and the difficulty some White South Africans had making sense out of the Huxtables' Americanness in a South African context:

> I remember someone saying that our problem was that our Blacks weren't like Cosby, and someone else saying that Cosby was Coloured, not Black. I think that most of my circle of White South Africans felt that if Blacks learnt to speak and live like the Cosbys then they would be okay.

Again, we see the coming together of several different methods for distancing *The Cosby Show* from White South Africans' racial views, including economic status, education, and racial classification. Just as the show was criticized in the United States for portraying only "safe," nonthreatening African Americans, some White South African viewers took the interpretation a step further, declaring African Americans as a whole "safe" when compared to Black South Africans. In this way the show could be used to justify the differences between formal legal treatments of race in the two countries: because Blacks in America are so civilized, the Americans can afford integration, whereas South Africa's tribalized Blacks require apartheid.

Jill, a thirty-two-year-old English-speaker, touches on nearly all of the interpretations discussed above, including the show's popularity among White South Africans:

> My family is White middle-class South African and my parents were, unfortunately, products of the apartheid system and at best "liberal"—in the worst sense of the word. I remember almost never missing a *Cosby Show*—

the whole family would sit down to watch and my parents even bought some Bill Cosby cassettes as a result of the popularity of the show.

Jill challenged her family on the seeming disjuncture between their love for *The Cosby Show* and their views on race in South Africa:

> By the time the show stopped and even at the tender and ignorant young age of fifteen I remember quizzing my dad on why he liked *The Cosby Show* but spoke disparagingly about Black people in South Africa. His response was that color was irrelevant as long as people were educated and the Cosby cast were clearly educated and were American—so they were okay. This weird hypocrisy and racist duality was one I heard expressed by other family members and friends—the same people who got really upset by *Roots* but made no connection with the treatment of Black people in South Africa!

The answers Jill received confirm many of the readings discussed earlier in this chapter, with significant overlap. In understanding these responses, she explicitly links class, race, and nationalism in the reaction of her family and friends to the political situation in South Africa:

> I think for a lot of White South Africans *The Cosby Show* was an example of how Black people could be, "given enough time and education"—they were a well-to-do family that spoke American English (not any other "native" language), had well-behaved children and made people laugh—in short, they were "okay" and nonthreatening in comparison to Black South Africans who were uneducated, did not all speak English, and were communists and terrorists to boot! Hence, to a degree, classism, American culture, and family values won out over racism—but only in the minds of White South Africans!

Jill's comments bring us full circle back to the larger political crisis around racialized identities in the mid- to late 1980s South Africa. Whereas both American and South African audiences may have viewed the Huxtables as "safe," the question of what kind of safety they represented remains. Although it may be difficult to overestimate the level of deep-seated racialized fear in the United States, South Africa was in the midst of an explosive State of Emergency. Race war, not race riots, was on the mind of South Africans at the time.[35] Within this context, White South Africans' difficulty in viewing the Huxtables through the same filter as Black South Africans— "communists and terrorists to boot!"—becomes quite understandable.

There is no shortage of ways in which White South Africans read *The*

Cosby Show. Each of these interpretations functioned within certain contexts and depended to some extent on political identifications themselves. Certainly each of these readings can make persuasive claims to validity. The most convincing claim regarding how White South Africans constructed meaning from *The Cosby Show* is in fact that there was no single meaning created from the program. Why, then, did *The Cosby Show*—or White South Africans' understanding of it—matter in South Africa?

The Social Phenomenon of *The Cosby Show*'s Popularity

The immense, and shared, popularity of *The Cosby Show* should indicate a new direction for analysis of the program and its importance in South Africa. Rather than turning to content analysis and attempting to discern what the "true" message of the show is or was, a better way to approach the program is to ask why so many South Africans, particularly White South Africans, possess such strongly held opinions about the show. What is it about *The Cosby Show* that caused such an investment in not only the show itself, but also in explaining why it was so popular?

The first and most obvious answer is the level of popularity itself. Very few cultural products create the kind of stir that *The Cosby Show* did, particularly over several years (distinguishing it from a mere fad). Not only was the program the most popular show on television, but it crossed over into the role of a cultural referent, a touchstone by which not only other shows but also real life events and characters were measured. Hall describes a similar kind of phenomenon in the United Kingdom around the drama *Dallas* (which, incidentally, ranked second to *The Cosby Show* in South Africa in the mid-1980s):

> At a certain moment the programme achieved a kind of popularity other than merely in terms of numbers of viewers. It had repercussions on the whole culture, the involvement of the viewers became of a different order. At a certain moment you could no longer avoid talking about the popularity of *Dallas* when people started using categories from it to help interpret their experiences.[36]

Hall continues to explain that, at the time of the interview from which this quote is taken, the show was still viewed by the same numbers, but was "no longer active in the collective cultural consciousness."[37] *The Cosby Show* had clearly become active in the collective cultural consciousness of the South African nation in the mid-1980s.

For a television program to be active in the collective cultural consciousness that Hall describes is no small accomplishment in any nation, but in the mid-1980s in South Africa it is astounding. The word "collective" is key, for the cultural consciousness of South Africans had been kept carefully separated and racialized by nearly forty years of apartheid and segregation before it. As indicated by quantitative measures, *The Cosby Show* was the first such phenomenon to enter into any kind of *collective* cultural consciousness across racial groups in South Africa, and it did so in the midst of the States of Emergency and the most polarized, violent moment in South African politics in nearly a century. Whether South Africans agreed on what *The Cosby Show* meant is of relatively little importance in comparison to the series' success itself.

What mattered was the fact that South Africans were not only captivated by a single television family—an African American family no less—but they were also fully aware of the Huxtables' popularity among their compatriots of different racialized groups. This awareness separates *The Cosby Show* phenomenon from the earlier fence posts of this project in crucial ways. Although Black South Africans watched TV1, it remained in both practice and White South Africans' perceptions an exclusively "White" channel, thereby managing to maintain the structured absence of Black South Africans in political and social life. Like TV1, TV2/3 remained the "Black" channel in spite of the fact that White South Africans occasionally played the role of tourist by surfing into Zulu. So while TV2/3 may have broken down part of the structured absence of Black South Africans, it nonetheless maintained the *perception* of apartheid's divisions, regardless of its White viewers and the restructuring of imagined subject positions that it helped instigate. *The Cosby Show* broke down these perceived divisions; it was the first program that nearly everyone watched, and nearly everyone knew that nearly everyone watched it.[38] As such, *The Cosby Show* became one of the first cultural experiences consciously shared across racial boundaries in South Africa. The shared popularity of the program therefore both reflected and accelerated a transnational rethinking of White South African identifications vis-à-vis the South African nation, which could perhaps now include Black South Africans.

In the context of the States of Emergency, it is quite possible that only a cultural product like a television show—perhaps specifically a comedy— would be able to enter the collective cultural consciousness, at least in an almost universally well-liked manner. Recalling Meyrowitz's work on electronic media, television is uniquely positioned to reach disparate audiences simultaneously and with relative equity. But even other forms of television programming have particular obstacles to achieving the kind of popularity of *The Cosby Show* in the mid-1980s.

As discussed earlier, the news and other actuality programming were too heavily controlled to allow any kind of departure, or even neutrality, from the National Party line, and tended therefore to alienate large numbers of South Africans. Indeed, the fact that *The Cosby Show* was described as "mere entertainment" in the SABC's *Annual Report 1987* may have allowed it not only to pass through otherwise reactionary SABC filters, but also given it a chance to enter viewers' homes with their political guard somewhat down.[39] Consider the reaction of Andrew, a thirty-four-year-old English-speaker, to the controversies around the program:

> I remember hearing a while back that there were some complaints in the U.S. about it not accurately portraying the lives of the average Black family. Not sure if that was true, but I couldn't understand what the big deal was, since it was meant to be entertainment, not current affairs.

Because it was entertainment, *The Cosby Show* was allowed into homes that may have resisted a similar show in another format. Likewise, the conversations that took place around it were not necessarily political. According to Anton, "My whole family [watched *The Cosby Show*]. People talked about it, like they did other programs, not to discuss weighty political matters or apartheid's demise or reform." Although the purpose of discussing the show was not to explore important political issues—perhaps even *because* of their lack of explicit political content—talking about the program gave South Africans a shared space with fewer constraints within which to revise and rehearse shifting South African identifications.

Even a television drama would have difficulty winning widespread adoration because of a greater difficulty in avoiding politically sensitive or painful topics. Television comedy has the advantage of giving us a certain form of pleasure—most often through laughter—that more serious dramas or actuality programming find more difficult to provide. Recall William's comments, quoted earlier, that the show

> made an impact on many White South Africans—to be able to identify with a Black family who lived a middle-class life and made them laugh—and the laughter was one of identifying with many of the issues and situations brought up in the show.

The importance of laughter and its associated pleasure in accepting the Huxtables is seconded by Alvin Poussaint, a child psychologist at Harvard and an advisor to *The Cosby Show*, who claimed, "This show is changing the white community's perspective of black Americans. It's doing far more to instill positive racial attitudes than if Bill came at the viewer with a sledge-hammer or a sermon."[40] Although one might argue that Poussaint over-states his argument, *The Cosby Show* demonstrates that television comedy was uniquely positioned to reach a mass audience across racial boundaries in spite of the highly polarized political situation.

Race, the Huxtables, and White South African Identifications

Race remains a crucial component in understanding both the popularity and the impact of *The Cosby Show* in South Africa. There is little likelihood such a program would have entered the collective cultural consciousness of the nation in as powerful and significant a way as it did if it were just an-other American sitcom featuring White characters. Even if another show had achieved this level of popularity, it would probably not have given shape to South African politics and culture to the same degree. However, race matters not because of some single, all-powerful message either in-tended by the producers or received by the audiences; rather, race matters in how White South Africans made sense of the pleasure they derived from the show.

Ang's work on *Dallas* focuses on the ways in which viewers gain plea-sure—sometimes "guilty" pleasure—by watching a specific television pro-gram.[41] Her emphasis on pleasure is useful for grasping the significance of *The Cosby Show*'s popularity among White South Africans. By denying the role of race in their enjoyment of *The Cosby Show*, many White South Afri-cans were required to make a crucial shift in their understandings of race that altered not only their views of Black South Africans but also their own subject positions and identifications. It remains unclear the extent to which *The Cosby Show* actually instigated this shift or merely reflected it; in all probability, both occurred to varying and overlapping degrees.

As we see in the quotes above, many White South Africans claimed the Huxtables as one of their own, or at least more like them, rather than draw-ing connections between characters on *The Cosby Show* and Black South Africans. In and of itself this may not seem terribly significant, but in the context of South Africa's highly racialized legal and political order, this re-quired delinking biological and cultural notions of race. In other words, their comfort with the Huxtables pushed many White South Africans away from a more essentialized biological understanding of race and toward a more cultural understanding of their power relationships with Black South Africans. White South Africans could only ignore the role of race in the show by *actively* denying a common racial identity between Bill Cosby and Black South Africans. In so doing, they also forced a rethinking of their own racial identifications and their biological versus cultural construction. The increasing pressure on the apartheid regime from European governments also fed into this shift, in that the moral rejection of apartheid by most of Europe left White South Africans unable to take for granted their "natural" racial kinship with Europeans. When compared to the racialized discourses around whether television should be introduced, interviewees' readings of *The Cosby Show* demonstrate a clear shift away from essentialized biological constructions of race toward a more class-based culturally and locally contingent creation.

Of course, cultural constructions of race can be every bit as oppressive as biological ones; this shift did not mark the end of racism in South Africa by any means. Likewise, the reinscription of race away from biology and onto class paved the way for many of the more pernicious continuities of apartheid throughout the democratic transition. This shift did, however, offer a way out of the crisis of will faced by White South Africans during the States of Emergency. For if someone of African origin like Bill Cosby could be educated and enculturated into such a charming and powerful individual, according to this logic, then perhaps so could Black South Africans. Hence Jill's observation above that White South Africans viewed Cliff Huxtable as what Black South Africans could become "given enough time and education." Race thereby ceased to be immutable, at least in the abstract. Indeed, formal apartheid became less practical under this conception of race because of difficulties in legislating such a concept, but informal segregation and the maintenance of political and social power through education and class remained quite plausible, perhaps even strengthened, thereby transforming the embarrassment of apartheid into a more internationally acceptable form of White supremacy.

"The 'Cosby Plan' for South Africa"

While Black South Africans were facing the most volatile and violent state repression in recent South African history during the mid- to late 1980s, White South Africans became increasingly disillusioned with the identifications and political structures that had served them for decades. As the States of Emergency pushed the nation into upheaval, the crisis of will that confronted the apartheid regime was accompanied by a crisis among White South Africans as they tried to make sense of their own identifications.

During this time the SABC attempted to avoid the turmoil completely, opting for heavily slanted news that presented no challenge to the government's perspective, along with light entertainment that ignored the racialized conflict consuming the nation. Amid the chaos, White and Black South Africans alike were invited into the home of the Huxtables. Across racial and language barriers, South Africans of all ilk shared their enjoyment of *The Cosby Show*—though for a wide variety of different reasons—and created a collective cultural consciousness around the program. In a political context becoming more and more polarized, *The Cosby Show* became a rare common ground for South Africans, even if it was infrequently invoked explicitly. *The Cosby Show* managed to enter into the collective consciousness of a nation that was otherwise being torn apart at the seams.

Throughout the many interpretations of the show, the interaction of race and popular entertainment combined to provide White South Africans with new options for imagining their relationship to Black counterparts. Sandra, a thirty-seven-year-old English-speaker, echoed the comments of many White South Africans when she said, "[The Huxtables] seemed a world away from reality and like no Black SA family." Yet despite distancing Bill Cosby from Black South Africans, her description still continued, "The only similarity was that they have the same dreams and desires we all have—Black or White." Like Sandra, Matthew, a twenty-nine-year-old English-speaker, "loved the Cosby Show. Thought it was great. To be honest, it never really hit me that they were Black—they were just an American family." Yet Matthew also noted that the entertainment format and his lack of awareness around race actually served to allow for a shift in his (and others') views regarding race: "Everybody I knew watched it, and I never recall hearing comments about race—so it seems to have been a good method of showing that Black people are just like White people."

The degree to which *The Cosby Show*'s popularity was caused by, or a symptom of, White South Africans' shift away from biological explanations of race is less important than the implications of that shift. In moving to a cultural understanding of race and racial divisions in South Africa, White South Africans began to uncouple biological race from formal political power in a manner that had never been done under apartheid or before, substituting a more explicitly class-based understanding of race in its stead. The result was the ability of White South Africans, for the first time, to imagine themselves within the same political system as Black South Africans, albeit only the "safe" ones.

In July of 1986, the *Wall Street Journal* featured a story titled "The 'Cosby Plan' for South Africa." According to the article, an Afrikaner named Carl Coetzer was proposing a complicated formula by which South Africans—Black and White alike—could receive a qualified franchise. Under Coetzer's "Cosby Plan," each South African could receive up to nine votes depending on his or her status regarding what Coetzer called "the three pillars of civilization"—education, work and ownership—along with a bonus vote for community leadership. According to Coetzer, this solved the problem of Black majority rule in South Africa because "The Cosbys of this world, irrespective of color, will vote for the Cosbys of this world. Then we won't have the rabble voting for some dictatorship like the rest of Africa."[42]

The thinly veiled classism of Coetzer's plan and its links to race, particularly in a nation with devastating unemployment and purposeful dispossession of land and education for its Black residents, is not difficult to detect.[43] Furthermore, there is no evidence that Coetzer's "plan" was ever more concrete than random ramblings to an American journalist. However, the nature of his plan illustrates the shift in racial identifications among White South Africans and the implications of that shift. No longer is *every* Black South African implicated in the *swart gevaar*, but instead only "the rabble." Black South Africans who are well educated, gainfully employed in a profession, own land, and involved in their communities were now welcome to vote; never mind the fact that apartheid had intentionally prevented the overwhelming majority of Black South Africans from attaining the first three of these four qualifications. Coetzer's plan is a call for "the Cosbys of the world, irrespective of color" to unite under the neoliberal banner. Thus White South African identifications had begun to shift away from being defined almost solely in opposition to Black South Africans, and the dismantling of the structured absence of Black South Africans in political as well as social life had become more plausible. Although Bill Cosby never stood for election in South Africa, the stage was set for the next fence post: it was a matter of just a few short years before another Black man—safe, charismatic, articulate, well educated, and professional in the eyes of White South Africans and the world—stepped through the gates of Victor Verster prison with every intention to run in a South African election.

CHAPTER SIX

I May Not Be a Freedom Fighter,
but I Play One on TV

In the final months of 1989, rumors surfaced that Nelson Mandela—the icon of the anti-apartheid struggle—was about to be released after more than a quarter of a century of incarceration. Other imprisoned leaders of the African National Congress (ANC), most notably Walter Sisulu, had been released to test the waters, and all indications pointed toward Mandela's imminent freedom. In preparing for this significant international news event, the press corps was faced with a considerable conundrum for visual media: no one was sure what Mandela looked like. Having been placed under the ban—which made it illegal for his picture or words to be published or broadcast in any form—the only images of Mandela available to the public during his time in prison had been made decades earlier. As Keyan Tomaselli and Arnold Shepperson put it, the structured absence of Mandela had made him "The Man with No Face."[1] In order to solve this dilemma, *Time* magazine used an artist to sketch how Mandela "should" look based on the famous photograph of Mandela and Sisulu in the prison yard of Robben Island, taken decades earlier. Ironically, the result bore little resemblance to the man who had spent twenty-seven years in prison and suffered through tuberculosis; instead, the image looked strikingly similar to Danny Glover, who had portrayed Mandela in an HBO miniseries three years earlier: I may not be a freedom fighter, but I play one on television.[2]

The structured absence of Black South Africans in conventional politics came crashing to a halt with Mandela's release and the unbanning of the various opposition groups. The immediacy of this change was evident not only in the media event of Mandela—the world's most famous political prisoner yet unrecognizable to almost everyone—walking out of prison and into the living rooms of people around the globe, but also in the sudden and striking changes in the SABC's programming. Just as it had in the early 1980s, the pendulum of the SABC's approach to current events once again swung from denial to an optimistic embracing of the nation's political future. For those who had lived through the States of Emergency, this shift was both a welcome relief and an ironic surprise.

The period of the so-called transition between 1990 and 1994 is neatly bookended by the release of Mandela from prison and his inauguration as the first democratically elected president of the Republic of South Africa. However, the tidy periodization of the transition belies both immense up-heaval and uncertainty within these years as well as substantial slippage and blurring of the boundaries between apartheid before 1990 and democracy after 1994. In the midst of this period, the SABC was one of the very first public institutions to undergo "transformation"—the catch-all phrase for moving apartheid-era institutions into a post-apartheid future. Indeed, because of its stranglehold on electronic media, grassroots activists and political elites alike saw the transformation of the SABC as a necessary pre-requisite for democratic elections. The role of television as both a site and a subject of contention during the dismantling of apartheid—the fourth and final fence post of this book—proves crucial to understanding South Africa's transition, sometimes referred to optimistically as a "negotiated revolution" or pessimistically as an "elite transition."[3]

The Release of Mandela as a Media Event

The media moment that nearly everyone—in South Africa and the rest of the world—remembers watching on television is Nelson and Winnie Mandela striding through the gates of Victor Verster Prison, outside Paarl in the Western Cape, and raising their fists in salute on February 11, 1990. Indeed, a leading British newspaper named the moment the second most important global media event of the twentieth century, superseded only by the Apollo moon landing.[4] Mandela's release provided a profound moment of transnational media flows emanating from, rather than arriving in, South Africa. This moment was preceded by five years of clandestine negotiations among various levels of the government, Mandela, the ANC, and other op-position groups, and set up by a speech given to parliament by F. W. de Klerk nine days previous, on February 2.[5] De Klerk's speech was given at the annual opening of Parliament—an event similar to the State of the Union address in the United States—less than six months after de Klerk took over the presidency of South Africa in a palace coup made possible by Botha's increasing intransigence following a stroke. Although the speech was promoted as a major statement of policy reform, expectations remained muted in part due to Botha's infamous "Rubicon" speech in 1985, which was also billed as a significant turning point in apartheid but fizzled into a "damp squib."[6]

De Klerk, however, dropped a bombshell; he declared in his opening statement that South Africa had been placed "irrevocably on the road of drastic change" and then proceeded to un-ban the ANC, the PAC, the SACP, and other opposition organizations, and stated his intention to release Mandela and other political prisoners in the imminent future. Although debates continue to rage over the relative weight to be given to de Klerk as an individual politician making a bold move versus the "inevitability" of such a decision due to structural and political pressures on the apartheid regime, there is no doubt that de Klerk's speech instigated a radical rethinking of the South African state and the racialized subject positions within it. In the words of journalist Allister Sparks, "He [had] demolished the old Afrikaner vision of a white South Africa, of a *volkstaat* that was theirs by divine right and without which they could not survive as a national entity."[7]

The significance of de Klerk's speech, which was televised nationally, was certainly not lost on lay people watching the proceedings. The reaction to the speech by Andries Treurnicht, the leader of the Conservative Party (CP), which had just risen to the level of official opposition in Parliament (i.e., the party with the second-highest number of seats), was particularly vivid for many people. Steven, a forty-year-old English-speaker, compared the speech to Mandela's release:

> Far more significant though was de Klerk's speech on February 2nd, 1990—Treurnicht looked like he would explode! That was when we realized that everything was different; it was a lot more talked about—the release was a bit disappointing.

De Klerk's speech made the growing estrangement between the National Party and the far-right wing of Afrikaner politics for all intents and purposes permanent.

The expectations that de Klerk's speech created for both Mandela's release and South Africa's political future is essential to understanding the release of Mandela as a media event. In *Media Events: The Live Broadcasts of History*, Daniel Dayan and Elihu Katz describe the media event as a "new narrative genre that employs the unique potential of the electronic media to command attention universally and simultaneously in order to tell a primordial story about current affairs."[8] They name several elements required of media events: they are an interruption to routine broadcasting; they are live; they are planned outside of the media; they are preplanned; they are presented with reverence and ceremony; and they enthrall very large audiences. These events have become the "high holidays of mass communication."[9] Had Mandela's release been sudden and unexpected, the anticipation of the event (which Steven hints at above) would not have risen to such a great degree.

The status of Mandela's release as a media event is significant because of media events' roles in shaping our collective consciousness. We talk about media events with our friends and colleagues at work or school, we remember where we were when they took place, and we position ourselves in relation to others according to our interpretations of them. As such, media events differ markedly from regular broadcast programming. Whereas we may discuss our favorite show with others the next day, we are far less likely to bring it up as a topic to spark conversation, or to remember the experience of watching it and how it made us feel years down the road.[10] In other words, media events and our understandings of them are far more likely to give shape to our ways of viewing ourselves and in relation to others.

According to Dayan and Katz, media events play a special role in fractured societies by providing a moment of common experience that transcends the daily divergence of our lives. Likewise, media events compel us to discuss a common issue, sometimes even providing common terminology with which to discuss it across large populations. Even if we completely disagree with one another's interpretations of such a media event, we talk about those disagreements differently. In other words,

> Even when these programs address conflict—as they do—they celebrate not conflict but *reconciliation*. This is where they differ from the daily news events, where conflict is the inevitable subject.[11] (emphasis in the original)

The sense of potential for positive change coupled with anxiety around Mandela's release was overwhelmingly evident in interviews. Vanessa, a thirty-five-year-old English-speaker, echoed the reactions of many:

> Yes [I watched Mandela's release], I have very positive, warm memories of the time . . . but at the same time realized it was a turning point in our history and I remember, as I watched it, wondering what the future held.

Marcia, a thirty-eight-year-old English-speaker, elaborated on Vanessa's concerns:

I remember there were bets being taken on how long he lived after coming out of prison. Luckily, we were all wrong and he is still alive today. It was a hard time. . . . Indoctrination is a hard thing to overcome, even when the truth is apparent, it is not always easy to accept. I was brought up believing Mandela was a terrorist. Although I know him to be one of the greatest leaders in the world, I still sometimes have a hard time believing him to be a saint, not a sinner.

In spite of the widespread anxiety among White South Africans ("suitably egged on by the right-wing, but of course it turned out to be unfounded," according to thirty-seven-year-old English-speaker Marc), the sense of hopefulness created by Mandela's release was powerful. After the violence and uncertainty of the States of Emergency in the mid- to late 1980s, the encouragement felt even by mainstream White South Africans at the time of Mandela's release is a testament to the distance traveled by White South African identifications in the previous five years. The volkstaat, whether dream or nightmare, had indeed been demolished in the eyes of most. William Beinart's authoritative history, *Twentieth Century South Africa*, depicts the aftermath of Mandela's release as "a wave of optimism . . . unleashed, the signal for symbolic reclaiming of the country."[12]

Just as it had played a role in earlier processes of identification, television also gave shape to these new hopes among White South Africans, in part through its ability to transform the release into a media event. Sandra, a thirty-seven-year-old English-speaker, expressed a similar sentiment to Beinart's when describing the release: "Uplifting . . . like it was a new and better beginning. I remember the celebrations in the streets and the uplifting scenes on TV." Although Mandela's release triggered widespread public celebrations in the streets, these joyous occasions were for the most part experienced by White South Africans through their television screens.

Once again, generational differences showed themselves in various White South Africans' responses to the release of Mandela. Over and over younger respondents described themselves celebrating while their parents dwelt in restless anxiety and their grandparents groused for the good old days. Steven related one of the more vivid of these tales:

My mother's mother was a lot more conservative than I had become—she had reacted to my becoming an objector with some vehemence, and said that "Nelson Mandela would be released over my dead body."[13] I was watching the [release] with several friends while 604 was playing; it had far better commentary than the TV.[14] My sister phoned me [as Mandela was getting into the car] to say that Gran had died. She had been ill, so her death wasn't unexpected, but the timing did give us something to talk about.

The broadcasting of Mandela's release was not without its own complications. His release came over an hour later than scheduled while his speech at Cape Town's Grand Parade was delayed several more hours, leaving the television commentators desperately trying to fill time but, like the rest of the nation, unclear what the current terms of engagement had become. The release was announced by the young news anchor Hendrik Verwoerd, the grandson of the assassinated prime minister of the same name known as the architect of modern apartheid, with the onsite reporter providing very little insight into the event itself. Anton, a thirty-six-year-old Coloured South African, said, "I can still remember Clarence Keyter's sparse commentary and found the SABC's shaky camera angles and lack of historical context and knowledge of the ANC as a movement as not impressive."

Looking back on that day almost ten years later, the producer of the SABC's coverage, André le Roux, attributed the SABC's less-than-stellar coverage of the event to "pressures from above" that made SABC reporters "too frightened to say anything that the authorities would not like."[15] He did not, however, elaborate as to what kinds of pressures were coming from above or how they were established to bring fear to reporters' coverage. In fact, following de Klerk's speech nine days earlier, it had suddenly become less clear to those at the SABC, even those wishing to conform to the desires of the National Party, exactly what was expected of them.

Nonetheless, the live broadcasting of Mandela's release conveyed a sense of collective importance, even beyond what his release would have otherwise garnered, simply by simultaneously reaching such a broad audience through television. As Dayan and Katz state, "These broadcasts integrate societies in a collective heartbeat and evoke a renewal of loyalty to the society and its legitimate authority" through the collective experience of participating in the media event.[16] In 1990 there was very little legitimate authority in South African society to be renewed; the media event of Mandela's release could be argued to have *established*, rather than renewed, legitimacy—or at least the potential for legitimacy—for the state.

The reality is messier, of course. Any given media event's impact may be permanent or fleeting, profound or superficial. The point is not that media events inevitably usher in a utopian era of integration and reconciliation, nor a closed system of hegemonic common sense. Yet, the ability of Mandela's release to penetrate the collective consciousness of South Af-

rica is due, in part at least, to its status as a media event. Whether each individual within the polity experiences the media event in the same way is
not irrelevant, but neither is it all-important. The very fact that each individual has the *potential* to experience the media event at all is what lends
the media event its power in shaping collective consciousness. People may
have vehemently disagreed about whether Mandela's release would impact
the country positively or negatively, but they were talking about South Africa as a single country, in some cases for the first time. While this clearly
does not lead to reconciliation in and of itself, it does represent the beginnings of a common if contentious imagining of both South Africa's past
and its future.

From Absent Signifier to Media Messiah

Mandela was perfectly suited for the role suddenly thrust upon him in the
beginning of the 1990s. He had the kind of genteel manner that White
South Africans found palatable, hardly the raging Stalinist with flesh in his
teeth that the "total strategy" had warned of for so many years. Likewise,
his stature as a man of the struggle had grown to mythic proportions during his time as "the man with no face," giving him massive support among
Black South Africans. However, the messianic expectations of Mandela
quickly became a potential liability as well as a benefit for both the ANC
and the nation's hopes for a peaceful transition to democracy. Rob Nixon's
book devotes an insightful chapter, titled "Mandela, Messianism, and the
Media," to the role projected onto Mandela following his release.[17] Nixon
makes two particularly important points that are supported by my research:
first, Mandela himself immediately recognized the danger of overshadow-
ing the ANC, and second, Mandela was able to carry the hopes and fears
of White as well as Black South Africans in part because his many years
under the ban had given him a personal presence that was a throwback to
another era.

Mandela began his speech on the Grand Parade by declaring himself
not a prophet but a servant of the people, and throughout the months after
his release he made declarations such as "I submit to the collective leadership of the ANC."[18] Likewise, his own autobiography—as well as other accounts of his secret negotiations while still in prison—often points to the
care with which he balanced his role as a leader with whom the government was negotiating while still maintaining his subservience to the collective leadership of the ANC-in-exile.[19] Indeed, Mandela had accepted
the ANC's strategy of making him and his release the focal point of the

international anti-apartheid movements only in response to a request by the ANC's leadership. He seems to have been remarkably free of the impulse to further his stature within the movement for his own gratification before, during, and after his time in prison. Nixon points out that this submission to collective leadership was more than just a personality trait; Mandela was coming out of a movement that had continually seen its leadership (and the leadership of its allies) removed from public life through the ban, imprisonment, and assassination. Some estimate that as many as 50,000 activists had been detained under the States of Emergency. "To concentrate power, talent, and hope in a prestigious few," Nixon says, "was simply to invite beheading."[20]

If Mandela's submission to the collective leadership of the ANC was both good strategy and a good fit with the remarkable emphasis on "consultation" that grew out of the UDF, MDM, and grassroots activism of the 1980s, his personality and mannerisms were also an excellent match for the task at hand. Not only was he *not* the firebrand who many had come to fear from the government's propaganda, but he was exceedingly polite and well mannered. As such, he harkened back to the era in which he was last a participant in public life: the 1950s. He responded to questions thoughtfully, not in the sound-byte of the 1990s, but in the considered and methodical way of interviews forty years previous. His manner was so clearly unselfconscious of the media age in which he found himself that it played particularly well to that very media. Mandela's lack of focus on the television cameras gave viewers the sense that he was sincere, thoughtful, and of course those double-edged adjectives for people of color, articulate and dignified.[21] As such, he reminded both Black Americans and South Africans of leaders from the heyday of both the American civil rights movement and the decolonization movements in Africa. Mandela was not the inheritor of these leaders' legacies, but rather a contemporary of Nyerere and Nkrumah, King and Malcolm X, suddenly transported into 1990. While these leaders had been considered firebrands during their own time, many were now viewed as tame compared to the more militant leaders of Black Power and Black Consciousness who had since been in the public eye.

The making of Mandela as a man above the slights and superficiality of politics in the televisual age was possible in large part to his erasure from public life through the use of the ban. Before his speech on the Grand Parade and subsequent interviews, Mandela had never before appeared on television. His famous speech in his own defense during the Rivonia Trial—more of a statement of defiance against apartheid than an argument for acquittal—was delivered months before King spoke of his dream on the Washington Mall.[22] Hence Mandela was reemerging as "a living martyr" long after the assassinations of Malcolm X and King "who embodied the spirit of those dead ones," according to Nixon. "Here was a voice from the past that was also a voice on the ascendant."[23] Had Mandela not spent nearly three decades outside of a media-saturated environment, it is highly unlikely that he would have retained the characteristics and mannerisms of the 1950s to the degree he had.

The implications of Mandela's structured absence while in prison go beyond what Nixon identifies as his seeming naïveté regarding a media-saturated public sphere. Mandela's absence also meant that he was insulated from having to take positions on the various controversies of resistance politics that had taken place in the previous three decades, leaving the luster with which he shone upon his release untainted by those controversies.[24] Furthermore, Tomaselli and Shepperson point out that his lengthy incarceration made him an "absent signifier," allowing widely divergent political agendas to project onto him what they wanted him to be.[25]

In this unusual context, Mandela entered the public arena in dramatic fashion, exploding the previously structured absence of Black South Africans on the political stage with a presence that filled the space created by the preceding decades of television and other cultural products. Mandela managed to fit perfectly Coetzer's "Cosby Plan" to provide a qualified franchise to "civilized" Black South Africans, as reflected by Mandela's surprising and persistent popularity among all South Africans, White and Black alike. His stature in the public consciousness shifted with amazing speed from the absent signifier, which could be read as both liberation hero and communist terrorist, into "a new and autonomous sign" that "now acted, had ways of doing and saying that the many aggregations that make up 'the audience' could hear for themselves . . . a fully developed, and still developing, sign in its own right."[26] Consider the impression Mandela made on Marike, a sixty-four-year-old Afrikaans-speaker:

I liked Mr. Mandela from the start. The way he spoke and all that. Calm and peaceful and not full of bitterness and hate. It's always been like that with him, even now. I can't say that about the other, new politicians and the new black government, that they give you that feeling of love and peace. But him definitely. For me that's still amazing, that he was in jail so long and came out without hate and bitterness and [did not try] to play people against each other. Yes, I liked him from the start.

In spite of Marike's hesitancy in extending her approval of Mandela to his beloved ANC and its current leaders, he nonetheless succeeded in bridging the gap between a White South African subjectivity forged in the strict separatism of apartheid and a newer identification that could imagine coexistence with a Black president. Over time, as Mandela voluntarily removed himself from leadership of the party and the government, that bridge appears to have held, albeit shakily, even as the messianic vision of the man has faded from the media spotlight. What was the role of television's communicative space in allowing Mandela to make the transition from absent signifier to autonomous sign, all the while remaining (or becoming) an acceptably safe and reassuring figure for White South Africans as their president?

The Institutional Transformation of the SABC

The release of Mandela and the un-banning of the opposition movements had immediate and serious implications for the SABC as an institution. The period between 1990 and 1994 was one of immense change in the content and the structure of the SABC, and yielded a profound impact in actuality and entertainment programming. The SABC was the first apartheid-era institution to be "transformed," even prior to the elections. The perceived power of broadcasting was so strong, in fact, that the transformation of the SABC joined the military and interim constitutional structures at the top of the list for negotiators.

In the 1980s the National Party had begun to privatize the various parastatals. These institutions, of which the SABC was one of many, had been a significant source of patronage and financial advantage in the Afrikaner community following the National Party's rise to power in 1948, serving a similar role to the civil service in other colonial and postcolonial African nations. With the government's attempts to reform apartheid in the 1980s, privatizing the parastatals became a method of entrenching the advantageous positions of White South Africans, particularly Afrikaners, within the institutions in anticipation of a more equitable political dispensation.

The 1987 government White Paper that proposed the privatization of most of the parastatals left the SABC untouched, "presumably because the broadcaster was seen as too important to the government's Total Strategy against black insurrection."[27] After de Klerk's landmark speech, however, the National Party quickly moved to alter the SABC before political transformations could occur. Named in March of 1990, the Task Group on Broadcasting in South and Southern Africa (referred to as the Viljoen Task

Group, after the chairman of both the task group and the SABC, Christo Viljoen) consisted of thirteen White men and included representatives of both the military and the intelligence bureau, underscoring the significance of broadcasting in the minds of the so-called securocrats of the apartheid regime.

Even before the Viljoen Task Group offered its final report, Viljoen announced the restructuring of both the SABC's organization and its channels in January 1991. In his detailed retelling of the transformations of the telecommunications industry, the press, and broadcasting, *Communication and Democratic Reform in South Africa*, Robert Horwitz summarizes the SABC's resulting television channels: a commercial White channel (TV1), a commercial Black channel (Contemporary Community Values Television [CCV], a combination of the former TV2/3 and TV4), and "a poorly accessible noncommercial public service channel in the American PBS mold" (National Network Television [NNTV], formerly TopSport Surplus).[28]

Although financial imperatives were given as rationalization for rethinking—and largely privatizing—the SABC, and though the SABC (like other parastatals) was certainly a bloated institution, the clear advantage for the National Party was twofold: to reduce the power of the SABC as a state broadcaster before it lost control of the institution, and to secure the financial control of commercial broadcasting for White South Africans. In Horwitz's words, "the changes contemplated for the broadcast sector were broadly consonant with the reform apartheid strategy of privatizing the parastatals as a subtle, largely hidden market-driven means of entrenching white dominance."[29]

As a result, the Mass Democratic Movement (MDM) "posted a fundamental procedural objection to the Viljoen Task Group: any restructuring of South African broadcasting could not be considered under the conditions of old-style secret deliberations by an elite white commission."[30] Under a great deal of pressure from several grassroots media-action campaigns (particularly the Campaign for Open Media [COM]), the future structure of broadcasting in general and the SABC in particular were forced out of the hands of the Viljoen Task Group and into the negotiations known as the Congress for a Democratic South Africa (CODESA).

The CODESA meetings, which included many parties but were dominated by the ANC and NP, were the site of the fundamental negotiations concerning an interim constitution and the procedures for South Africa's first fully representative elections. That transforming the SABC played a role in these negotiations gives testament to the importance placed on broadcasting during the transition. During the first CODESA meetings, an agreement was reached to create an independent regulatory board over both broadcasting and telecommunications. Yet the importance of broadcasting became even clearer with the suspension of the CODESA talks following the Boipatong Massacre, before the initial agreements could be acted upon.[31] With CODESA on hold and the telecommunications sector unable to agree among themselves on a way forward, the Multi-Party Negotiating Council—a kind of executive committee of the CODESA groups that met between the two CODESA congresses—agreed to move forward on broadcasting alone.[32] Horwitz outlines the thinking behind this prioritization of transforming the SABC:

> Long a National Party instrument, [the SABC] had to be transformed into a neutral institution in order for free and fair elections to take place. No challenger to the National Party could contemplate running an election campaign if broadcasting . . . remained in the NP's pocket. The power of the state broadcaster to set the agenda, to deride and undermine the opposition, to discourage voting, and especially to foment confusion and violence, was considerable. More than that, broadcasting is voice, the ability to communicate and state grievances, to share ideas and experiences, to challenge reigning orthodoxy on a national scale—precisely those forms of interaction and representation from which the black majority had been shut out for so many decades.[33]

The Multi-Party Negotiating Council therefore agreed to create the Independent Broadcasting Authority (IBA), effectively splitting the regulation of broadcasting and telecommunications.[34] The creation of the IBA established for the first time in South African history an agency independent of both the SABC and the government that was ultimately responsible for broadcasting, including the awarding of licenses and the hearing of complaints. The growing consensus around an independent regulator for broadcasting was only logical. "Every political party could see the danger if its opponent obtained control of the medium," Horwitz tells us. "The ANC was fearful of continued NP control of broadcasting *before* the election; the NP was fearful of the possibility of ANC control of broadcasting *after* the election" (emphasis in the original).[35]

Before the IBA came into being, however, the term of the current SABC board was ending in March of 1993. Again, under intense pressure from grassroots groups and a threat from the Media Workers Association of South Africa (MWASA) labor union to strike—which would have effectively shut down the SABC—the NP minister of home affairs accepted a significantly more open process, proposed by the Campaign for Independent Broadcasting (CIB), for selecting the new SABC board.[36] Though not without its own share of controversy, particularly de Klerk's rejection of the well-known professor and writer Njabulo Ndebele as the chair, the new board was nonetheless received as a significant step forward. With the appointment of a diverse and relatively representative board at the SABC, chaired by ANC member Ivy Matsepe-Casaburri, and the passage of the Independent Broadcasting Authority Act of 1993, broadcasting became the first sector of South African social or political life to create the formal structures for transformation, even before the first vote was cast by a Black South African.

Actuality Programming on the SABC

Important changes were in fact taking place at the SABC before the formal restructuring of the institution itself, particularly in its production of actuality programming. While individuals in the news division realized that the terms of engagement had changed, the NP realized that their hopes for a favorable negotiated settlement relied on the acceptance of the ANC as a valid negotiating partner among White South Africans. The NP was in a particularly tricky situation, needing to normalize relations with the ANC while simultaneously weakening the organization for the elections. This created a new openness in actuality programming at the SABC that in turn led to an explosion of discussion shows, most notably *Focus* and *Agenda*, where representatives of the ANC and the NP debated the various issues around negotiations. In addition to the ANC and the NP, other parties were often invited to join the shows—particularly the CP, in order to distance the NP from the White right wing, and the Inkatha Freedom Party (IFP), in order to provide a supposed alternative to the ANC for Black voters. The SABC thereby attempted to reflect the recent and future changes in the political dispensation while still favoring, though much more cautiously, the National Party.

These shows received a very large audience and respondents—both Black and White—were no exception. Liso, a thirty-one-year-old African said, "After 1990 the political debates which raged on in our television did inform my political thinking." In spite of the fact that Liso had already been politicized in the 1980s, he nonetheless said he gained political perspective from "*Agenda* and news. Political debate at this stage was more than central to my life so any other program was a waste of time. They sharpened my political *noûs*." Likewise, Anton remembered that *Agenda* was where "for the first time ANC/SACP leaders and others debated on television" which indicated to him that changes were taking place.

White South Africans also recalled the discussion shows as a major shift in SABC actuality programming. William, a thirty-eight-year-old English-speaker, said, "[I would watch] the half-hour news analysis programs they would have, often interviews with government and ANC politicians," though he also recalled "the usual frustration with politicians avoiding issues and bad interviewers." Yet even in this common complaint regarding the quality of these shows and a more mundane dislike of politicians or irritation with self-evident questions, a profound shift toward politics within institutional means is evident. Even though the ideological and strategic positions often represented on these shows were extremely contentious, they nonetheless took place in a far less volatile context than extrainstitutional politics in the 1980s. After years of hearing how terrifying the terrorists of the ANC and its affiliated organizations were, White South Africans were now seeing not only Mandela but also Joe Slovo (the head of MK), Chris Hani (the general secretary of the SACP), and other ANC cadres sitting down to thoughtful, if intense, policy conversations with ministers in the government.

Some of these shows even provided an opportunity for South Africans to find humor in the intensity of their political situation. No single media personality supplied this more than Pieter-Dirk Uys or, more accurately, his alter-ego Evita Bezuidenhout. As the conservative Afrikaner matriarch Evita, known as "the most famous White woman in South Africa," the cross-dressing Uys managed to build a career caricaturing in flesh and blood the many players in South African politics, even during the States of Emergency. In the early 1990s, Evita became a household name for her irreverent jabs to all sides. Phillip, a twenty-eight-year-old English-speaker, recalled:

> Focus had a lot of panel discussions about what was happening in the country. . . . I remember Evita Bezuidenhout on Focus with Pik Botha [then the foreign minister] taking the piss out of the apartheid government and the changes. That was hilarious.

Paul also said that "Pieter-Dirk Uys (of Evita fame) was the best—he ripped off everyone from PW to Mandela. His shows displayed the lighter side of it all."

Political talk and analysis shows were not the only actuality programming to make a comeback in the early 1990s. The changes in newsgathering at the SABC, combined with the momentousness of events themselves in South Africa at the time, also led to a resurgence of daily television news consumption. The vast majority of my respondents described a massive increase in their news viewing habits during this period. Across the board, the SABC was seen as providing a less-biased—though far from unbiased—picture of current events. For instance, Sylvia described the shift as follows:

> In the early '90s [news coverage] got a little better as by then we were on a road to democracy and the media started giving a more unbiased view of the news . . . not totally so, but at least not as bad as in the past. With Mandela's release the news became even more unbiased and for the first time it felt as if the train to democracy was moving too fast to stop and the media played along.

Likewise Matthew, a twenty-nine-year-old English-speaker, said he "[watched the news] at least two to three times a week. Good coverage—I could notice the Nationalist bias starting to wane." Anton described himself as a "news junkie" during this period because "it was important to witness the changes of the SABC on air. The programs were still largely stale and clumsy, but at least now they tried more." Liso also watched the news "daily and in all the different languages," describing it as "very heated political debate punctuated by extreme violence."

The irony of the changes in the SABC's ideology surrounding the news was certainly not lost on White South Africans, regardless of whether they celebrated or bemoaned the changes themselves. Andrew, a thirty-four-year-old English-speaker, said, "I remember thinking how ironic it was that the same presenters who once were telling us how evil the ANC was were now extolling their virtues!" The inclusion of Black South Africans in political debates and news generation was nothing short of a sea change in the history of South African television. Unlike any other period in this study, the years between 1990 and 1994 were the only time during which nearly all my respondents named actuality programming as among the most important and memorable shows on television.

Although this newfound importance would have been impossible without the ideological changes at the SABC mentioned above, it would be a mistake to attribute all of actuality programming's significance to these changes. As with *The Cosby Show* and the media event of Mandela's release, the shared nature of actuality programming during the transition—not only made possible but actively created by television as a medium—played at least as important a role as the content of the political debates themselves. South Africans had been sharing—mostly unawares—the communicative space of television for fifteen years; now that space had finally become both explicitly shared and politicized for the first time, a crucial step for making the political imaginary of sharing the nation a reality. Transnational media flows had also been moving through South Africans' living rooms for a decade and a half, but now those flows were experienced as explicitly more reciprocal and inclusive across national boundaries as well as within the country

Investigative Reporting and Integrated Entertainment on M-Net

Although M-Net was still not broadcasting news, the political changes in South Africa freed the cable channel, like the SABC, to become much more innovative in its programming. Two M-Net programs in particular proved to be not only groundbreaking at the time of the transition, but also foretold the future of much of the programming on SABC in two very different genres. M-Net presented South Africa's first in-depth investigative reporting show that was not obviously slanted in favor of the government, *Carte Blanche*, while they also created a new soap opera that featured an integrated cast, *Egoli*. Marcia, a thirty-eight-year-old English-speaker, echoed earlier reception of *The Cosby Show* in her reactions to these two shows, saying:

> I thought [M-Net] was brilliant—it had wonderful soaps (*Egoli*) which did more for race relations than anything else I remember. I also remember their documentary program *Carte Blanche,* which was the first time South Africans saw some real issues on their screen.

The repercussions of these shows, even though they were limited to the pay service, have continued to give shape to programming in South Africa today.

Carte Blanche, designed in the mold of *60 Minutes* (sometimes airing segments from that show), joined the news analysis programs on the SABC as one of the most-mentioned programs during this period among interviewees. Although it rarely tackled the issues of the transition itself, it nonetheless provided "interesting and enlightening programming."[37] According to Marcia:

> *Carte Blanche* was not so much a racial program as an honest program. It dared to show things we had never seen before—child abuse, animal cruelty, racial issues, all sorts of things our press had shielded us from over the years.

It started off as very hard-hitting, and quite scary. I avidly watched it but was generally quite worried about what the content would be. It showed us townships, violence, worker abuse on farms, lack of schooling for farm children, etc. Things we had never seen growing up in apartheid.

Following the censorship of apartheid, and the States of Emergency in particular, any information could quickly come to seem profound. Interestingly, Marcia also incorporates a generational analysis into the significance of *Carte Blanche*:

I think it gave younger people ammunition when arguing with family members who would never accept the changes. I believe it allowed us more freedom of ideas and speech—if they would speak honestly, then perhaps we could, too.

Once again, shifts in how White South Africans viewed themselves and South African politics impacted younger people differently than others.

In addition to *Carte Blanche*, which continues to air on M-Net today, the pay service also introduced an innovative new soap opera called *Egoli*, titled after the indigenous name for Johannesburg, literally "place of gold." Marcia describes the show's significance while again emphasizing a generational aspect:

I think *Egoli* was great for race relations because it was the first "fun" program I remember to have mixed relationships, integrating Coloured, Indians, Blacks and Whites into one community as equals. When I reached an age that I realised that Whites were not better people than Blacks, and there was a great injustice being done, I still wasn't in a social position to even experiment with these ideas. The only Black people I mixed with were the maid and the gardener. I went to a White school, White college and eventually worked with mostly White people. *Egoli* showed a social mix I never really experienced in South Africa. In South Africa I never had a Black, or even a Coloured, friend, because I never met any!

Like *Carte Blanche*, *Egoli* continues to air on M-Net today, and both shows have spawned many imitators on SABC. *Egoli* in particular gave shape to a new, specifically South African strategy for transforming televisual entertainment: not only did it depict a wide variety of South Africans socializing and working together, it portrayed the mix of South African languages in a complex and inventive way. *Egoli* and shows that followed it feature several languages spoken over the course of a given episode, often in a single sentence, with subtitles sometimes providing translation. For an American watching South African entertainment television, it can be a surprising mix of sounds and sights, whereas South Africans watching American television in the 1990s sometimes described the experience as watching apartheid-era programming, with its relative lack of interaction among characters of different races, languages, and cultures.[38]

Making Meaning Out of Violence

In spite of the "miracle" of South Africa's negotiated revolution, it did not come without significant bloodshed—a point often forgotten or minimized in the celebrations of the South African transition. To borrow Liso's phrase above, the political debates of 1990 to 1994 were often punctuated with extreme violence. Though the examples are too numerous to itemize here, I will highlight three illustrations during this period in which television played either a significant or intriguing role in making meaning out of violence for White South Africans: the bloody fighting between the ANC and the IFP; the assassination and funeral of Chris Hani; and the so-called Battle of Bophuthatswana.

Violence between the ANC and the IFP

By far the greatest loss of life during the supposedly peaceful transition took place in warfare between the ANC and the IFP, which began primarily in KwaZulu/Natal, spread to the townships of the Rand, and occasionally spilled over into other areas of the country. Nearly 12,000 people were killed as a result of this particular strain of political violence between 1985 and 1997, with the bulk of the murders taking place between 1990 and 1994. Often portrayed in the press as a kind of atavistic, so-called black-on-black violence, the causes and consequences of this violence are far too complex to do justice here.[39] What makes the violence noteworthy for this work is its use as the subject of a controversial television miniseries aired on SABC titled *The Line*.[40]

The Line opens with a scene that had become all too familiar to South Africans in the early 1990s—a militant opening fire in a crowded commuter train. The frequent shootings on commuter trains during this period became a hallmark of the random violence clearly intended to disrupt the negotiations and the ANC's position within them. Such attacks often led to retaliation killings by ANC members, creating a cycle of violence that claimed thousands of lives in the years leading up to the elections. The hero of *The Line* is a young ANC member trying to carve out a workable life for himself when he witnesses the shooting—carried out by an IFP member—and is therefore implicated in the conflict. His dilemma is whether and how to respond.

What made *The Line* controversial was not only its portrayal of the ANC in a highly favorable light vis-à-vis the IFP, but a far more contentious issue: the IFP shooter turns out to be in cahoots with the South African police, acquiring both weapons and support from a local officer. As such, the miniseries—though fictional—lent credence to the claims of the ANC that the violence between themselves and the IFP was fomented by a "third force," namely the state's security forces. As Anton recalls, the screening of the series "led to a long debate about whether the SABC could show [the conflict] as the film suggested, contrary to main White opinion, that the state was complicit in the violence."

Overwhelming evidence that has since surfaced, particularly during the hearings of the Truth and Reconciliation Commission, indicates that the security forces were indeed involved in training, funding, and supplying the IFP militants, though the exact extent of their involvement remains murky. De Klerk and the government at the time vehemently denied the involvement of a third force that was intentionally destabilizing the situation, thereby allowing the NP to proclaim itself as the provider of security and order. Hence, the airing of *The Line* represented not only a bold move on the part of the SABC, bringing a powerful and controversial drama about the realities of Black South Africans' lives to television, but also a watershed in the presumptive control of the NP and the government over the SABC.

Chris Hani's Assassination and Funeral

On the morning of April 10, 1993, Chris Hani was assassinated outside his home in the predominantly White working-class suburb of Johannesburg that he was trying to integrate. Hani was the secretary-general of the SACP, former MK chief of staff, and considered by many to be the heir apparent to the leadership of the ANC. He was without a doubt the most popular ANC politician among Black South African youth, and his killing by a member of the neo-Nazi Afrikaner Weerstandsbeweging (AWB) threatened to instigate massive retaliatory violence.[41] This fear was heightened when a well-known member of the CP, Clive Derby-Lewis, was arrested days later for conspiracy in connection with the assassination.

The ANC took two steps to quell the potential for descent into the all-out race war that so many had predicted for so long. The first was to call for a week of rallies and demonstrations across the nation in order to supply an outlet for the overwhelming anger of so many activists.[42] The second was for Mandela to personally address the nation on the SABC the night of the assassination. In his speech, Mandela chose to highlight that it was an Afrikaner neighbor of Hani's who had taken down the license plate of the killer's getaway car, leading to his arrest:

> Tonight I am reaching out to every single South African, black and white, from the very depths of my being. A white man, full of prejudice and hate, came to our country and committed a deed so foul that our whole nation now teeters on the brink of disaster. A white woman, of Afrikaner origin, risked her life so that we may know, and bring to justice, this assassin. . . . Now is the time for all South Africans to stand together against those who, from any quarter, wish to destroy what Chris Hani gave his life for—the freedom of all of us.[43]

The strategy to highlight the race of the Afrikaner woman was widely hailed as a key instance of encouraging racial reconciliation at a moment when Mandela could have tried to exploit circumstances to gain the upper hand in negotiations. Likewise, Mandela's choice to emphasize the foreign origins of the assassin (who was a Polish immigrant) rhetorically pits a nation united across racialized identifications against a threat posed as at least partially external, even though later evidence tied the assassin to Derby-Lewis and very domestic political conflicts.

Mandela's speech was mentioned by countless interviewees as a crucial turning point in their view of South Africa. Rather than being addressed by the president of South Africa—de Klerk—the nation saw Mandela providing leadership on television. The SABC's recognition of Mandela as the most influential leader at that decisive moment had a profound impact on South Africans' understandings of their nation. As Anton put it, Mandela's broadcast to the nation proved that "de Klerk had lost control of the situation." Although the elections were still a year away, Mandela had become the de facto leader of the media(ted) nation in a time of crisis. And only television could provide the kind of communicative space—immediately accessible, widely shared, and visually emotive—required for the moment.

The SABC followed Mandela's address with the decision to air Hani's funeral live and in its entirety from the FNB Stadium in Soweto. For those who had lived through the political funerals of the 1980s—often the scene of huge demonstrations and overt resistance to the state that would never have appeared on live television—the broadcasting of one of the largest and most volatile political funerals of all was nothing short of astounding. Not only was it an acknowledgment of the importance of Hani, the ANC, and the SACP, but it was also a rare opportunity for these organizations to present themselves unedited and at length.[44] The SABC's response to Hani's assassination and funeral reflected a very different perspective on television, one in which the concerns of Black South Africans garnered far greater attention than had been the case prior to 1990.

Mandela's speech and the live airing of Hani's funeral—media events in their own right—highlight the crucial role of television as a medium in making meaning out of the extensive violence in South Africa during the transition period. Television did more than provide a method for distributing Mandela's message of reconciliation in a moment of fear and apprehension; it collapsed the distance between Mandela and his audience to create the shared communicative space within which he was able to provide reassurance to the nation, in its entirety. Likewise, the airing of Hani's funeral provided the space for communal mourning, thereby helping to diffuse some of the fierce anger generated by the assassination. Without the visual power, simultaneous broadcasts, and unique communicative space of television, Hani's death might have instigated far worse violence.

The Battle of Bophuthatswana

During the television news services on the evening of Friday, 11 March 1994, viewers not only in South Africa but all over the world watched in horror a scene in which a black man in the uniform of the former Bophuthatswana Police, armed with an R4 rifle, shot dead three white men, who were part of a group of members of the Afrikaner Weerstandsbeweging which had that day invaded the Mmabatho/Mafikeng area, as they lay wounded next to the vehicle in which they had been travelling.[45]

So begins the introduction of the "Commission of inquiry into the incidents that led to the violence in the former Bophuthatswana on 11 March 1994, and the deaths that occurred as a result thereof," better known as the Tebbutt Commission Report. The sensational image described above was beamed live around the world through cable news stations including CNN and was also shown live on the SABC. Family members of one of the men reportedly watched the scene from their living room without previous knowledge that their husband and father had even gone to Bophuthatswana to fight for the AWB.

Throughout the transition period, the threat of armed resistance from the White right wing was often invoked as a warning; the prospect of a coup that would bring the transfer of power to a halt was perceived to be a very real possibility. This fear gained credence with Hani's assassination in April of 1993 and again in the following month with the formation of the Afrikaner Volksfront, part paramilitary organization and part political party dedicated to the idea of a volkstaat. Fears of insurrection were heightened by the fact that the leader of the organization was General Constand Viljoen, a former chief of the South African Defence Force who had left the military amid accusations of third force involvement.

In the beginning of March 1994, these issues came to a head in the supposedly independent homeland of Bophuthatswana (often referred to simply as "Bop"). On March 4, with less than two months before the scheduled South African election, Bophuthatswana president Lucas Mangope announced that his homeland would not participate. This set off enormous demonstrations and civil unrest threatening Mangope's government. Six days later, on March 10, Mangope requested assistance from Viljoen and his "Boere People's Army" to prop up the collapsing administration of Bophuthatswana. Mangope also spoke with the leader of the AWB, Eugene Terre'Blanche, on the same day. Although Terre'Blanche claims that Mangope asked for his assistance as well, Mangope told the Tebbutt Commission that he did not.[46]

The next day members of both the Volksfront and the AWB arrived, though with drastically different methods and agendas. The Volksfront came full of military discipline and awaited orders from Viljoen, whereas the AWB entered the homeland helter-skelter and created havoc. Before Viljoen could organize his troops, the AWB had already engaged the Bophuthatswana Police and Defence Forces, now in open insurrection toward Mangope, in what became known as the Battle of Bophuthatswana. The battle, however, was short-lived, with the shootings of the wounded AWB militants slumped against their Mercedes providing an exclamation point to a thorough routing of the AWB. The swagger of the far right was reduced to the impotent ranting of defeated weekend warriors.

In addition to the deposing of Mangope, which restored the participation of Bophuthatswana in the general elections, the most important and immediate political fallout from the Battle of Bophuthatswana was Viljoen's decision to participate in the elections under the banner of a new party called the Vryheidsfront ("Freedom Front" in Afrikaans, or VF-FF). However, the significance of the Battle of Bophuthatswana was to be found more in the de-fanging of the far right's threat of a military coup to topple the transition. The defeat of the AWB at the hands of disorganized, under-trained, and ill-equipped Bantustan security forces left such threats sounding particularly hollow. The fact that this particular revolution was, in fact, televised—in gruesome and gory detail, no less—gave the AWB's defeat a symbolic significance far beyond its military implications.

Many scholars have pointed to the televising of the Battle of Bophuthatswana as the turning point in the transition, leaving White South Africans disgusted, fearful, and unwilling to contemplate armed resistance to the transition, paving the way for the elections.[47] In contrast, I argue that these causal arrows interpreting the AWB's televised failure should be reversed. Rather than causing a newfound distaste among White South Africans for opposing democratization, this reticence had already taken hold among White South Africans due to the shifts in identifications described in the previous chapters of this book. Only with this distaste toward armed resistance already in place would White South Africans interpret the AWB's failure as they did—the bumbling idiocy of those on the wrong side of history—rather than as a betrayal by the National Party to provide sufficient support for their incursion into Bophuthatswana. White South Africans made meaning from the Battle of Bophuthatswana not primarily through the inhumanity of the Bophuthatswana police officer, though that was certainly part of the discourse, but more significantly through the dismissal of the AWB as ineffectual and, more important, not representative of White South Africans. The crisis of will that typified the mid- to late 1980s had come full circle, building not only hesitation toward the armed maintenance of apartheid, but will toward a negotiated settlement that included a formally nonracial state apparatus.

The Inauguration of Mandela

The first truly democratic election in South Africa fell quickly into place following the AWB's highly visible failure in Bophuthatswana and Viljoen's decision to join the electoral process, with the final obstacle being overcome when Chief Buthelezi of the IFP also chose to participate at the last possible moment.[48] Although the AWB did set off a handful of car bombs during the elections, the voting was surprisingly uneventful. The intimidation

and violence many had anticipated at polling places never fully material-
ized. Mandela himself described the power of the images broadcast during
the four days of polling:[49]

> Great lines of patient people snaking through the dirt roads and streets of
> towns and cities; old women who had waited half a century to cast their
> first vote saying that they felt like human beings for the first time in their
> lives; white men and women saying they were proud to live in a free coun-
> try at last. The mood of the nation during those days of voting was buoyant.
> The violence and bombings ceased, and it was as though we were a nation
> reborn.[50]

The images of Black South Africans voting for the first time became iconic
in the worldwide press, once again placing South Africa at the center of
transnational media flows for a brief moment. After several more days of
counting the votes, the ANC won—as expected—with a nearly two-thirds
majority (62.6%).

Because the election took place over several days and in hundreds of locations, it provided less of a media event to mark the end of the transition
than did the more television-friendly inauguration eleven days later, on
May 10. Nearly all South Africans gathered with friends and family in front
of a television set for the inauguration of Mandela as president of South Africa, in a ceremony that—like all inaugurations—utilized the many trap-
pings of state power to invoke the government's legitimate authority. Although the international news gave the inauguration far less time than the
elections themselves, the SABC carried the event in its entirety.

As an exercise in image making, the inauguration was an overwhelming success. Many respondents described a sense of allegiance toward
the government that they had not felt in some time, if at all. Margaret, a
forty-year-old English-speaker, described the experience of many younger
White South Africans watching the inauguration:

> A large group of friends came over to watch and we drank champagne and
> celebrated. We stood for the national anthem which is probably the first time
> I ever did that in SA.

Three scenes in particular stood out for those I interviewed: the location itself, the flyover by South African Defence Force jets, and the presence of
many world leaders at the ceremony. The ceremony took place in the cur-
vature of the Union Buildings, which form a semicircle of red brick on a

bluff overlooking the city of Pretoria. Built in the tradition of British colonialism and modeled after the government buildings in New Delhi, India, the Union Buildings form a striking vision of power, particularly on a beautiful, clear autumn day like the one on which the inauguration took place. To see Mandela atop the hill, framed by the Union Buildings, proved an enduring image of fortunes reversed for many White South Africans.

Immediately following Mandela's inaugural address, a number of military aircraft flew in formation low over the Union Buildings, followed by five Impala fighter jets trailing plumes in the colors of the new South African flag: black, green, gold, red, and blue. The symbolism of South African military power saluting the founder of MK was not lost on either the audience in Pretoria or watching on television. According to Mandela, who chose to end his own autobiography of 115 (albeit very short) chapters with one on the inauguration, the military flyover "was not only a display of pinpoint precision and military force, but a demonstration of the military's loyalty to democracy, to a new government that had been freely and fairly elected."[51]

By far the most significant image was the presence of more world leaders in South Africa than had ever set foot in the country previously. "It was a good day for South Africa," Marcia said, "and for the rest of the world's opinion of South Africa." Sylvia echoed this sentiment, saying, "I remember how nice it was to see the world finally accepting SA back in the fold and how great it was to see that Mandela's years of suffering had a happy ending." Phillip also described the inauguration as "a great moment. Castro, Clinton, Arafat, and all of the other global leaders all in Pretoria. I remember the praise singers (a feature of Mandela's public appearances at that time) and Mzwakhe Mbuli," concluding his account with an ambivalent, "I was proud, I guess." Such ambivalence typified respondents' accounts of watching the inauguration: at once exciting, hopeful and exhilarating, but also carrying a sense of the unknown and a certain amount of anxiety over what would happen in the future.

The inauguration of Mandela provided more than just a convenient symbolic bookend for the nation's transition to democracy. It also became a remarkable media event that marked the reinclusion of South Africa into the international community. The inauguration not only marks a partial endpoint for the dramatic changes set in motion by Mandela's release and the un-banning of the ANC, but also brings us full circle back to the beginning of this book and White South Africans' growing sensitivity to their pariah status in the rest of the world. While the Apollo moon landing found South Africans "twiddling the dials on their wirelesses," unable to take part in that global moment of media awe, Mandela's release from prison and subsequent inauguration brought South Africans back into the world not only as participants in media events but also as the heroic subjects of such events.[52]

Television after Apartheid

For three years prior to his release, Mandela had been going on excursions with his warders into the malls, streets, and beaches of the Western Cape. By all accounts, the government was attempting to acclimate him to life outside of prison and the changes that had taken place since his incarceration began. In spite of Mandela being in many public places during these excursions, no one ever recognized the most famous political prisoner on earth. Like the story of the *Time* image of Mandela in anticipation of his release, the apartheid regime's success at erasing his countenance from public consciousness is a forceful testament to the power of the ban and the structured absence of Black South Africans from conventional political life.

During the second half of 1989 and the first half of 1990, the structured absence of Black South Africans collapsed in rapid and dramatic fashion, with profound implications for both political and social life. Not only did White South Africans observe many of these changes through their television sets, but the very nature of television itself also underwent significant modifications in the process. Although the altered mediascape of South Africa may seem in hindsight inevitable or predetermined, it in fact took shape—like the new political dispensation itself—in the midst of a highly contentious and contingent struggle. The years between 1990 and 1994 were highly volatile and innovative ones for both South African television and the society in which it operated.

South Africa's transition to democracy has been heralded as a miracle, though it was an extremely difficult and traumatic as well as exciting time. South African television played a crucial role in the transition process, not only by mediating the experience for many White South Africans through news and other actuality programming, but also by providing the communicative space through which South Africans could reimagine and assert themselves as a single nation. Television provided this space in grand scale through media events like Mandela's release and his inauguration as well as on a much smaller scale through programs such as *Egoli* and Evita Bezuidenhoudt's unsparing satire. Meanwhile television's structures—particularly the SABC—led the way into the transformation faced by all of apartheid's institutions in the 1990s and beyond.

South African television's role in the transition cannot and should not be understood apart from its presence in the social and political life of the nation prior to 1990. Each of the specific elements examined in this chapter has been given shape by the historical trajectory of South African television and other media formed by the fence posts of 1976 and the Soweto Uprising, the early 1980s and attempts at reform, and the States of Emergency in the mid- to late 1980s. The sudden obsession with actuality programming during the democratic transition was in part the result of such programs' lack of legitimacy and meaning in earlier eras, just as the significance of explicitly political events and debates resurfaced after decades of being largely relegated to the cultural realm under apartheid. And the ways in which White South Africans made meaning out of specific moments during the transition—including Mandela's release, acts of political violence, and the election, among others—was bounded by earlier shifts in their identifications made possible in part by South African television.

The transition of 1990 to 1994 is in many ways the culmination of the struggle against apartheid. Yet just as the struggle continues in many important ways under the democratically elected government of post-1994 South Africa, so also does the legacy of Black South Africans' structured absence continue—though in a transmuted form of White supremacy—today. Likewise, White South African identifications continue to shift in order to accommodate the changing subject positions of racialized individuals within the "new" South Africa and the nation within a global political and economic context. I now turn to summarizing the main themes of the book while briefly looking toward the continuing implications of this history for understanding media, democratization, and the multiple ends of apartheid in the context of ongoing transnational media flows.

Television and the Afterlife of Apartheid

> Speaking from the perspective as one who was disenfranchised . . . for me a
> rough and ready distinction . . . was to be drawn between those [media] who
> supported and those who were against apartheid. The former [were], mostly
> but not exclusively, Afrikaans and the electronic media . . . largely mouth-
> pieces of the ruling elite, hardly ever the watchdogs one had hoped for the
> public.[1]

Archbishop Emeritus Desmond Tutu used these words to introduce the
Truth and Reconciliation Commission of South Africa's (TRC)special hearings on mass media during apartheid in September of 1997.[2] The hearings were hosted free of charge by the SABC at its headquarters in Auckland
Park, Johannesburg, in a visible public relations move to adjust the past
identification of the SABC as an Afrikaner and National Party stronghold.
As Tutu points out, the electronic media under apartheid—both radio and
television—were almost completely controlled by the SABC, and as such
provided precious little outlet for explicitly political communication outside the bounds of apartheid ideology.

Nothing in this book disputes either the fact of electronic media's domination by the ruling party under apartheid or the damage done to public
discourse as a result of that domination. The paradox is that even in the
midst of the profoundly authoritarian and repressive mediascape of South
Africa, wherein television was arguably the most carefully controlled and
censored feature of that mediascape, television simultaneously became a
contested, limited site of renegotiating White South African identifications
that made possible a rethinking of the nation. The SABC's censorship, manipulation of facts, and outright triumphalism of apartheid not only de-
stroyed the quality of meaningful political discourse on television, but also

helped to create "an environment in which human rights abuses could take place" as described by television critic John van Zyl.[3] Likewise, while he is referring to the owners of private sector mass media, the words of Jon Qwelane—a well-known journalist, talk-show host (on both radio and television), and publisher—are equally applicable to the SABC and electronic media:

> Did the media owners, by their endorsement of Botha's madness, not help to delay the day of liberation? Can it be correctly said that the blood of those who were murdered by Botha's police and soldiers, in the name of total onslaught, is on the hands of the media owners? I say it can.[4]

While Qwelane's stinging critique applies to almost all of the mediascape of late-apartheid, it is not the *entire* story of that mediascape. Much of the programming provided ample fodder for apartheid ideology and those who believed in it, but television also provided an unheard-of communicative space that was shared—at first in an unsuspecting way but later explicitly—by all South Africans within reach of its signal. Without discrediting concerns regarding free speech and the content of television, I emphasize the ways in which this shared communicative space allowed for new processes of identification for White South Africans to form, processes that became crucial in moving the nation from apartheid to a more democratic dispensation. Television played an ambivalent role under apartheid regarding the normative ideal of democracy, simultaneously serving as a mouthpiece of apartheid oppression and as a communicative space within which White South Africans were able to move beyond the static identities constructed through apartheid ideology. Television under apartheid embodied the nature of hegemony as a high-stakes, contested process with powerful capabilities of repression as well as fissures and gaps that could be exploited to create resistance to that same hegemony. What are the implications of this process, spanning the four fence posts explored in *Starring Mandela and Cosby*, for both post-apartheid South Africa and broader themes of transnational mediascapes and democratization?

Structured Absence and Television under Apartheid

The South African government actively structured television's absence prior to 1976 in an attempt to preserve apartheid ideology and along with it White South African, particularly Afrikaner, identities. By incorporating leftist critiques of cultural imperialism into the Christian Nationalism of apartheid, the regime projected onto television a wide variety of characteristics seen as threatening to static White South African identities and the White supremacy on which they were largely based.[5] Not unlike the structured absence of Black South Africans themselves from shared political and social life, this absence allowed for a reconstruction of the concept of television that fit with the hopes and fears of apartheid ideology far more seamlessly than the actual medium itself.

Even before it was introduced, television was viewed as a foreign entity that would inevitably tie South Africa more closely to the rest of the world. While this international connection did not fit with the defiant isolationism of apartheid at the time, it did speak to the growing cosmopolitan desires of many White South Africans. Whether viewed as a status symbol or a threat, the presence of television in the country was expected to open the nation to outside influences. This history shows that television did indeed create stronger ties to the outside world, most significantly through the communicative space formed by television and transnational media flows, from *The Cosby Show* to the Olympics and even moments where those flows were blocked, such as the Apollo moon landing. And these flows were not only moving into South Africa, but also from South Africa to the rest of the world; coverage of protests against apartheid garnered increasing coverage in news programming around the globe, and South Africa became a symbolic stand-in for all sorts of tropes in cultural production—from the heroic freedom-fighter to the evil Afrikaner—in the imaginaries of international culture industries.

As White South Africans "finally" tuned in to TV1, they found themselves inhabiting a worldwide communicative space. For some this led to feelings of insignificance in the grand scope of things, for others embarrassment at the supposedly backward nature of South African television and, by association, society. But the experience of television as a communicative space led White South Africans to incorporate a much larger frame of reference into their own processes of identification, to move from what Jan Nederveen Pieterse calls an inward-looking territorial culture toward an outward-looking translocal culture.[6] Jonathan Hyslop asserts that exactly such a shift took place in South Africa, and that television was central to that shift: "For all but the most recalcitrant whites, explaining themselves to imagined external interlocutors became a central concern. Nothing did so much to create this desire for accounting than the coming of television in 1976."[7]

Although TV1 was "White television" in its content and its imagined audience, Black South Africans nonetheless tuned in, transgressing the segregated information systems more easily maintained by print and even radio. "Just as the segregation of blacks and whites in neighborhoods, transportation, and the workplace has proved impractical," wrote journalist Steven Mufson in the 1980s, "apartheid in television hasn't worked out as planned."[8] This incursion into White South African social life was less immediately apparent than the linking of White South Africans to international contexts, but it was the first indication that the structured absence of Black South Africans would be weakened by television. Likewise, the concurrence of the Soweto Uprising with the introduction of television would lead to the politicization of this new communicative space, thus challenging the exclusion of Black South Africans from political as well as social life.

The reforms of P. W. Botha's government in the early 1980s, coupled with the advent of "Black television" in the form of TV2/3, further diminished the structured absence of Black South Africans. Whereas the tricameral parliament and the Koornhof Bills recognized limited political agency for Black South Africans, TV2/3 broadened the communicative space shared by all South Africans. Neither TV2/3 nor the tricameral parliament managed to regain legitimacy for the apartheid regime; instead, they consolidated active resistance to apartheid and provided a space in which White South Africans began to reconstruct their processes of identification and imagine a post-apartheid future. My research demonstrates that the communicative space of television was shared more actively than previously imagined. White South Africans reshaped their assumptions regarding Black South Africans, along with their own identifications formed in relation to those assumptions. Although the content of TV2/3 may have misled White South Africans, even increasing many stereotypes and misconceptions, the space of television proved to be an essential element in (re)shaping processes of identification. Though still officially excluded from the nation's political and social life, Black South Africans had crossed into White South Africans' lives in informal ways that would be nearly impossible to rescind.

The breakdown in the hegemony of apartheid among both Black and White South Africans led the state, as Gramsci claims it often does, to rely increasingly on direct force to maintain apartheid and to declare the States of Emergency.[9] Precipitated in large part by the failure of reforms—including the launch of TV2/3—to win legitimacy for apartheid, White South Africans experienced a crisis of will regarding their investment in and commitment to apartheid. This crisis of will was instigated in part by the restructuring of White South African imaginaries as they attempted to reconcile their shared presence with both Black South Africans and the international community through the communicative space of television. With the stakes being raised day after day, the SABC retreated into a seemingly detached reality while progressive politics, stymied by the draconian measures of the States of Emergency, reinvented itself in both the cultural realm and in an increase in extrainstitutional political action.

The popularity of *The Cosby Show* in this historical conjuncture can be understood only by taking into account both the communicative space of television and its impact on White South Africans' construction of potential post-apartheid identifications. Regardless of whether *The Cosby Show* was interpreted by viewers as supportive or critical of apartheid ideology, its massive popularity made it the first cultural product to be fully shared, *along with an awareness that it was shared,* in the inhabited communicative space of South African television by the entire nation. *The Cosby Show* thus serves as an important watershed in the history of Black South Africans' structured absence in the nation. The show's popularity marks the last vestige of that formal exclusion, as evidenced by some White South Africans' implausible explanations of its popularity as completely disconnected from race. Yet that popularity also marks the beginnings of an explicit inclusion of Black South Africans within the polity and a reformulation of White supremacy along the lines of culture and class rather than biology. This reformulation made formal apartheid more difficult to justify while preserving the potential for more internationally acceptable forms of racialized domination. In retrospect, the popularity of *The Cosby Show* in the midst of the States of Emergency appears as the writing on the wall heralding both the demise of formal apartheid and the nascent reinscription of a South African nationalism that crossed previous racial divides even as it (re)constructed a more subtle racial project.

The paradoxical visibility of Bill Cosby and structured absence of Nelson Mandela during this third fence post framed both individuals as cultural icons, even as Mandela remained "the man with no face."[10] With the release of Mandela and other political prisoners and multiparty negotiations toward a more democratic political system beginning in 1990, the structured absence of Black South Africans in both the political and social life of the nation was dismantled rapidly. Just as it was central in setting the stage for South Africa's transition to democracy, television played a crucial role in giving shape to that transition, as both a site and an object of contention. South African television most closely approximated the ideal of a democratic public sphere during this time, though it still fell far short of that ideal. It did, however, provide an outlet for political debate and introduced South Africans (in the seemingly personal way that only television can do) to the leaders of the opposition movements, who had been demonized by the press for so many years. Throughout this process, Mandela was able to shed the perception that he was a communist and terrorist, assuming the mantle of the educated, reasonable, moderate bargaining partner required for a negotiated transition. In this limited sense, Nelson Mandela became to politics what Bill Cosby had already become on television—a nonthreatening, reassuring Black presence that allowed White South Africans to rethink their processes of identification.

Although televisual content became essential to public deliberation during the momentous years leading up to the election of 1994, the communicative space formed by television remained a crucial contribution of the medium during this period as well. Without television's ability to broadcast media events, several of the key turning points during the transition—Mandela's release from prison, his address to the nation after Chris Hani's assassination, and his inauguration, to name just a few—would not have shaped the social imaginary of the new South African nationalism in the way that they did. As the leader of the ANC stood on the steps of the Union Buildings with world leaders sitting before him, SADF fighter jets above him, and the television cameras of the world pointing toward him, the history of television in South Africa came full circle. The medium once reviled for its international influence served as witness to the re-entry of the nation into the international community and its legitimacy as a constitutive juncture within transnational media flows.

Communicative Space and Television in South Africa

This history of television differs significantly from the way it most often appears in studies of South African media, whether from the perspective of political economy or with primary concerns around freedom of the press. Most scholars have described television's appearance as an extension of National Party and apartheid ideological hegemony, understood as a trait to be possessed in greater or lesser degrees, as it already existed in SABC radio. These accounts view the changes between 1990 and 1994—particularly the institutional transformation of the SABC that culminates in 1993—as the most significant historical cleavage to be examined. While South African scholars often diverge on the state of mass media after 1994, very few challenge this view of television's history prior to the transition.

In contrast, this work views the introduction of the medium in 1976 as a significant event worthy of analysis in its own right for making sense of democratization in South Africa and elsewhere. By taking television seriously as a technological form as well as paying attention to its content, I draw attention to the impact of communicative space on shifting White South African identifications and their subsequent importance in the political events of late-apartheid South Africa. As such, this work is centrally concerned with identifying the historical continuities across the transition that may be masked by other approaches.

Because processes of identification operate on a less instrumental level than do conventional politics, the critical-rational discourse of the public sphere and mass media's impact on that discourse are for more easily recognized than the kinds of changes I have examined here. Thus the most common analysis of SABC television follows the logic of Tutu's quote at the beginning of this chapter: electronic media were mouthpieces of the apartheid regime. The concept of communicative space allows us to see that television under apartheid impacted the normative project of democracy in both positive and negative ways. At the same time that the apartheid regime's control over broadcasting was drastically curtailing public discourse while maintaining the structured absence of Black South Africans in conventional politics, the communicative space formed by television was breaking down that same structured absence in the national imaginaries of South Africans.

In no way should this argument be viewed as providing an excuse for those in control of apartheid television, since the normatively positive results of television were nearly all unintentional, whereas the negative results of its introduction were nearly all intentional. However, this is not an argument for technological determinism. While the concept of media-generated communicative space travels across multiple locations, time periods, and forms of media, the specific shape of that space is socially constructed by those who inhabit it during a given historical conjuncture.[11] This book reminds us to look for such communicative spaces; it does not predict what those places will look like.[12]

By delaying television's presence in the country after it had become technologically and commercially feasible, and by introducing it as a full-fledged, national, state-of-the-art system, South Africa provides an unusually compelling situation for before-and-after studies.[13] In spite of their fears of the international influence that television might bring, the construction of televisual space adopted by the SABC was exactly that—adopted. The SABC structured their broadcasting into very similar elements as television elsewhere, with brief religious invocations at the beginning and the national flag and anthem at the end of the day's broadcast, children's educational programming, situation comedies, news, documentaries, religious programming, movies, sports and, eventually, advertisements.[14] Jésus

Martín-Barbero describes a similar process involving the adoption of North American models of television in Latin America. Instead of emphasizing the political economy or ideological content of the model, he claims that "the heart of the model lies in the tendency to constitute, through television, a single public, and to reabsorb the sociocultural differences of a country."[15] Thus what Raymond Williams first identified as the "flow" of television, and the construction of televisual space that it created in South Africa, developed in part from contingent transnational media flows of both content and form circulating globally.[16]

South African television therefore needs to be examined within the specific context of the nation's political and social life and also with an eye to processes of globalization. Apartheid was a particularly insidious form of totalitarianism, maintaining power through explicitly racialized ideology by linking national identity to race in this specific way. While apartheid penetrated the realm of identity in a far more explicit way than elsewhere, it nonetheless is best understood as part of a broader ideoscape of White supremacy. As Appadurai indicates, the "action" in globalization lies in the intersections of how one -scape, such as the ideoscape of White supremacy, both constitutes and is constituted by its intersections and disjunctures with transnational flows within many other -scapes, not only mediascapes and the overlapping technoscapes of technological forms, but also finance-scapes (global flows of capital) and ethnoscapes (global flows of people and their identifications). Taking Appadurai's insights and grounding them in a particular time and place should not tether us to that temporal location as either a case study to be universalized or an exceptionalist moment, but rather help us in understanding both the material and the metaphorical contingencies of global flows. This book has therefore focused on disjunctures and reinscriptions between mediascapes and ideoscapes in late-apartheid South Africa (while not discounting the impact of other -scapes).[17] With the removal of meaningful political discourse through the repressive apparatus of the state, White South Africans' identifications, particularly as they related to politics, had little room to develop outside of the racialized state except through those avenues created by transnational (and, in the case of TV2/3, intranational) media flows. Thus the social construction of communicative space through the medium of television provided a far more important place within which identifications could be revised and rehearsed than might be the case in a different location. Television allowed South Africans to inhabit a shared place—created through both transnational and translocal processes—like no physical space in the nation could provide.

White South African Identifications, Demobilization, and Democracy

This space was necessary for White South Africans to revise and rehearse new identifications that could incorporate an understanding of themselves within the same polity as Black South Africans. Because of apartheid's success at structuring the absence of Black South Africans, several shifts in identification were necessary for White South Africans to be able to create a political imaginary that included their compatriots. White South Africans' experiences of television heightened their awareness of the international community and their exclusion from that community. Likewise, images of White and Black were shared in the communicative space formed by the medium of television, particularly following the introduction of TV2/3, thereby altering South Africans' understandings of the "other" as well as themselves. By the mid-1980s, the popularity of *The Cosby Show* among White South Africans indicated openness to affinity and equality for their Black counterparts, at least in the abstract.

These experiences made a wider range of identifications available, undermining the salience of White South Africans as denizens of an isolated outpost of civilization on the tip of the continent and the world, dependent on White supremacy for survival. Although this identity was not completely abandoned, its subversion by new identifications opened through the communicative space of television diminished White South Africans' willingness to support the more extreme elements of the apartheid regime. Opposition to the liberation movements was thus demobilized, smoothing the way for the end of formal apartheid. Each of these shifts in identity had taken root sufficiently by 1994 for White South Africans to contemplate and then to participate in formal political equality through democratic elections.

Without each of these shifts in White South Africans' ways of thinking about themselves and their role in the nation, the possibility of armed resistance to the democratic changes would have been significantly greater. Such resistance could, in turn, have greatly constrained the options and strategies of the two lead organizations in the negotiations, the African National Congress and the National Party, along with the other parties involved. The surprisingly peaceful transition to majority rule, which caught so many academic and political analysts of 1980s South Africa off guard, might have been easily derailed by violent resistance to apartheid's end among a greater number of White South Africans.

The demobilization of this resistance is testament to the shifts in White

South African identifications that had occurred in the previous quarter century. As Hyslop correctly asserts, "Analysts of white political behaviour in the eighties and nineties consistently overrated the depth of the middle-class's investment in racial ideology and underrated its commitment to individually defined self interest."[18] White South Africans in 1994 were less invested in the racial ideology of apartheid than in their increasingly middle-class-identified aspirations, but the political move toward a democratic dispensation was instigated and driven by the social movements opposed to apartheid. Without the pressure generated by these movements, White South Africans would have had little motivation to overturn the status quo and their privileged position within it:

> There was nothing necessarily in the logic of the new identities that whites were taking on that was incompatible in theory with a racially segregated society. But once internal opposition and external pressure threatened the access of whites to their desired consumer life styles, there was little question that they were willing to abandon or revise their racial ideologies.[19]

While both White and Black South Africans were involved in resistance movements, this work has concentrated on shifting identifications among the less overtly political collective of White South Africans. In other words, while many individual White South Africans had formed far more radical political identifications (both to the right and the left) than those examined here, the larger question of demobilized resistance requires a focus on mainstream White South African identifications as a group.

These changing processes of identification should not be understood as instrumental or voluntary with a linear progression toward a goal as the end result, but rather as an ongoing, contingent process of negotiating one's view of the nation in relation to one's self, often operating below the surface of daily life. White South Africans did not consciously set off one day to reconcile their own processes of identification with the possibility of democracy, nor did they respond to the democratic imperative by intentionally reinscribing White supremacy into a post-apartheid political dispensation; they simply engaged with and responded to the circumstances of their lives under apartheid.

The End(s) of Apartheid

A final, crucial distinction remains to be made. While my research has shown that the communicative space created by television had a positive impact on the normative project of democracy, this same research has shown a much more ambivalent role for that space in the normative project of eliminating racism. The end of formal apartheid was undoubtedly an enormous victory for antiracism. Alister Sparks claims that de Klerk's speech "was to race relations everywhere what the collapse of the Berlin Wall was to communism. It signaled the end of the world's last racial oligarchy."[20] Even if this is so, the end of formal apartheid was not a final victory against White supremacy, either in South Africa or globally. Thus the end of formal apartheid is only a single end in the midst of the multiple trajectories of apartheid, many of which categorically have not met their demise.

Throughout the period I have examined, the structured absence of Black South Africans from the lives of White South Africans slowly eroded, partially because of the communicative space of television. The importance of this space rests largely on its shared nature. Had apartheid television succeeded in segregating the communicative space of television, it seems highly unlikely that White South African identifications would have undergone the changes they did. But while the very act of sharing communicative space may break down structured absence, it does not automatically follow that this act also breaks down racism. Presence does not necessarily breed equality, or even understanding.

In each of the fence posts I have examined, the maintenance of White supremacy can be identified along with the dismantling of structured absences and the modification of White South African processes of identification. After television was introduced in 1976, the structures of "White" television reinscribed racialized difference and power into the structure of channels as well as content. Even as White South Africans tuned in to TV2/3 in the early 1980s, the sense they gained of individuality and agency among Black South Africans was tempered by the caricatures of Black South African life on the channel. In order to make meaning out of *The Cosby Show* in the mid- to late 1980s, White South Africans reconstituted racism as a cultural—rather than biological—construct, closely tied to class and education. Through our final fence post, negotiations for a democratic South Africa, racism was reconstituted in the economic and cultural realms, even as politics moved toward a more equitable dispensation.

If racism depends on the operation of power over another, then the newly enacted democratic constitution of South Africa, one of the most progressive in the world, safeguards Black South Africans against many of the forms of racism to which they were subjected under apartheid. The legal establishment of human rights in South Africa does indeed go a long way toward dismantling the racism of apartheid. Nonetheless, having struggled for and finally achieved equality in the political and legal arenas, and having made a great deal of progress in the cultural and economic arenas as well, South Africa still faces onerous challenges ahead. Overcoming racism's legacy of apartheid in South Africa remains, like surmounting White supremacy everywhere, an uphill battle. If we understand apartheid as a racial project with cultural and economic as well as political and legal aspects, then indeed, as the title of John Pilger's controversial 1998 documentary declares, apartheid did not die.

Looking to the Future, Dealing with the Past

Coming to terms with the apartheid past while simultaneously building a democratic future is now the enduring task of all sectors of South African society. While this process was certainly accelerated—in terms of activity and public focus—in the first several years following 1994, recognizing these processes as ongoing, incomplete, and at times contradictory remains imperative. Three high-profile events aimed at the transformation of the South African mediascape that took place in the first six years after the 1994 elections are therefore worth brief consideration at the conclusion of this book: the Truth and Reconciliation Commission of South Africa's (TRC) institutional hearings on mass media under apartheid; the relaunch of SABC TV; and the South African Human Rights Commission's (HRC) hearings on racism in the media.

One of the most important and certainly the most visible effort toward coming to terms with the nation's apartheid past has been the TRC, established by an Act of Parliament to deal with gross violations of human rights—defined as killing, abduction, torture, or severe ill-treatment—that occurred between 1960 and 1994. The TRC received unheard-of coverage from both the domestic South African and the international press. For better or worse, the TRC became the symbol and lightning rod for the "new" South Africa's attempt to both look back and move forward. The TRC drew on many sectors of South African civil society in order to pursue its goals. As I argue elsewhere, no sector developed as symbiotic a relationship with the TRC as did South African mass media.[21] Without mass media—particularly broadcast media—the TRC's much-heralded process of providing a public platform for victims of gross violations of human rights would have been severely limited by constraints of physical time and space to only those present at any given hearing. Likewise, the oft-mentioned goal of forging a common national history of the apartheid era would have been impossible even to contemplate without mass media's ability to dissemi-nate the work of the TRC in the form of a media event.[22]

Nowhere did the complexities of the relationship between South Afri-can mass media and the TRC become as clear as during the special hear-ings of the TRC on the media. Mass media became one of the institutions of apartheid that was to be examined as a whole, allowing the TRC to move beyond its strict mandate regarding individual gross violations of human rights and toward a more systemic and structural analysis of apartheid's op-pression. In his opening remarks at the media hearings, Tutu asked, "How do you stretch the whole notion of culpability?"[23] In other words, the hear-ings were intended to question not only whether apartheid-era mass media had been directly responsible for gross human rights violations, but also whether they helped create an atmosphere within which such violations could more easily occur. During the hearings, mass media found them-selves playing several roles at once, reporting on the hearings while also being placed in the spotlight as both victims and perpetrators (in the well-known though oversimplified dichotomous terminology common to TRC hearings) of apartheid. Unfortunately, the institutional hearings on mass media strayed little from the discourse of freedom of expression, thus fail-ing to expose either the systemic forms of media control under apartheid or more complex social processes like those discussed in this book.

Another attempt at dealing with apartheid's mediascape was the South African Human Rights Commission's (HRC) hearings on racism in the media. Prior to the hearings, held in March 2000, the HRC commissioned and published a report titled *Faultlines: Inquiry into Racism in the Media* that attempted to make the kind of critique of contemporary media that was not able to occur in the TRC hearings regarding apartheid-era media.[24] Crit-ical of mass media, particularly newspapers owned by White South Africans or international corporations, *Faultlines* was immediately met with cries of censorship from the press. Indeed, the HRC hearings brought to the fore one of the most prominent tensions in post-apartheid mass media: on the one hand, mass media have been called on to participate in the building of the nation, while on the other, mass media (especially the press corps) have seen their role as that of the fourth estate, a watchdog critical of the govern-ment regardless of who is in power.

This dichotomy often operates as coded language for deeper claims around racism and media. The post-apartheid South African mediascape is undoubtedly far more pluralistic than it was before 1994, yet both the ownership and the operation of mass media remains largely in the hands of White South Africans or foreign investors. In this context, calls for media to join in nation-building are often veiled accusations that the press is racist and that it unduly criticizes the government, now controlled by the Black South African majority. Likewise, the press's at-times-premature cries of censorship often divert attention from valid criticism of racism within media. By accepting this dichotomy in the *Faultlines* report, which utilized highly criticized research methodologies, the HRC hearings rapidly descended into a repeat performance of the same kinds of posturing that had already been taking place in the press, focusing almost entirely on a freedom of the press approach to understanding media.[25] As a result, those voices concerned with more subtle, systemic, and complex understandings of racism in mass media were lost in the din.[26]

Even before the TRC attempted to uncover the workings of apartheid media or the HRC examined that legacy in current expressions of racism in mass media, the IBA and the SABC continued the process of restructuring the institutions of broadcasting in South Africa. Following the 1994 elections, the IBA proposed that a mixed system of broadcasting be instituted that included public, private, and community broadcasting. Like the creation of the IBA and the restructuring of the SABC board before the elections, this proposal and its subsequent modification and acceptance by Parliament resulted from a highly contentious process that involved political parties, media organizations, and media activists.[27]

In the altered mediascape of post-apartheid South Africa, then, broadcasting is no longer solely controlled by the SABC. In addition to several commercial radio stations and M-Net (including its subscription-based digital satellite television service, DSTV, launched in 1995), there is one national free-to-air television channel called e.tv, launched in October 1998 and licensed to the Midi consortium through a black empowerment scheme.[28] Midi is a partnership of several labor union investment funds and others, originally including a 20 percent share for AOL/Time Warner. These additions to private-sector broadcasting have coincided with an explosion of community radio in South Africa, though many of the stations struggle to survive, as well as some fledgling attempts at community television.

In spite of this growth in both commercial and community broadcasting, the SABC remains by far the largest and most powerful broadcasting institution in South Africa. Following its relaunch in February 1996—an audacious, televised, highly criticized affair held in an airport hangar during which the guests of honor arrived on a South African Airways 747 jet—the SABC itself became a mixed system in many ways. The new SABC has three free-to-air television channels, one of which (TV3) carries primarily imported English-language sitcoms and dramas in order to draw in more substantial advertising, thereby cross-subsidizing the other two channels, TV1 and TV2. The latter two channels are more public service-oriented than TV3 and more often broadcast in indigenous South African languages, though all eleven official languages of the nation are represented to varying degrees. This trend toward a mixed system has continued with the SABC's more recent ambitions to become the central player in continental media with the creation of SABC Africa, designed for export to other parts of sub-Saharan Africa and beyond, along with other potential forays into regional and subscription television.

Given both the successes and the failures of these early attempts to deal with apartheid's legacy in mass media, how can the current mediascape of South Africa best be understood and addressed in the long term? Did the years immediately following the elections of 1994 represent the last, best chance to significantly alter the South African mediascape, with media matters now settling into more established patterns? Political economy approaches to post-apartheid mass media have yielded some interesting and important debates, particularly regarding black empowerment schemes, as have analyses of affirmative action and the hiring practices of media corporations since 1994.[29] Yet none of these treatments are able to provide a complete view, much less offer a way forward from the legacy of apartheid. Controversies have continued to proliferate regarding freedom of the press, with South Africa dropping in the global press freedom rankings issued by Reporters sans Frontières from sixteenth in 2002 to a low of forty-fourth in 2006 (before recovering to a six-way tie for thirty-sixth, along with the United States, in 2008).[30] Conflict around the ANC government's broadly conceived antipornography bill and accusations of blacklisting certain political commentators at the SABC in 2007, the tit-for-tat suspensions of the SABC's CEO Dali Mpofu and head of news Snuki Zikalala in 2008, and the near-complete meltdown of the SABC board and administration in 2009 all indicate that the South African mediascape, particularly the public broadcasting sector, remains in flux.

Perhaps the most important point in the debates surrounding the current state of the South African mediascape lies in definitions of the buzz word "transformation." Each commentator comes to the issue with his or her own, often-unspoken ideas about exactly what transformation would or should look like.[31] It comes as little surprise, then, that the resulting analyses are often far apart in their conclusions. Agreement on such a definition seems highly unlikely. The answer lies not in finding the definitive analysis of South African media and apartheid's afterlife within it, but rather in the *process* of analysis and political contention itself.

The restructuring of broadcasting in South Africa was "in most respects, a successful transformation" according to Horwitz.[32]

> These mixed systems should be viewed . . . not as a less than satisfactory compromise, but as a positive good. And this process [of political reform] . . . should not be viewed as 'compromised,' but rather as a vibrant, sometimes messy and conflictual but productive interplay between participatory and electoral democratic forms.[33]

Though Horwitz is referring only to a specific case of transformation in the new South Africa, herein lies the best hope for the future of South African media, as well as South African society as a whole: that the *process* of participatory democracy will slowly but steadily overcome the devastating legacy of apartheid and the racialized identifications it reified. Just as democracy was lived out in the resistance movements long before it became the political system of the nation, a racialized authoritarianism and extreme economic inequality continues in most parts of South African life beyond the political transition. This work shows that while issues of freedom of expression, censorship, institutional structures, and ownership are important, they are not the only concerns worthy of consideration. Without taking into account the specific nature of various media's social formation of communicative spaces, we are likely to either misinterpret—or miss entirely—the ambivalence and potential for unintended outcomes of television and other media in a democratic South Africa and beyond.

The Transnational Future of Communicative Spaces

Why should we care about television? Even if television mattered in late-apartheid South Africa, can the lessons from that experience be applied to a global mediascape that has become increasingly fractured through the decreasing viewership of broadcast television, displaced by sources of entertainment such as narrowcasting (through niche channels on satellite or cable television and user-driven internet navigation), Web 2.0, and the convergence of media technologies?[34] If an analysis of media and democratization in South Africa needs to be grounded in that particular time and place, does that leave any insights applicable only to that context?

As television scholar John Hartley has pointed out, in spite of many prognostications that television is on its last legs, it remains "the most popular pastime ever."[35] Although television—particularly broadcast television—no longer holds a near-monopoly on forms of televisual entertainment, it still retains a dominant position in most mediascapes around the globe, including and especially in areas outside North America and Western Europe, where new media and subscription television have not yet penetrated the mediascapes to the same degree. So while television's role in social life is undoubtedly shifting, it is certainly not diminished. Indeed, the increasing attention to more specialized and converging media may leave television as the predominant communicative space that is actively *shared* across broad social differences in real time, thereby increasing its significance even as the frequency of that sharing is enacted less often.

A close analysis of the communicative space created by television in late-apartheid South Africa—and particularly the counterintuitive dynamics made possible within that space—raises the question: what kinds of communicative spaces are being generated through social engagement with other media in other times and other places? And what are the implications of those other communicative spaces, equally grounded in their particular contexts, for normative projects that transect the globe such as democracy and the defeat of White supremacy? Rethinking our understandings of historical and geographic specificity as a complex articulation of local and global flows should cut us free from the sense that concepts only travel across those specificities if they map directly onto one another. If we take seriously the approach I advocate in this book—that we approach the question of hegemony lived within communicative spaces not as one of degrees of dominance to be possessed but as a set of problematics and processes—then the preceding analysis should open up more questions than it answers. Indeed, it is perhaps the most important contribution that scholarship can make: to provoke new and better questions.

POSTSCRIPT

I think myself and everyone know much more about each other today than we did in earlier years. I think Black people know more about Whites, and Whites more about Blacks, and Coloureds and Indians. I mean there are people in some parts of the country who don't know Indians at all, and don't have contact with them at all, because they are mostly in Natal, now also in other cities, but not really in the rural areas. And now you know lots more about them because you watch TV and see and hear about everyone in the country and across the world. Yes, I think we've learnt a lot about each other.

—Marike, sixty-four-year-old Afrikaans-speaker

NOTES

INTRODUCTION

1. Like many others, I adopt the approach of identifying all those denied full rights under apartheid (i.e., those of African, Indian, or so-called Coloured [mixed-race] descent) as Black. White comes to identify those South Africans of British and other descent whose primary language is English, and those known as Afrikaners, of primarily Dutch and other European descent who immigrated to South Africa in the first decades of the nineteenth century and earlier. If referring to any of these groups specifically, I use the more precise term. These identities were the bedrock of South African social and political structures throughout the apartheid era, and their histories both preceded and extend beyond the apartheid era itself. Of course, these divisions are never clean-cut, and many individuals transgressed their imposed ethnic identities; however, the exceptions were relatively few and far between in the highly antagonistic and racially charged South Africa politics. I adapt the use of uppercase first letters of words denoting ethnic and racial groups from the work of Crenshaw and DuBois in order to avoid the naturalizing of these socially constructed categories, a particularly necessary distinction in apartheid South Africa. Kimberlé Crenshaw, "Race, Reform, and Retrenchment: Transformation and Legitimation in Antidiscrimination Law," *Harvard Law Review* 101 (1988): 1332 n. 2; W. E. B. DuBois, "That Capital 'N,'" in *The Seventh Son: The Thought and Writings of W. E. B. Dubois*, ed. Julius Lester (New York: Random House, 1971), 12, 13.
2. Thanks to Jon Hyslop of the University of the Witwatersrand for first bringing these facts and their possible relationships to my attention. See the acknowledgments for more details.
3. My use of the term *identifications* is discussed in the next chapter.
4. See chapter 3 for further discussion of the relationship between television and the Soweto Uprising.
5. Personal conversation with anonymous individual, August 1998.
6. The term "shifting selves" comes from the title of Herman Wasserman and Sean Jacobs, eds., *Shifting Selves: Post-Apartheid Essays on Mass Media, Culture and Identity* (Cape Town: Kwela Books, 2003).
7. As a result, most White South Africans would have done the majority of their television viewing in homes after the first couple of years of television, whereas Black South Africans (especially those of African and mixed descent) would have watched

television in *shebeens* (bars; see n. 3 in chapter 3) or on street corners and in shops prior to the mid-1980s. Although television sets have become more affordable, these trends still persist, though to a lesser extent, today. See chapter 3 for a more detailed discussion of these issues.

8. Steve Mufson, *Fighting Years: Black Resistance and the Struggle for a New South Africa* (Boston: Beacon Press, 1990), 182.

9. I fully recognize that many White South Africans stretched beyond these political identifications and supported far more radical political parties and ideologies; however, these remained a small percentage of the overall White population. This book, then, seeks to trace the identity shifts among the more politically mainstream supermajority of White South Africans.

10. Arjun Appadurai, "Disjuncture and Difference in the Global Cultural Economy," *Public Culture 2,* no. 2 (1990): 1–24. See also Appadurai, *Modernity at Large* (Minneapolis: University of Minnesota Press, 1996).

11. Michael Omi and Howard Winant, *Racial Formation in the United States: From the 1960s to the 1990s* (New York: Routledge, 1994).

12. Manuel Castells, *The Rise of the Network Society* (Oxford: Blackwell, 1996), 5.

13. Appadurai, "Disjuncture and Difference," and *Modernity at Large.* My appreciation goes to Ruth Teer-Tomaselli for helping me to initially form the metaphor of "fence posts."

CHAPTER ONE

1. On the public sphere, see Jurgen Habermas, *The Structural Transformation of the Public Sphere: An Inquiry into a Category of Bourgeois Society* (Cambridge, Mass.: MIT Press, 1989); Nancy Fraser, "Rethinking the Public Sphere: A Contribution to the Critique of Actually Existing Democracy," in *Habermas and the Public Sphere,* ed. Craig Calhoun (Cambridge, Mass.: MIT Press, 1992), 109–42. On the implications of television, see Ien Ang, *Watching Dallas: Soap Opera and the Melodramatic Imagination* (New York: Methuen, 1985); James Lull, ed., *World Families Watch Television* (Newbury Park, Calif.: Sage Publications, 1988); Jésus Martín-Barbero, *Communication, Culture and Hegemony: From the Media to Mediations* (London: Sage, 1993); Joshua Meyrowitz, *No Sense of Place: The Impact of Electronic Media on Social Behavior* (New York: Oxford University Press, 1985).

2. Kate Crehan, *The Fractured Community: Landscapes of Power and Gender in Rural Zambia* (Berkeley: University of California Press, 1997); Crehan, *Gramsci, Culture and Anthropology* (Berkeley: University of California Press, 2002); Gillian Hart, *Disabling Globalization: Places of Power in Post-Apartheid South Africa* (Berkeley: University of California Press, 2002). For more on Gramsci's conceptualization of hegemony, see Antonio Gramsci, *Selections from the Prison Notebooks of Antonio Gramsci, 1891–1937,* ed. and trans. Quintin Hoare and Geoffrey Nowell Smith (New York: International Publishers, 1971).

3. Hart, *Disabling Globalization,* 26.

4. Joshua Gamson, *Freaks Talk Back: Tabloid Talk Shows and Sexual Nonconformity* (Chicago: University of Chicago Press, 1998).

5. Quoted in Julie Salamon, "An Evolving Vision in Black and White," *New York Times,* February 1, 2002, E1.

6. Ibid.

7. The Broederbond was a quasi-secret society of conservative Afrikaner leaders that had suffused both the state bureaucracy and legislative bodies in one of the most im-

pressive "stealth" takeovers in history. The Broederbond's role in twentieth-century South African politics is quite significant. See Dunbar Moodie, *The Rise of Afrikanerdom: Power, Apartheid, and the Afrikaner Civil Religion* (Berkeley: University of California Press, 1975); Ivor Wilkins and Hans Strydom, *The Super-Afrikaners: Inside the Afrikaner Broederbond* (Johannesburg: Jonathan Ball, 1978).

8. For examples of earlier treatments of mass media under apartheid, see William A. Hachten and C. Anthony Giffard, *The Press and Apartheid: Repression and Propaganda in South Africa* (Madison: University of Wisconsin Press, 1984); John M. Phelan, *Apartheid Media: Disinformation and Dissent in South Africa* (Westport, Conn.: Lawrence Hill, 1987). For examples from those who focus on framing contests within social movement theory, see David A. Snow and Robert D. Benford, "Master Frames and Cycles of Protest," in *Frontiers in Social Movement Theory*, ed. Aldon D. Morris and Carol McClung Mueller (New Haven: Yale University Press, 1992); William A. Gamson and David S. Meyer, "Framing Political Opportunity," in *Comparative Perspectives on Social Movements: Political Opportunities, Mobilizing Structures, and Cultural Framings*, ed. Doug McAdam, John D. McCarthy, and Mayer N. Zald (Cambridge: Cambridge University Press, 1996). For a classic treatment of this approach through visual perception, which has been used by those who focus on representations of gender, violence, or sexuality within both feminist theory and family values' campaigns, see John Berger, *Ways of Seeing* (London: British Broadcasting Corporation, 1972); also see the website of the Center for Media Literacy, "Violence in the Media," http://www.medialit.org/focus/viol_home.html. Don Bogle's work walks an unusual line regarding representation. Although most of his publications focus on typologies of representation of African Americans on television or in films, he nonetheless (as evidenced by the previous quote) acknowledges a more complicated relationship between representations and audience responses.

9. Louis Althusser, "Ideology and Ideological State Apparatuses (Notes towards an Investigation)," in *Lenin and Philosophy and Other Essays*, trans. Ben Brewster (New York: Monthly Review Press, 1971). The concept of structured absence figures heavily in Keyan Tomaselli, Graham Hayman, Abner Jack, Nofikile Nxumalo, Ruth Tomaselli, and Nhlangla Ngcobo, "Square Vision in Colour: How TV2/3 Negotiates Consent," in *Broadcasting in South Africa*, ed. Ruth Tomaselli, Keyan Tomaselli, and Johan Muller (Bellville: Anthrops, 1989); and Ruth Tomaselli, "The Politics of Discourse and the Discourse of Politics: Images of Violence and Reform on the South African Broadcasting Corporation's Television News Bulletins, July 1985–November 1986," Ph.D. dissertation in cultural and media studies, University of Natal. Although I use the term in a similar way to these authors, I am using it in a less literary manner and applying it to a much broader time period in South African television.

10. Althusser, "Ideology and Ideological State Apparatuses."

11. Michel Foucault, *Discipline and Punish: The Birth of the Prison* (New York: Vintage, 1995).

12. Sarah Nuttall, *Entanglement: Literary and Cultural Reflections on Post-Apartheid* (Johannesburg: Wits University Press, 2009). While Nuttall rightly points to the ways in which White and Black South African lives have always been entangled in sometimes surprisingly intimate and often shockingly violent ways, the concept of structured absence refers to the lived understandings of those lives. In other words, while the reality of South African social life has always been deeply entangled, as Nuttall explores, the perceptions of those lives as profoundly separate and different was made possible through structured absences.

13. See Jésus Martín-Barbero, "The Processes: From Nationalisms to Transnationalisms," in *Media and Cultural Studies Keyworks*, ed. Meenakshi Gigi Durham and Douglas M. Kellner (Oxford: Blackwell, 2001). Though referring to film and radio in Latin America, Martín-Barbero describes a similar dynamic on page 638 as "[giving] the people of the different regions and provinces their first taste of the nation."

14. See, for example, Appadurai, "Disjuncture and Difference"; David Harvey, *The Condition of Postmodernity* (Oxford: Blackwell, 1989); Anthony Giddins, *Consequences of Modernity* (Cambridge: Polity Press and Stanford University Press, 1990); Castells, *Rise of the Network Society*.

15. Appadurai, "Disjuncture and Difference."

16. Meyrowitz, *No Sense of Place*.

17. This should not, of course, imply that the decoding of the communication (i.e., the interpretation of the message) is uniform across these—or other—identifications.

18. Meyrowitz, *No Sense of Place*, 117.

19. Meyrowitz's assumption of North American and Western European contexts include an emphasis on the nuclear family, the assumption that television (both sets and signals) is ubiquitous, and a focus on primarily market-driven rather than primarily state-driven systems of production, to name only a few.

20. Televisuality, n.d., The New School, http://www.newschool.edu/mediastudies/tv/ (hereafter Televisuality).

21. Ibid., http://www.newschool.edu/mediastudies/tv/channel2/page1.html.

22. Ibid., http://www.newschool.edu/mediastudies/tv/channel4/page1.html.

23. Ibid., http://www.newschool.edu/mediastudies/tv/channel5/page1.html.

24. Ibid.

25. See, e.g., Eiko Ikegami, *The Taming of the Samurai: Honorific Individualism and the Making of Modern Japan* (Cambridge: Cambridge University Press, 1995); Harrison C. White, *Identity and Control: A Structural Theory of Social Action* (Princeton, N.J.: Princeton University Press, 1992); Roger V. Gould, *Insurgent Identities: Class, Community, and Protest in Paris from 1848 to the Commune* (Chicago: University of Chicago Press, 1995).

26. Eiko Ikegami, *Poetry and Protest: The Rise of Japanese Civility through Network Revolutions* (New York: Cambridge University Press, 2002); Benedict Anderson, *Imagined Communities: Reflections on the Origin and Spread of Nationalism*, 2nd ed. (London: Verso, 1991).

27. Habermas, *Structural Transformation of the Public Sphere*.

28. On the positive effects of television see, e.g., Marshall McLuhan, *Understanding Media: The Extensions of Man* (New York: McGraw-Hill, 1964). On the negative effects of television see, e.g., Guy Debord, *The Society of the Spectacle* (Detroit: Black and Red, 1967); Jean Baudrillard, *In the Shadow of the Silent Majority* (New York: Semiotext[e], 1983). Regarding the conditions under which television is consumed, for instance, monitoring television tends to be far more public and participatory (in the sense of audience members interacting with each other or shouting back at the screen while watching) outside of North America and Western Europe.

29. Hart, *Disabling Globalization*, 34, 37. Appadurai may also be vulnerable to this critique. Doreen Massey, *Space, Place and Gender* (Minneapolis: University of Minnesota Press, 1994); Henri Lefebvre, *The Production of Space* (Oxford: Wiley-Blackwell, 1991).

30. Hart, *Disabling Globalization*, 13, 14.

31. Jan Nederveen Pieterse, "Globalization as Hybridization," *International Sociology* 9, no. 2 (1994).

32. *All in the Family* was only broadcast much later in South Africa, unlike its short-lived sequel.

33. Paul Gilroy, "British Cultural Studies and the Pitfalls of Identity," in *Cultural Studies and Communications*, ed. James Curran, David Morley, and Valerie Walkerdine (London: Arnold, 1996). According to Hall, "Since they have not been superseded dialectically, and there are no other, entirely different concepts with which to replace them, there is nothing to do but to continue to think with them—albeit in their detotalized and deconstructed forms, and no longer operating within the paradigm in which they were originally generated": Stuart Hall, "Introduction: Who Needs 'Identity'?" in *Questions of Cultural Identity*, ed. Stuart Hall and Paul du Gay (London: Sage, 1996), 1.

34. Gilroy, "British Cultural Studies and the Pitfalls of Identity," 383, 387.

35. See, in particular, Jonathan Hyslop, "Why Did Apartheid's Supporters Capitulate? 'Whiteness,' Class and Consumption in Urban South Africa, 1985–1995," *Society in Transition* 31, no. 1 (2000): 36–43, and Hyslop, "Why Was the White Right Unable to Stop South Africa's Democratic Transition?" in *Africa Today: A Multi-disciplinary Snapshot of the Continent in 1995*, ed. Peter F. Alexander, Ruth Hutchison, and D. M. Schreuder (Canberra: Australian National University, 1996), 145–65. This possibility of depoliticization was also central to Gilroy's work on identity. See, for instance, Gilroy, "British Cultural Studies and the Pitfalls of Identity," 384.

36. Courtney Jung, *Then I Was Black: South African Political Identities in Transition* (New Haven: Yale University Press, 2000).

37. It is worth noting that the provision of separate amenities (i.e., the segregation of passenger cars on trains, buses, bathrooms, beach access, and so on) were often marked by signs that said "Europeans Only" and "Africans Only," as well as "Whites Only" and "Non-Whites Only."

38. Shula Marks and Stanley Trapido, eds., "Special Issue: Social History of Resistance in South Africa," *Journal of Southern African Studies* 18, no. 1 (March 1992). See chapter 6 for more information about Uys.

39. A total of 107 interviews were conducted with ninety-two individuals, with five individuals being interviewed twice, in 2000 and 2003, and five individuals being interviewed three times, in 2000, 2003, and 2006.

40. I recognize that many of the people of color in South Africa, particularly those identified by the apartheid regime as Coloured or Asian, speak Afrikaans or English as their first language as well. Likewise, nearly all Black South Africans speak multiple languages, often including fluency in either English or Afrikaans. While this system of identifying respondents in the text is far from perfect, it seems necessary in order to provide a bit more nuance within the predominant group of respondents, that is, White South Africans. Of the ninety-two individuals formally interviewed, the breakdown of self-identification is as follows: 32 White English-speaking; 50 White Afrikaans-speaking, 1 White fully bilingual, 5 African, 3 Coloured, and 1 Asian. In this context, "White fully bilingual" does not refer to fluency in these languages as an adult, since many White South Africans, particularly Afrikaners, are fluent in both Afrikaans and English, but to this particular individual's self-identification of his cultural upbringing as being fully located within both English-speaking and Afrikaner cultures, with one parent each from Afrikaans- and English-speaking families.

41. If the interviewee's language of choice was Afrikaans, my limited Afrikaans skills dictated that the interview be conducted and translated by research assistants.

42. Rowland Atkinson and John Flint, "Accessing Hidden and Hard-to-Reach Populations: Snowball Research Strategies," *Social Research Update* 33 (Summer 2001): 1–4.

43. Of the 92 individuals interviewed, 43 were men and 49 were women. Twenty-eight grew up with television from their earliest memories, 35 recalled the introduction of television as "part of my growing-up years," and 29 were adults in 1976. See n. 40 for the distribution of English and Afrikaans speakers.

44. Thirty-three respondents were interviewed in Durban or the surrounding area, 23 were interviewed in or around Johannesburg, 17 were interviewed in or around Cape Town, 6 were interviewed in Pietersburg, 4 were interviewed in Port Elizabeth, 3 were interviewed in Bloemfontein, and 2 were interviewed in Kimberly. An additional four respondents were "interviewed" over multiple exchanges on e-mail. The location of the interview does not, of course, mean that the interviewee has lived his or her entire life in that area; the larger cities, in particular, tend to draw people from smaller towns in the surrounding area and beyond. Thus, the experiences of the interviewees draw on a broader array of locations than indicated in this distribution. Nonetheless, these interviews should be understood as primarily drawing out experiences from cities and towns rather than rural areas.

45. See Keyan G. Tomaselli and Arnold Shepperson, "The Absent Signifier: The Morphing of Nelson Mandela," in *Cultural Icons*, ed. Keyan G. Tomaselli and David Scott (Walnut Creek, Calif.: Left Coast Press, 2009), 29, for a discussion of similar generational markers in White South Africans' responses to Nelson Mandela as a cultural icon. According to Tomaselli and Shepperson, a cultural icon needs to gain resonance across at least three generations to claim continuity as an icon.

46. Ien Ang, *Living Room Wars: Rethinking Media Audiences for a Postmodern World* (New York: Routledge, 1991), 47.

47. Ibid.

48. Ibid., 52.

CHAPTER TWO

1. Rob Nixon, *Homelands, Harlem, and Hollywood: South African Culture and the World Beyond* (New York: Routledge, 1994).

2. This has, of course, shifted in the past couple of decades with the costs of media production being greatly reduced by video and digital editing technologies, as well as the costs of distribution through websites like YouTube.

3. Although apartheid was not officially codified until the early 1950s under the National Party government, legal segregation and its accompanying exploitative racial state policy preceded apartheid throughout South Africa's history and the discovery of these natural resources.

4. See Carin Bevan, "Putting Up Screens: A History of Television in South Africa, 1929–1976," MHCS dissertation, University of Pretoria, Pretoria, 2008, viewed June 24, 2009, http://upetd.up.ac.za/thesis/available/etd-05212009-182219/, particularly chap. 3, for an extended discussion of the cost of television and its role in preventing the National Party from instituting a national service before 1976.

5. *Verkrampte* refers to the more conservative branch of the National Party, as opposed to the less conservative *verligte* (in Afrikaans, literally "enlightened"). The *verkrampte* are considered to have wielded control of the National Party from the time of its

political ascendancy in 1948 until the assassination of Prime Minister Verwoerd in 1966.

6. When the term *Nationalist(s)* appears with an uppercase *N*, it refers to the National Party and/or its supporters; if a lowercase *n* is used, it refers to the ideology of nationalism and its related terms. I emphasize the use of *relatively*; in spite of being to the left of the Nationalists, the UP consistently supported the underpinnings of apartheid if not all of its specific elements.

7. Nixon, *Homelands, Harlem, and Hollywood*; Bevan, "Putting Up Screens."

8. Nixon, *Homelands, Harlem, and Hollywood*, 59, 60.

9. See William Beinhart, *Twentieth Century South Africa* (Oxford: Oxford University Press, 1994); Monica Wilson and Leonard Thompson, eds., *The Oxford History of South Africa*, 2 vols. (Oxford: Clarendon Press, 1971); Dunbar Moodie, *The Rise of Afrikanerdom: Power, Apartheid, and the Afrikaner Civil Religion* (Berkeley: University of California Press, 1975).

10. Until recently, the South African War was known as the Anglo-Boer War, or simply the Boer War. Boer literally means "farmer" in Afrikaans, but is often used to refer to the Afrikaners as a whole, at times in a derogatory way, at other times neutrally.

11. The irony of this political and cultural isolation, largely self-imposed, should not be lost on students of the Cold War, since South Africa remained a powerful military force supported by the West in Southern African Cold War conflicts.

12. Quoted in Nixon, *Homelands, Harlem, and Hollywood*, 52. *Bantu* literally means "the people" in many African languages; in South Africa, it was originally used as an indication of an individual or group being African, but the term came to be viewed as pejorative by Africans when associated with state policy. During the Black Consciousness Movement, Bantu Steve Biko attempted to reclaim the term as a positive one, although the controversy continues to this day.

13. For a theorization of the flip side of the structured absences I explore here—the intimacy of "entanglement" among South Africans—see Nuttall, *Entanglement*.

14. Quoted in Nixon, *Homelands, Harlem, and Hollywood*, 53, 60.

15. Quoted in ibid., 66.

16. Although Biko's name appears in publications in many different iterations, I use "Bantu Steve Biko" in deference to the same usage by the Steve Biko Foundation.

17. Quoted in Nixon, *Homelands, Harlem, and Hollywood*, 66.

18. See n. 5 above.

19. Nixon, *Homelands, Harlem, and Hollywood*, 63. Also see McLuhan, *Understanding Media*.

20. Nixon, *Homelands, Harlem, and Hollywood*, 63.

21. Ibid.

22. Graham Hayman and Ruth Tomaselli, "Broadcasting Technology as an Ideological Terrain: Some Concepts, Assumptions and Problems," in *Broadcasting in South Africa*, ed. Tomaselli, Tomaselli, and Muller, 65.

23. Nixon, *Homelands, Harlem, and Hollywood*, 69.

24. Bevan, "Putting Up Screens."

25. I pluralize movements in order to indicate that, although they shared the goal of ending apartheid, the many organizations were far from unified in either ideology or tactics.

26. Nixon, *Homelands, Harlem, and Hollywood*, 68; Tomaselli, Tomaselli, and Muller, eds., *Broadcasting in South Africa*.

27. Nixon, *Homelands, Harlem, and Hollywood*, 70.
28. Ibid.
29. See Ruth Teer-Tomaselli, "The Mediazation of Culture: John Thompson and the Vision of Public Service Broadcasting," *South African Journal of Philosophy* 13, no. 3 (1994): 124–32.
30. Not surprisingly, the ANC and other groups also identified the SABC as the first government institution requiring transformation as political power began to change hands in the first half of the 1990s, addressing this need even prior to the first democratic elections in 1994. See chapter 6 for more details.
31. This is not to say that the SABC failed to serve as a government mouthpiece under earlier governments; particularly during World War II, the SABC did indeed heavily favor the interests of the Smuts administration—particularly its support for the Allies. However, the level of explicit government propaganda connected to the SABC was less significant prior to 1948.
32. Nixon, *Homelands, Harlem, and Hollywood*, 64.
33. Several scholars have pointed out that, ironically, the paternalism of Radio Bantu did indeed "protect" these indigenous cultures, in the sense that the indigenous language was maintained and encouraged, along with so-called traditional music, drama, folklore, and so on. Hachten and Giffard, *The Press and Apartheid*, 221. See also Robert B. Horwitz, *Communication and Democratic Reform in South Africa* (New York: Cambridge University Press, 2001), 66. The tensions between the invented traditions (see Terrance Ranger and Eric Hobsbawm, eds., *The Invention of Tradition* [New York: Cambridge University Press, 1983]; see in particular Ranger's chapter in the volume, "The Invention of Tradition in Colonial Africa") of tribal life and more cosmopolitan Black life in the cities was ongoing during this time in South African history. Nonetheless, these cultural practices have been preserved to a greater degree than they might otherwise have been, considering the loss of many of these practices in other indigenous cultures subjected to large-scale media systems.
34. Hayman and Tomaselli, "Broadcasting Technology as an Ideological Terrain," 2.
35. For more details, see Isabel Hofmeyr, "Building a Nation from Words: Afrikaans Language, Literature and Ethnic Identity," in *The Politics of Race, Class and Nationalism in Twentieth Century South Africa*, ed. Shula Marks and Stanley Trapido (New York: Longman, 1987).
36. SAAN became Times Media, Ltd., in 1987, while the Argus Group was bought by Independent Newspapers, Ltd., in 1994. *Nasionale Pers* was originally the voice of the relatively *verligte* Cape NP, whereas Perskor resulted from mergers of three separate companies—Voortrekker Pers, Afrikaanse Pers, and Dagbreek Pers, all of which operated as voices of the *verkrampte* Transvaal NP—between 1962 and 1971.
37. Horwitz, *Communication and Democratic Reform in South Africa*, 48.
38. Les Switzer, "Introduction: South Africa's Alternative Press in Perspective," in *South Africa's Alternative Press: Voices of Protest and Resistance, 1880–1960*, ed. Switzer (Cambridge: Cambridge University Press, 1997), 2.
39. Although the alternative press came to play a crucial role in the politics of the late 1970s and the 1980s, its influence was minimal in the years preceding the initiation of television. For more details, see ibid.
40. Truth and Reconciliation Commission of South Africa (TRC), *Truth and Reconciliation Commission of South Africa Report*, vol. 4 (Cape Town: Juta, 1998), chap. 6, para. 9, 112 (hereafter TRC, *Report*).
41. Ibid., para. 22.

42. Biko was arrested for breaking his banning order by having traveled outside the vicinity of his home. It was during this arrest that he was beaten to death.
43. See Nelson Mandela, *Long Walk to Freedom* (London: Abacus, 1995), 633–35. See also chapter 6 of this book for further exploration of the ban and Mandela's role in the period between 1990 and 1994.
44. Bevan, "Putting Up Screens."
45. This delay was due to the SABC's insistence on waiting for the next generation of televisual technology in order to institute a nationwide, color, state-of-the-art service and to avoid the costly conversion from black-and-white to color. See the introduction of the next chapter for further information.
46. For an overview of the political process model, which is often referred to in terms of political opportunity structures, see Doug McAdam, Sidney G. Tarrow, and Charles Tilly, *Dynamics of Contention* (Cambridge: Cambridge University Press, 2001); see also McAdam, McCarthy, and Zald, *Comparative Perspectives on Social Movements*, 1996.
47. Tomaselli et al., "Square Vision in Colour," 153.
48. Ibid.
49. Quoted in Keyan Tomaselli and Ruth Tomaselli, "Between Policy and Practice in the SABC, 1970–1981," in *Broadcasting in South Africa*, ed. Tomaselli, Tomaselli, and Muller.
50. Carpignano et al. describe the importance of live telecasts in terms of the "common occurrence it represents. It is, in other words, the act of watching simultaneously that makes the event, and the presence of the audience has as much to do with the outcome of the live event, as the presentation provided by the televisual apparatus"; The Televisuality Collective, http://www.newschool.edu/mediastudies/tv/channel6/page1.html. For further exploration of the significance of media events, see Daniel Dayan and Elihu Katz, *Media Events: The Live Broadcasting of History* (Cambridge: Harvard University Press, 1992). Also see chapter 6.
51. Nixon, *Homelands, Harlem, and Hollywood*, 73.
52. Ibid., 74.
53. Bevan, "Putting Up Screens," 64.
54. See, e.g., Anderson, *Imagined Communities*, 122, 123. Although Anderson's argument is based on print media, he does view radio and television as an extension of that media, rather than something entirely different.

CHAPTER THREE
1. Tomaselli et al., "Square Vision in Colour," 175 n. 3.
2. It seems plausible to also postulate that the artificially high cost of television sets was a mechanism by which the apartheid regime could prevent television from reaching a wider population, whether by design or happenstance.
3. A *shebeen* is an unlicensed bar, often operated out of an individual's home in the townships. Shebeens are frequently informal gathering points for township communities.
4. Interview with Marc, thirty-seven-year-old English-speaker.
5. *Dominee* is the Afrikaans word for a clergyman (along with *predikant*) and most often refers to a minister in the Dutch Reformed Church of South Africa (NGK).
6. Soweto is, in fact, named according to its location relative to Johannesburg: SOuth WEstern TOwnship.
7. Personal conversation, April 1998.

8. From the SABC's 1976 *Annual Report*, p. 15, quoted in Horwitz, *Communication and Democratic Reform in South Africa*, 70. For more on the SABC's refusal to produce a documentary on the unrest, see Tomaselli and Tomaselli, "Between Policy and Practice in the SABC," 101, 111.

9. While his young age may help explain Steven's response to the Soweto Uprising, these kinds of more impressionistic responses were consistent among older respondents as well.

10. C. Rogerson and K. Beavon, "Towards a Geography of the Common People in South Africa," quoted in Alan Lester, "Introduction: Historical Geographies of Southern Africa," *Journal of Southern African Studies* 29, no. 3 (2003): 595–613, 601.

11. Tomaselli and Tomaselli, "Between Policy and Practice in the SABC," 134.

12. Ibid., 115.

13. See, e.g., Tomaselli, Tomaselli, and Muller, eds., *Broadcasting in South Africa*.

14. Nixon, *Homelands, Harlem, and Hollywood*, 160. Though the SABC could still import older British television programming, almost all current programming—with the exception of documentaries and sports—was inaccessible as a result of the boycott.

15. Although Hyslop, in "Why Did Apartheid's Supporters Capitulate?," asserts that the Equity boycott was relatively unimportant, many of the respondents indicated that they were aware of the boycott and my archival research indicates a large number of newspaper reports bemoaning the boycott. So while the Equity boycott may not have increased the influence of U.S. cultural products, my research indicates that it did carry a symbolic significance for White South Africans' sense of their isolation from the rest of the world.

16. Ibid. Some shows were also imported from other English-language countries in the commonwealth such as Australia, New Zealand, and Canada, but these countries had a far less-developed television production system—particularly in the late 1970s—than did the United States, leading to both fewer and more expensive products coming out of them.

17. In 1994, for instance, the average cost for the SABC to produce a drama in their own studios was ten times the cost of an imported drama, while a local drama produced outside the SABC cost twenty times more than an import; Horwitz, *Communication and Democratic Reform in South Africa*, 152. Though these figures are more recent than the time period I am examining here, they nonetheless reflect the extreme disparity in cost for imported versus locally produced programming.

18. Hyslop, "Why Did Apartheid's Supporters Capitulate?," 40.

19. See chap. 1, n. 40, for a discussion of what bilingualism means in this context.

20. Hyslop, "Why Did Apartheid's Supporters Capitulate?," 39.

CHAPTER FOUR

1. Although the term *Frontline States* is not always used consistently, it generally refers to those countries immediately bordering South Africa, namely Botswana, Mozambique, Swaziland, and Zimbabwe. Because Namibia was under South African control until 1990 it is not usually included, whereas Angola—the site of a civil war in which South African troops were heavily involved—is included. In addition, most accounts include Zambia as a Frontline State. Lesotho is most often excluded from the category because it is completely surrounded by South Africa, thereby effectively cutting off its border to outside access without permission to cross either South African territory or airspace.

2. Many respondents described international news during this time as designed explic-

itly to tell White South Africans that other locations around the globe were really in much worse shape than South Africa.

3. Most recently, e.g., in debates in the United States around the (second) Iraq War and the need for political versus military solutions.

4. For studies of WHAM, particularly in relation to media, see Tomaselli, "Politics of Discourse and the Discourse of Politics"; Keyan G. Tomaselli and P. Eric Louw, "Disinformation and the South African Defence Force's Theory of War," *Social Justice* 18, nos. 1/2 (1991): 124–40; Keyan G. Tomaselli and P. Eric Louw, "Militarization, Hegemony and the South African Media, 1976–1986," *In Con-Text* 2 (1989): 27–47.

5. Botha's nickname—"Die Groot Krokodil," or The Big Crocodile—also gives some indication of Botha's leadership style.

6. Much of the information currently known about the NSMS comes from testimony before the TRC or through court records from the prosecution of infamous members of the security apparatus such as Eugene de Kock.

7. African National Congress, "ANC Submission to the Truth and Reconciliation Commission," 1996, http://www.geocities.com/CapitolHill/5013/trcall.html; TRC, *Report*.

8. Ineke van Kessel, *"Beyond Our Wildest Dreams": The United Democratic Front and the Transformation of South Africa* (Charlottesville: University Press of Virginia, 2000), 49.

9. For a thorough history of the UDF, see ibid; and Jeremy Seekings, *The UDF: A History of the United Democratic Front in South Africa, 1983–1991* (Athens: Ohio University Press, 2000). Also see their reviews of each other's books and the resulting discussion on the South African history electronic discussion group "H-SAFRICA," run through H-Net, which is archived at http://www2.h-net.msu.edu/~safrica/.

10. In the 1983 elections for the municipal councils, a mere 21 percent of the potential electorate voted, while the 1984 elections for the House of Delegates (representing Indians) drew only 16 percent of possible voters and the elections for the House of Representatives (representing Coloureds) drew 19 percent of potential participants; van Kessel, *"Beyond Our Wildest Dreams,"* 23, 25. These numbers are all the more striking when compared to the overwhelming participation in the 1994 elections.

11. Tomaselli et al., "Square Vision in Colour." Though the study was conducted at Rhodes University, the lead author was at the University of Natal at the time of publication.

12. For a thorough and convincing deconstruction of the concept of "tradition" as a static and ingrained source of authority, see Ranger and Hobsbawm, *Invention of Tradition*.

13. Tomaselli et al., "Square Vision in Colour," 174.

14. Quoted in ibid.

15. Each of these are indigenous to Southern Africa, with the Nguni languages including Zulu (the most common first language among South Africans) and Xhosa, while the Sotho languages include Northern and Southern Sotho among others.

16. Because of this inconsistency in naming, and because I deal with TV2/3 as a single entity, I refer to TV2/3 as singular rather than plural.

17. This theme proves particularly ironic, given the system of Bantu Education that was explicitly designed to prepare Black South Africans for no more than the most menial of jobs.

18. Tomaselli et al., "Square Vision in Colour," 157. The term "manufacturing consent" comes from Edward S. Herman and Noam Chomsky, *Manufacturing Consent: The Political Economy of Mass Media* (New York: Pantheon, 1988), and was made popular

through the well-known video recording by the same name featuring the two authors. For a sampling of Chomsky's work, see Noam Chomsky, *The Chomsky Reader* (New York: Pantheon, 1987). Also see Michael Parenti, *Inventing Reality: The Politics of the Mass Media* (New York: St. Martin's Press, 1986); Stuart Hall, *Representation: Cultural Representations and Signifying Practices* (London: Sage, 1997).

19. Tomaselli et al., "Square Vision in Colour," 174. See also the transcripts from the TRC's hearings on mass media under apartheid, held September 15 to 17, 1997, during which several witnesses gave testimony to the funding disparity between TV1 and TV2/3; Truth and Reconciliation Commission of South Africa (TRC), unpublished transcripts of special hearings on the media, held September 15–17, 1997, http://www.truth.org.za (consulted June 8, 1998).

20. Tomaselli et al., "Square Vision in Colour," 174.

21. Ibid., 154.

22. The authors are quoting from John van Zyl, "Competence in Popular Culture: the Deep Structure of Mass Communication," *Communicatio* 8, no. 1 (1982): 54.

23. Tomaselli et al., "Square Vision in Colour," 175.

24. Meyrowitz, *No Sense of Place*, 75, 76.

25. Stuart Hall, "Encoding/Decoding," in *Culture, Media, Language*, ed. Stuart Hall, Dorothy Hobson, Andrew Love and Paul Willis (London: Hutchinson, 1980). In post-apartheid South Africa there are eleven official languages; prior to 1994, these languages were not official due to the fragmentation of the state into Bantustans and more generally the structured absence of Black South Africans in the public sphere.

26. For further explication of the presentational versus the representational nature of television, see The Televisuality Collective, n.d., http://www.newschool.edu/media studies/tv/channel5/page1.html. Also see Catherine Celebrezze's use of "presentational electricity" in her "Television Time and Space: A Social History of the Present," Ph.D. diss., Department of Sociology, New School for Social Research, New York.

27. Meyrowitz, *No Sense of Place*, 75, 76. Meyrowitz also explores a much more subtle way in which print media further divides those who speak the same language, e.g., children, through specialized language. He uses the example of rarefied academic terminology as a way in which print can exclude even readers familiar with the language being used (78).

28. Ibid., 80.

29. While this is changing somewhat with pay-per-view television and, to a lesser extent, cable television, the distinction between television's relationship with the product itself compared to print remains apropos. Ironically, the viewing of taboo topics on the Internet, as the medium becomes capable of handling faster speeds of data transfer and therefore more sophisticated media, both benefits from the ephemeral quality of electronic media and reintroduces the fear of "getting caught" through electronic fingerprints left on personal computers. In any case, South African television was at this time solely free-to-air and therefore Meyrowitz's analysis remains accurate.

30. Meyrowitz, *No Sense of Place*, 81.

31. Ibid., 83.

32. This is another trend that we currently see being revived in new media, with its convergence of visual and textual codes and its greater volume of information, leading

to increasing "narrowcasting" and self-selection of audiences, tending to gravitate toward content that reaffirms rather than challenges an individual's own viewpoint.

33. This paradox is the core of Gamson's *Freaks Talk Back* discussed in chapter 1.

34. Meyrowitz, *No Sense of Place*, 88.

35. Ibid. These quotes and statistics are quite dated, given the 1985 publication date of Meyrowitz's book. However, the phenomenon remains significant regardless of subsequent changes in the specifics.

36. Ibid., 87.

37. There are, of course, exceptions to this assertion, including religious groups like the Amish and activist groups like those behind Kill Your Television. The degree to which these groups are outliers to mainstream views of television make them the exceptions that prove the rule.

38. See, e.g., McLuhan, *Understanding Media*.

39. My searches of the SABC archives unearthed no evidence of expectations that White viewers would ever tune in to TV2/3, and the AMPS data surprisingly took no measure of White viewers of TV2/3, whereas it did measure Black viewing of TV1.

40. I am indebted to my colleague Crispin Thurlow for this analogy, which fits well with his own research on elite tourisms and the discourses of luxury. See, e.g., Adam Jaworski, Crispin Thurlow, Sarah Lawson, and Virpi Ylänne-McEwen, "The Uses and Representations of Local Languages in Tourist Destinations: A View from British TV Holiday Programmes," *Language Awareness* 12, no. 1 (2003): 5–29.

41. Jaworski et al., "Uses and Representations of Local Languages."

42. Tomaselli et al., "Square Vision in Colour," 166.

43. Ibid., 168.

44. Ibid., 158.

45. Mandla Langa, "The Writing Was Always on the Wall, but Where Were the Reporters?" *Rhodes Journalism Review* (May 1997): 13–19. Langa was a prominent leader of the ANC-in-exile and also served as the chairperson of the Independent Broadcasting Authority (IBA) before it was subsumed into the ICASA (see chapter 6 for more information on the formation of the IBA).

46. See, e.g., Ruth Frankenberg, *Displacing Whiteness: Essays in Social and Cultural Criticism* (Durham, N.C.: Duke University Press, 1997); Ruth Frankenberg, *White Women, Race Matters: The Social Construction of Whiteness* (Minneapolis: University of Minnesota Press, 1993); David Roediger, *Towards the Abolition of Whiteness* (London: Verso, 1995); Eric Lott, "Love and Theft: The Racial Unconscious of Blackface Minstrelsy," *Representations* 39 (Summer 1992). For a classic treatment of this process within postcolonial theory, see Edward Said, *Orientalism* (New York: Vintage Books, 1979); see also Ann Laura Stoler, *Race and the Education of Desire: Foucault's* History of Sexuality *and the Colonial Order of Things* (Durham, N.C.: Duke University Press, 1995). It is worth noting that whiteness studies—like media studies—often takes as a given the context of North America or Europe. Thus the idea of (re)discovering Whiteness as a particular rather than universal identity does not apply very well to South Africa, since White South Africans have always been acutely aware (and fearful) of their minority status within the country, even as they lived that identity as a social default. As a result, the structuring of Black South Africans' absence had to be a much more active process—and is therefore more striking in some ways—than in North America or Europe.

47. For example, several respondents mentioned being raised in a racist viewpoint, then

altering that viewpoint at university—which would (not incidentally) have been during the 1980s and early 1990s for these particular individuals.

CHAPTER FIVE

1. Van Kessel, *"Beyond Our Wildest Dreams,"* 37.
2. Quoted in ibid.
3. Ruth Tomaselli, "Politics of Discourse and the Discourse of Politics." Tomaselli also does an excellent job of analyzing the discourses created and mobilized by SABC News during the states of emergency, utilizing parallel constructs of violence and reform to demonize both the then-banned ANC and opposition movements within the country, in order to shield television viewers from the unfolding political conflict.
4. Hall, "Encoding/Decoding."
5. Van Kessel, *"Beyond Our Wildest Dreams,"* 52.
6. Patrick Bond, *Elite Transition: From Apartheid to Neoliberalism in South Africa* (London: Pluto Press, 2000).
7. See, in particular, Jonathan Hyslop, "The Prophet Van Rensburg's Vision of Nelson Mandela: White Popular Religious Culture and Responses to Democratisation," *Social Dynamics* 21, no. 2 (1995): 23–55; and Hyslop, "Why Did Apartheid's Supporters Capitulate?"
8. Public address, University of Washington Bothell, April 24, 2008.
9. See, e.g., the documentary by Lee Hirsch, dir., *Amandla! A Revolution in Four-Part Harmony*, 2002, distributed by Artisan Pictures.
10. In addition to the many Black musicians who popularized a wide variety of anti-apartheid songs, which employed varying degrees of analogy to veil their messages at times, the rise in popularity of White and/or integrated bands with anti-apartheid themes like the Kalahari Surfers and Juluka (and its progeny, Johnny Clegg and Savuka) is notable during this time. Likewise, the drama productions of the People's Experimental Theatre, Workshop 71, the Junction Avenue Theater Company, and even the more mainstream Market Theatre provided a significant outlet for multiracial cultural production. For more details see chapter 4 of Mufson, *Fighting Years*.
11. Although mentioned less often by respondents, it seems reasonable to suspect that the role of White South Africans, particularly Afrikaners, as "bad guys" in Hollywood genre films—whether specifically about South Africa, as with *Cry Freedom*, or more generally as rough-and-tumble, unethical mercenaries—also contributed to their sense of international rejection during this time. White South Africans continue to be cast in these roles by Hollywood, most recently in the mini-series *Diamonds* (2009) on U.S. television.
12. Gramsci, *Selections from the Prison Notebooks of Antonio Gramsci*.
13. Tomaselli et al., "Square Vision in Colour," 168.
14. Ibid.
15. See Julia Kristeva, *The Kristeva Reader* (New York: Columbia University Press, 1986).
16. Ien Ang, *Watching Dallas: Soap Opera and the Melodramatic Imagination* (New York: Methuen, 1985).
17. Tomaselli, "Politics of Discourse and the Discourse of Politics."
18. M-Net relied on purchased programming—like HBO and other early cable channels in the United States—because it produced very little of its own programming. Although the SABC sometimes aired decades-old British programming produced before the Equity Ban was put into place, M-Net eschewed such outdated material.

19. Horwitz, *Communication and Democratic Reform in South Africa*, 69.
20. Daan P. van Vuuren, Elirea Bornman, Gerhard Mels, and Mariette van Vuuren, "Children's Perceptions of and Identification with the Social Reality of the *Cosby Show*: A Comparison between the USA and South Africa," *South African Journal of Psychology* 20, no. 2 (1990): 70, 71.
21. This is not, of course, to imply that the racial atmosphere of the United States was not also highly charged in the mid-1980s, but rather that the specific context of South Africa had particular intensity and a unique form of politicization at the time.
22. Hall, "Encoding/Decoding." Note here that I am referring to popular understandings and television criticism in the popular press, rather than academic analyses.
23. Ibid., 138.
24. Donald Bogle, *Blacks in American Films and Television: An Encyclopedia* (New York: Garland Publishing, 1988).
25. Linda Fuller, *The Cosby Show: Audiences, Impact, and Implications* (Westport, Conn.: Greenwood Press, 1992), 111. Any critiques I offer here are regarding Fuller's work rather than the work of the graduate student. Fuller's own survey in South Africa was both brief and the kind of research for which glamour magazines are infamous: a readers' poll that required initiation on the part of the participant. Fuller made contact with the survey participants through a query published in two South African newspapers. Thus Fuller's results, while interesting, need to be understood within the limited nature of her methodology.
26. Because I did not formally interview this individual, I do not have the more detailed information that is available from interviewees.
27. Quoted in Fuller, *The Cosby Show*, 110. Fuller is here describing the graduate student's analysis (see n. 25 above). Interestingly, in spite of intense searches of the SABC archives and countless discussions with media professionals in South Africa, I have been unable to find any evidence of discussion or controversy around *The Cosby Show*'s purchase for airing on SABC. It almost seems as if the show somehow slipped under the radar of the SABC, not an unheard-of occurrence, and was chosen only because of its immense popularity in the United States at the time of purchase.
28. Respondents repeatedly referred to the fictional family in *The Cosby Show* as the Cosbys rather than as the Huxtables, which was the name of the fictional characters. While this undoubtedly comes in part from the incongruity between the names of the show and the characters, it also indicates the remarkable degree to which the characters of the show came to be understood as "real" by audiences and conflated with the actors who portrayed them, particularly Bill Cosby himself.
29. Ibid., 133.
30. Personal correspondence, June 5, 2002.
31. For an example of what a more integrated television program may look like, see the next chapter, particularly the section regarding South African shows such as *Egoli*.
32. Quoted in Fuller, *The Cosby Show*, 113.
33. Ibid.
34. Ibid.
35. Incidentally, the final broadcast of *The Cosby Show* in the United States took place on April 30, 1992—one day after the not-guilty verdicts were returned in the case of the officers accused of beating Rodney King, setting off the Los Angeles Riots which continued to burn during the showing of the farewell episode.
36. Quoted in Ang, *Watching Dallas*, 5.
37. Ibid.

38. While I recognize that a couple of Fuller's respondents quoted in the previous section seem to deny that Black South Africans watched or enjoyed *The Cosby Show*, AMPS data clearly contradicts the respondents' claims.

39. South African Broadcasting Corporation (SABC), *Annual Report 1987* (Johannesburg: SABC, 1987). Fuller cites a study performed through funding from the SABC itself, which compared the show's popularity and impact on children in South Africa compared to children in the United States. According to Fuller, the paper concludes that "for South African children, the show's popularity can better be explained as 'mere entertainment' rather than as a model for cultural transformation" (Fuller, *The Cosby Show*, 112). However, Fuller was working of a draft of the paper (as listed in her citation) that was published as Daan P. van Vuuren, Elirea Bornman, Gerhard Mels, and Mariette van Vuuren, "Children's Perceptions of and Identification with the Social Reality of the Cosby Show: A Comparison between the USA and South Africa," *South African Journal of Psychology* 20, no. 2 (1990): 70–79. When published, the final paragraph of the paper read, "The present study indicates that the popularity of *The Cosby Show* might be more than 'mere entertainment' (SABC, 1987) and that it could be used by children in South Africa, particularly black children in cultural transition, to be a model for their own behaviour." I do not know whether Fuller misread the draft copy or the authors changed their conclusion in subsequent drafts, but the article as a whole makes careful claims based on quantitative data that are appropriately limited and do not approach questions of whether *The Cosby Show* had a role in transforming South African society. Of note for my research, though, is the authors' focus on children's degrees of identification with the Huxtable characters. Although their conclusions are appropriately tentative, the authors do approach the question of identification as relevant to the popularity and importance of *The Cosby Show*.

40. Quoted in Fuller, *The Cosby Show*, 133, from Harry F. Waters, "Cosby's Fast Track," *Newsweek*, September 2, 1985, 54.

41. Ang, *Watching Dallas*. Ang's work builds on the work of David Morley and many others. See David Morley, *The "Nationwide" Audience: Structure and Decoding* (London: BFI, 1980); and John Fiske, *Television Culture* (London: Routledge, 1987).

42. Steven Mufson, "The 'Cosby Plan' for South Africa," *Wall Street Journal*, July 30, 1986, 17.

43. It is also worth noting the similarities between this plan and the various obstacles to black voter participation in the Jim Crow South of the United States, such as voting tests and property requirements.

CHAPTER SIX

1. Tomaselli and Shepperson, "The Absent Signifier," 26.

2. My appreciation goes to Keyan Tomaselli for first relating this story to me in personal conversation; he has subsequently published a more in-depth analysis of this story in ibid. See 32–33 in particular.

3. This latter phrase, "Elite Transition," is the title of Patrick Bond's influential book: Patrick Bond, *Elite Transition* (Pietermaritzburg: University of Natal Press, 2000).

4. Bonny Schoonakker, "SA Takes a Big Step into TV History," *Sunday Times*, September 19, 1999, 5.

5. See Allister Haddon Sparks, *Tomorrow Is Another Country: The Inside Story of South Africa's Road to Change* (New York: Hill and Wang, 1995), for a short but compelling account of these negotiations, as well as Mandela, *Long Walk to Freedom*.

6. Sparks, *Tomorrow Is Another Country*, 5. The speech was dubbed the Rubicon speech

because it closed with the words, "We are today crossing the Rubicon. There can be no turning back," referring to Julius Caesar's pivotal crossing of the Rubicon River, thereby defying his opponents and eventually claiming control of the Roman empire. Although Botha's rhetoric matched the pre-speech publicity of significant changes in the apartheid regime, the actual policies put forth both in the speech and in subsequent months by the National Party amounted to little change. For more details and an analysis of the speech (which was actually repeated, though not verbatim, at the opening of Parliament in 1986), see Daniel Daran, Ansuya Chetty, Jeanne Prinsloo, and Mark Allison-Broomhead, "The Visual Role of 'the Rubicons' as Part of the Reform Strategy: The Beginning of the End of Apartheid," paper presented at the 1986 Conference of the Association of Sociology in Southern Africa at the University of Natal, http://www.nu.ac.za/cms/socialsemiotics/socialsemiotics .asp?ID=9.

7. Sparks, *Tomorrow Is Another Country*, *Volkstaat* literally means, in Afrikaans, "People's State." The term was used in the early days to refer to the whole of South Africa. As it became apparent that some form of democratic rule would come to pass, *volkstaat* referred to the idea of reserving a large geographic segment of South Africa that would become an independent homeland for White South Africans, particularly Afrikaners.

8. Dayan and Katz, *Media Events*, 1.

9. Ibid.

10. As such, media events are often recognized as such retroactively, after their persistence in the collective imagination has withstood intervening years; likewise, some attempts at constructing media events fail to "stick," either because they fail to capture the collective imagining at the time or they lose their salience over the long term.

11. Ibid., 8.

12. William Beinart, *Twentieth Century South Africa* (Oxford: Oxford University Press, 1994), 252.

13. Steven is referring to becoming a conscientious objector and joining the End Conscription Campaign (ECC), refusing to serve his military time during the States of Emergency. Such objectors faced both jail time and harsh persecution among both prisoners and civilians.

14. From the beginning of television in South Africa, radio stations would occasionally simulcast the audio portion of television programs, sometimes as a cheaper way of dubbing programs. Many interviewees recalled listening to programs on the radio before they had a television set in order to understand what their friends would be talking about the next day at school or work. The habit of listening to radio for audio while watching television for visuals was thus formed for many individuals. 604 was Capital Radio, which broadcast from the supposedly independent homeland of the Transkei into the Witwatersrand area. Capital Radio, like Bop-TV and Channel 702 (television and radio, respectively, broadcast from Bophuthatswana), was technically independent from the SABC and developed a reputation for better news coverage in the late 1980s, though only nominally better. The independence of broadcasting in the homelands was, like the independence of their governments, significantly curtailed and only by permission of the South African government.

15. Quoted in Schoonakker, "SA Takes a Big Step into TV History," 5.

16. Dayan and Katz, *Media Events*, 9.

17. Nixon, *Homelands, Harlem, and Hollywood*.

18. Ibid., 183, 184, 189.
19. Mandela, *Long Walk to Freedom*; Sparks, *Tomorrow Is Another Country*.
20. Nixon, *Homelands, Harlem, and Hollywood*, 185. This also coincides with many social movement theories that emphasize that, particularly in situations of extreme state repression, social movements are more likely to succeed if they have a "polycephalous" leadership structure that can survive the removal of any given leader or organization.
21. Nixon joins others in pointing out that the amazement of both White South Africans and the domestic and international press that Mandela was "dignified" stems, at least in part, from a form of racist bigotry, "as if they had been expecting, all along, Idi Amin to come crashing in"; Nixon, *Homelands, Harlem, and Hollywood*, 185.
22. The Rivonia Trial (sometimes also called the Second Treason Trial) was the trial during which Mandela, Sisulu, and many other leaders of the ANC were sentenced to their very long prison terms, many for life. It was called the Rivonia Trial because most of the leaders were arrested while meeting on a farm in Rivonia, and many of the documents submitted as evidence were seized at that time. Mandela himself, however, had been living underground previous to that time and was arrested on lesser charges before the raid at Rivonia, but was then charged and tried with the other Rivonia defendants for treason. For excerpts from his speech during the trial, see Mandela, *Long Walk to Freedom*, 432–38.
23. Nixon, *Homelands, Harlem, and Hollywood*, 188.
24. Indeed, according to Nixon, de Klerk felt he had made a mistake by maintaining the exile of Sam Nujoma, the Namibian resistance leader, until just prior to elections, thus leaving "too little time to demythologize him in the eyes of the populace"; ibid., 179.
25. Tomaselli and Shepperson, "The Absent Signifier."
26. Ibid., 38.
27. Horwitz, *Communication and Democratic Reform in South Africa*, 117.
28. Ibid., 118. TopSport Surplus, or TSS, was only available beginning in the early 1990s in the area around Johannesburg known as the PWV (for Pretoria-Witwatersrand-Vereeniging) and featured, as the name implies, only sports programming.
29. Ibid.
30. Ibid., 129.
31. The Boipatong Massacre took place on June 17, 1992, when thirty-nine unarmed ANC supporters were killed in the township of Boipatong, apparently by IFP supporters in collusion with the police.
32. Horwitz, *Communication and Democratic Reform in South Africa*, 140.
33. Ibid., 18.
34. The IBA was initially intended to be an interim body to ensure impartiality during the elections, after which a permanent regulatory body would be instituted by a democratically elected parliament; see ibid., 148. The regulatory division between telecommunications and broadcasting has since been rescinded, with the merging of the IBA and the South African Telecommunications Regulatory Agency (SATRA) to form the Independent Communications Authority of South Africa (ICASA) in July 2000.
35. Ibid., 141.
36. Ibid., 143. The CIB was an umbrella group of thirty-seven other groups, including the Campaign for Open Media and many media-related labor unions.
37. Anton, for instance, said that "[*Carte Blanche*] focused on soft/lifestyle issues related

to the White community and rarely covered representative/institutional politics."
The quote is from an interview with Margaret, a forty-year-old English-speaker.

38. Personal conversation with Keyan Tomaselli, August 1998.

39. For an insightful account of the press coverage of this violence (though it deals primarily with print rather than broadcast media), see Lesley J. Fordred, "Narrative, Conflict and Change: Journalism in the New South Africa," Ph.D. diss., Department of Social Anthropology, University of Cape Town (UCT). This is also the source of the figure of 12,000 killed. Fordred is now on the faculty at UCT.

40. "The Line" is actually the name of the first of the three episodes. Taken as a whole, the miniseries is officially titled *In a Time of Violence* and distributed as such in the United States, but South Africans almost without exception refer to the entire series as *The Line*.

41. The insignia of the AWB is a black, three-pronged version of a swastika on a white circle in a red flag—clearly intended to invoke the Nazi regime.

42. Mandela, *Long Walk to Freedom*, 731.

43. Ibid., 730.

44. In a particularly astounding moment during the televised funeral, in the midst of the anger and bitterness surrounding Hani's assassination, Tutu led the crowd to wave their hands in the air while saying, "We are all God's children—black and white." For an exchange about this incident between Tutu and poet/journalist/ author Antjie Krog, see Antjie Krog, *Country of My Skull: Guilt, Sorrow, and the Limits of Forgiveness in the New South Africa* (New York: Times Books, 1998).

45. Tebbutt Commission, "Commission of Inquiry into the Incidents That Led to the Violence in the former Bophuthatswana on 11 March 1994, and the Deaths That Occurred as a Result Thereof," South African Government documents, 1998, http:// www.polity.org.za/govdocs/commissions/1998/tebbutt/tebbutt1.html.

46. Ibid.

47. Sparks, for instance, casts the Battle of Bop as the crucial turning point in the runup to the elections; Sparks, *Tomorrow Is Another Country*. In a related debate, Guy Berger has named these images as signaling that "whites had had their day, and the active newsmakers were black South Africans"; Guy Berger, "Towards an Analysis of the South African Media and Transformation, 1994–1999," *Transformation* 38 (1999). While I clearly recognize the symbolic importance of these images vis-à-vis racial power in South Africa, to name this moment as one in which Black South Africans are forever established as the most important newsmakers in South Africa ignores the continuing tendency of mainstream media—particularly newspapers, most of whose readership remains predominantly White—to provide disproportionate coverage of events and individuals associated with White South Africans' lives. Likewise, this particular image obviously tends toward the common narrative in White-controlled media of Black "newsmakers" as atavistic criminals outside the rule of law. See n. 29 in the conclusion for references on an extended debate between Berger and Mashilo Boloka and myself on this and other issues of post-apartheid transformation in mass media

48. The IFP's decision to join came so late that the ballots had already been printed, so a sticker was added to the bottom of the ballot to accommodate Buthelezi's candidacy.

49. The four days were April 26–29, 1994. The first day, April 26, was reserved for the elderly, the disabled and others, so most histories of South Africa mark April 27 as the date of the election.

50. Mandela, *Long Walk to Freedom*, 743.
51. Ibid., 747.
52. Nixon, *Homelands, Harlem, and Hollywood*, 73. See also chapter 2 of this book.

CONCLUSION

1. TRC, unpublished transcripts.
2. I describe the TRC in more detail later in this chapter.
3. Quoted in TRC, *Report*; see also TRC, unpublished transcripts.
4. Quoted in TRC, *Report* 4, chap. 6, para. 75.
5. The scholar most closely associated with cultural imperialism is Herbert Schiller. For one example of his work, see Herbert Schiller, *Invisible Crisis: What Conglomerate Control of Media Means for America and the World* (Boulder, Colo.: Westview Press, 1996). "Christian Nationalism" is the name often applied to apartheid ideology, particularly the more abstract or theological elements that provided the moral justification for the social engineering of apartheid.
6. Pieterse, "Globalization as Hybridization."
7. Hyslop, "Why Did Apartheid's Supporters Capitulate?," 39.
8. Mufson, *Fighting Years*, 182. Mufson goes on to point out that by 1986 approximately one-quarter of those watching TV1 were Black South Africans, while "TV4 appealed to people of all races."
9. Gramsci, *Selections from the Prison Notebooks of Antonio Gramsci*.
10. See Tomaselli and Shepperson, "The Absent Signifier," for both their use of "the man with no face" in reference to Mandela and an extended analysis of the semiotic meanings of cultural icons more generally in the volume as a whole, Tomaselli and Scott, eds., *Cultural Icons*.
11. As in the introduction, see Castells, *Rise of the Network Society*, 5, for a discussion of the "false problem" of technological determinism. In addition to these concerns, we must keep in mind that the exact form of a given media technology is also the result of social processes and should not be taken as a naturalized given. For an example of scholarship that exposes the social forces that have shaped television as we understand it today, see Celebrezze, "Television Time and Space."
12. I use the words *space* and *place* intentionally, invoking the distinctions common in critical human geography between space as an abstracted, conceptually neutral ideation and place as a more historically and geographically specific construct. As such, identification of place requires being attuned to what cultural studies scholars describe as a specific historical conjuncture.
13. The Human Sciences Research Council (HSRC), a governmental parastatal for social science research, recognized this potential and instituted a large-scale study of television's affects, including sections on race relations and violence. Having initiated this study in 1971 when the SABC's intention to introduce television was announced, they created baseline data that they then compared to parallel data collected in 1976 and again in 1981. Although the potential for such a study was immense, both the effects-theory orientation of the study and the ideological alliance of the HSRC with the apartheid regime marred the findings. In the words of Pieter Conradie, one of the researchers, the study found "that television had very little effect" except for a slight increase in violence among children who were already socially susceptible to violent behavior; interview with Conradie, April 2000.
14. As a public-service broadcaster, the SABC did not air television advertisements for the first two years. It eventually proved impossible to maintain the public broad-

caster only on license fees, which were often difficult to collect, so advertising was introduced in 1978.

15. Jésus Martín-Barbero, *Communication, Culture and Hegemony: From the Media to Mediations* (London: Sage, 1993), 179.

16. For the classic treatise on televisual flow, see Raymond Williams, *Television: Technology and Cultural Form* (London: Wesleyan University Press, 1992). For an excellent (and more recent) explanation and development of the concept, including its connections to televisual space, see Televisuality, http://www.newschool.edu/media studies/tv/channel7/index.html.

17. For instance, the racial project of apartheid, not to mention television in South Africa, would never have been sustainable without the legacy of colonial exploitation and the mineral wealth of the nation—an excellent example of global flows with what Appadurai would call financescapes. Likewise, Appadurai's ethnoscapes—the movement of people—played a significant role as well, through the broadening international awareness of apartheid from the migration of Black South Africans to North America, Western Europe, Eastern Bloc, and other African nations; White South Africans' back-and-forth travel to and from European and North American destinations, particularly the United Kingdom; and the immigration of White Rhodesians following the decolonization of that country, which was then renamed Zimbabwe.

18. Hyslop, "Why Did Apartheid's Supporters Capitulate?," 40. This quote comes from a longer passage that asserts the centrality of middle-class self-interest had its origins in U.S.-produced television: "When many of them designated themselves as 'middle class' they seemed by this to signify participation in certain styles of consumption, the parameters of which were defined primarily by television images of American suburbia. This was crucial to the decline of active support for apartheid."

19. Ibid.

20. Sparks, *Tomorrow Is Another Country*, 10.

21. See Ron Krabill, "Symbiosis: Mass Media and the Truth and Reconciliation Commission of South Africa," *Media, Culture and Society* 23 (2001): 567–85, for a much more detailed reading of the TRC and its relationship to media, including the TRC's special hearings on mass media.

22. This goal of the TRC, whether seen as the positive unification of a divided nation or the negative reinscription of nationalism, is deemed by many to be largely unachieved.

23. TRC, unpublished transcripts.

24. South African Human Rights Commission, *Faultlines: Inquiry into Racism in the Media* (Johannesburg: South African Human Rights Commission, 2000). For a critique of *Faultlines*, see Keyan Tomaselli, "Faulting *Faultlines*: Racism in the South African Media," *Ecquid Novi* 21, no. 2 (2000): 157–74.

25. For one of the many harsh critiques of *Faultlines*, see Tomaselli, "Faulting *Faultlines*."

26. See, e.g., Sean Jacobs and Thabani Masuku, "Opinion on the Human Rights Commission's Hearings into Racism in the Media," Institute for Democracy in South Africa (IDASA) opinion paper, IDASA, Cape Town, 2000; Lynette Steenveld, "Theoretical Considerations in the Study of Racism in the Media," submission to the South African Human Rights Commission, 2000.

27. See Horwitz, *Communication and Democratic Reform in South Africa*, for perhaps the most thorough treatment of this process.

28. In most cases, the commercial stations are former SABC radio stations that have been

sold to commercial interests. Black empowerment schemes are methods of transferring ownership of various corporations, parastatals, and so on, either in part or in whole, to Black South Africans. One of the main debates surrounding black empowerment revolves around the extent to which such schemes benefit Black South Africans as a whole, as opposed to benefiting a small new elite class of Black South Africans. See n. 29 below.

29. Farhana Goga, *Towards Affirmative Action: Issues of Race and Gender in the South African Media* (Durban: Centre for Cultural and Media Studies and UNESCO, 2000), available at: http://ccms.ukzn.ac.za/index.php?option=com+content&task=category &sectionid=16Uid=73&Itemid=86. For an extended debate on black empowerment schemes and other issues of the political economy and transformation of post-apartheid media, see Keyan Tomaselli, "Ownership and Control in the South African Print Media: Black Empowerment After Apartheid," *Ecquid Novi* 18, no. 1 (1997); a critique of Tomaselli in Berger, "'Towards an Analysis of the South African Media'"; a response from myself and a colleague, Gibson Mashilo Boloka and Ron Krabill, "Calling the Glass Half Full: A Response to Berger's 'Towards an Analysis of the South African Media and Transformation, 1994–1999," *Transformation* 43 (2000); and finally a retort to our response, Guy Berger, "Response to Boloka-Krabill," *Transformation* 43 (2000).

30. See Reporters sans Frontières' website at http://www.rsf.org/. See also Steve Mbogo, "Journalists: Progress Needed Toward Press Freedom in Africa," *World Politics Review* (May 3, 2007).

31. Boloka and Krabill, "Calling the Glass Half Full."

32. Horwitz, *Communication and Democratic Reform in South Africa*, 176.

33. Ibid., 21.

34. Henry Jenkins, *Convergence Culture: Where Old and New Media Collide* (New York: New York University Press, 2006).

35. John Hartley, *Television Truths* (Oxford: Blackwell, 2008), 1.